INTO THE UNKNOWN

Best regards,

Susan SB Schwartz

INTO THE UNKNOWN

◆

THE REMARKABLE LIFE
OF
HANS KRAUS

Susan E.B. Schwartz

iUniverse, Inc.
New York Lincoln Shanghai

INTO THE UNKNOWN
THE REMARKABLE LIFE OF HANS KRAUS

iUniverse books may be ordered through booksellers or by contacting:

iUniverse
2021 Pine Lake Road, Suite 100
Lincoln, NE 68512
www.iuniverse.com
1-800-Authors (1-800-288-4677)

ISBN-13: 978-0-595-35752-9 (pbk)
ISBN-13: 978-0-595-80229-6 (ebk)
ISBN-10: 0-595-35752-0 (pbk)
ISBN-10: 0-595-80229-X (ebk)

Printed in the United States of America

Into the unknown
with a few small soft-iron pitons and a hemp rope,
*boldness, and **big** cojones.*

Climbing author, Dick Williams,
describing Hans Kraus in the mountains

So far ahead of his time;
it will take fifty years for others to catch up.

White House doctor, Dr. Gene Cohen,
describing Hans Kraus in medicine

To my husband John.
A thoroughly remarkable man.

Contents

Part II   *NEW YORK 1938–1949*

Part VI   CONCLUSION: THE STORY BEHIND THE
          STORY 1994–1996

Advance Acclaim for INTO THE UNKNOWN

"Kraus was back doctor to all kinds of stars, athletes, politicians, show business personalities, even journalists. Anyone who was anyone went to Kraus."
Mike Wallace

"I kept turning the pages. This story has it all—adventure, death in the mountains, universal father-son conflict, celebrities, never before revealed Kennedy secrets, a charismatic and complex subject. Schwartz is a born story teller who weaves it all together in a darn good read."
James P. McCarthy, past President, American Alpine Club

"A terrific book. A fascinating and important medical story, but also an exciting read for doctor, climber or layperson. Kraus was one of the great, unheralded medical pioneers of the 20th century, and Schwartz's book shines a deserved light on his breakthrough contributions—which could save the U.S. billions of dollars in evaluating and treating back pain. On top of that, what a life he led! Truly remarkable!"
Norman Marcus, MD, past-President, American Academy of Pain Medicine; Director, Norman Marcus Pain Institute; and Associate Clinical Professor, New York University School of Medicine.

"A gripping story of idealism, adventure, and one man's indomitable spirit. It is inspiring to read about Hans Kraus, who was resolved that a single man could make a big difference."
Norbu Tenzing Norgay, son of Tenzing Norgay, who summitted Everest with Sir Edmund Hillary.

"Bravo! Schwartz does an excellent job of portraying a life that could have been scripted by Hollywood. A great account of a great old school adventurer, who led his life with passion, wit, and unswerving determination. We need more books like this."
James M. Clash, Adventurer columnist, Forbes Magazine, and author of To the Limits

"Hans is a legendary figure in rock climbing, but until I read Schwartz's book, I didn't realize the passion and grandeur of his exploits both in and out of the mountains. From life as a pioneering rock climber, to the struggles of a medical pioneer ahead of his time, as well as the previously unrevealed details about life in the inner circle of Kennedy's Camelot, Schwartz has taken a climbing story and elevated it to a higher plane. I started reading it from a climber's perspective and finished with a vision of a man with a most extraordinary life, told through this book in the most compelling way."
Robert Mads Anderson, Everest Guide and author of Seven Summits Solo and To Everest Via Antarctica

"Beautiful and touching. Hats off to a great piece of writing!"
Matt Samet, Rock and Ice Contributing Senior Editor

Acclaim for the Man

"A real friend."
Katharine Hepburn,
in a 1996 note to the author.

"I wish I could have known you years ago."
John F. Kennedy to Hans Kraus in 1962,
overheard and reported by his personal secretary, Evelyn Lincoln.

"Even though I have never met Hans Kraus. I feel as though I know him...*Every* climber at the Gunks knows Hans."
Arthur Sulzberger, Jr.,
Contemporary Shawangunks rock climber.

"Hans has always been a hero of mine."
Yvon Chouinard, Founder and President of Patagonia, Inc,
legendary rock climber.

"You will always remain on the top of the list by those who dearly loved and worked with the President."
John F. Kennedy's Chief White House doctor, George Burkley,
in a note to Hans Kraus, dated 11/30/63.

"An aura of energy about the man...Sizzle and spunk, exuberance, confidence, great physical strength, high-voltage enthusiasm, bursting vitality."
Sports Illustrated feature article, 6/15/81.

"*Cojones* so big, he needed a bag to carry them around."
James P. McCarthy, past American Alpine Club president.

"(Kraus' routes) represent great moments in American climbing. They are proud, committing and were, for their respective periods, groundbreaking."
Rock and Ice Magazine, 12/04.

PREFACE

✦

The Side of a Cliff, Two Hundred Feet above the Ground

✦

1965, Shawangunk Mountains, New York State

He was hanging there, in the air.

Air was everywhere. Above, below, ahead. To the left and right. Seemingly against logic, wherever he looked—hundreds of feet of sheer, open air. The wind whipped at his face, hawks swooped below his feet, and he felt serene and at peace.

At sixty, he was very much in his prime. After all, how many men—of any age—could crank a one-arm pull-up or full split like he still could? Or climb such a fearsome, overhanging, exposed rock wall, such as the rock buttress from which he now dangled?

Steep and jutting sharply from the cliff, the buttress looked unscalable, unattainable; or, as the guidebook put it, like a journey "into the unknown." Perched on a hillside, to a climber dangling off its side, the buttress felt even higher than its footage, and colder, windier and wilder than anywhere else on the cliffs. And seemingly against logic, it offered complete exposure—air on four sides.

Experts warned: "Its 'psychological grade' is several notches harder than its climbing difficulty grade." What did they say, then, to the sixty-year-old man dangling from its side?

He had been the first, nearly a quarter of century before, to scale the rock buttress—wearing sneakers, tied to a hemp rope little better than laundry line. Years passed before anyone else dared try. Even after climbers had specialized, safer gear, the buttress remained a climbing test piece, entitling bragging rights.

One climbing expert shook his head and marveled, "His *cojones* are so big, he needs a bag to carry them in." The man's reputation continued to grow with the years. When climbers spotted him on the hiking trail below the cliffs, they murmured and pointed in excitement.

"There he goes, that's him."

"Is it? Are you sure?"

"Yes, yes, see!"

They looked closer.

"It is! It is!"

"That's Hans Kraus!"

Yet climbing was just one part of Kraus' remarkable story. During the week, Hans Kraus led a separate, equally remarkable life outside the mountains, pushing into other unknown territory.

Twenty-nine years later, it was 1994, and I was recently elected to the American Alpine Club Board of Directors and wrote regularly for adventure magazines. When the climbing magazine *Rock and Ice* asked me to feature Hans Kraus (1905–1996), I was thrilled.

A Shawangunks climber myself, I knew that the 5'6" Kraus was a giant in the sport of rock climbing; first in his native Dolomites in Italy, then, after moving to the U.S. in 1938, in the world famous Shawankgunk Mountains of New York. What I did not know was that Kraus was also a giant outside of the mountains as well.

In 1963, *Time Magazine* had compared Kraus to three towering scientific luminaries who changed human existence forever—the inventors of the polio vaccine, Jonas Salk and Albert Sabin, and the inventor of the smallpox vaccine, Edward Jenner. So what was Kraus' remarkable medical breakthrough?

The answer is startlingly simple:

Exercise!

It was Kraus, based on his landmark research during the 1940's at Columbia Presbyterian Hospital in Manhattan, who first linked exercise and health. *Exercise,* he would explain to dubious audiences, *plays a crucial role in almost all aspects of health. Lack of exercise causes many diseases,* he would warn, citing obesity, high blood pressure, heart disease, arthritis, depression, diabetes, back pain, and many cancers. *Exercise even cures some of these diseases,* he would continue to skeptical looks, occasional guffaws, sometimes outright laughter.

Kraus also sadly predicted the current U.S. health crisis—epidemic obesity, which is poised in 2005 to replace smoking as the leading cause of preventable death[1] and to shrink the U.S. population lifespan for the first time in 200 years.[2]

In the 1950's, Kraus created sensation, controversy, and headlines, as he exhorted Americans to exercise. While Kraus is largely unknown to Americans today—except for thousands and thousands of adoring former patients and fellow climbers—in his day, Kraus was big news. When President Eisenhower invited Kraus to the White House in 1955, the event was covered by the major newspapers and magazines. (*Sports Illustrated*, for instance, ran a feature article, separate cover story, and two-page photographic spread). Throughout the rest of the decade, Kraus and his fitness campaign were front-page news—even the *Sports Illustrated* cover of August 1957.

Yet not only did Americans resist Kraus' exercise message—painfully clear today—amazingly, many declared themselves insulted. Some even went as far as to call Kraus a Nazi! (Ironic, considering that the Trieste-born Kraus was part Jewish, and fled the Nazis for New York.)

But until Kraus retired at age eighty-nine, his practice boomed. Kraus treated many for free, as well as a blue chip roster of Nobel scientists, Olympic athletes, royalty, millionaires, movie stars, and U.S. presidents, like John F. Kennedy. In fact, the complete story of Kennedy's back has never before been told, since Kraus had never previously let anyone read his White House medical records on Kennedy.

While researching the *Rock and Ice* article, I realized that a 3,000-word magazine piece could never capture Hans Kraus' complex and remarkable life. I vowed to write it as a book. My motivation, as readers will see in the book's conclusion, was as much personal as literary. But first I had to make sense of Kraus' seemingly two distinct lives in the mountains and medicine.

In the course of the ten years of researching and writing this book, I came to see that they were, in fact, two halves of a seamless whole. The glue was a searing boyhood tragedy when Kraus was sixteen years old. From it, he drew the strength to face his wealthy, domineering father, define meaning in his life, and live life on his own terms.

Pushing into the unknown, both in the mountains and in medicine, was Kraus' way of making sense of what had happened and dealing with his lifelong guilt: In the mountains, the physical and emotional commitment of hard climbing brought Kraus numbing relief from his emotional pain. In medicine, the satisfaction of healing others' physical pain brought him the closest he knew he could ever come to finding something like atonement and redemption.

When Hans Kraus set off at age ninety, on that last, ultimate journey into the unknown, he died a fulfilled man, in his own bed, surrounded by his family and wife of thirty-eight years, at peace, in control, knowing he touched the lives of thousands and thousands and thousands of people for the better.

Throughout it all, he never lost his trademark wit, verve, passion, or sense of purpose. Or his youthful zest of meeting challenges head-on, chin-up, eye-to-eye, with dignity and unswerving honesty. Hans Kraus led a remarkable life, and he did it with a remarkable soul.

Not to mention that bag of remarkable *cojones*.

PART I
EUROPE 1878–1938

1

Rudi's Son

✦

1878–1921, The Hapsburg Empire

In the sunset glow of the Hapsburg Empire, at the turn of the last century, a young man named Rudi Kraus sought his fortune. Nicknamed *Schöne Rudi* in his youth for his striking dark looks and strapping physique—*schöne* in German means beautiful—he was coming of age during exciting and unsettling times.

The century of Rudi's birth saw more sweeping, fundamental changes than during all the previous centuries of human history combined. Telephones, telegraphs, photographs, and phonographs. Steam engines, automobiles and electricity. X-rays that peered into the body and Freudian analysis that peered into the mind. New ideas such as Darwinism that rethought man's place in nature, Marxism and Socialism that rethought man's place in society, and thermodynamics and electro-magneticism that rethought man's place in the universe.

Ambitious young people felt that the rules of old Europe were changing and that new opportunities were out there for the smart, bold or lucky. Rudi Kraus intended to be among them.

Born in 1878 in a small town in the Sudentenland, Rudi had more than good looks going for him. An early championship bike racer, Rudi had won a race from Trieste to Vienna peddling the fashionable "high wheeled bike"—the type sporting a huge front wheel and small rear wheel. But Rudi was as ambitious as he was athletic. Rudi's father owned a grocery store in Pilsen, but Rudi had bigger ideas. After high school, Rudi migrated to Fiume, a bigger city with bigger potential. There he found a job as a junior shipping clerk, saved his money, and dreamed of starting his own company.

As it was common practice for university students and young professionals in Fiume, Rudi rented a spare room in the house of a local family of shopkeepers. His landlords, the Schlessingers, had a young daughter of marriageable age. Ella also happened to be smart, lively, practical, and pretty—all in all, an ideal help-mate for a man like Rudi. It didn't take long for the two young people to fall in love. Rudi and Ella married in 1904, and the next year moved to the "big city"—Trieste.

Sometimes described as a cross between Vienna and Venice, the beautiful and moody Adriatic port city of Trieste was basking in its heyday as the crossroads of the Hapsburg Empire. A designated "free port," Trieste was the commercial hub for all of central Europe and Asia. Like other great cities in other times, it was prosperous and bustling with possibility.

Karl Marx derided Trieste as a capitalist center teeming with a motley crew of speculators.[3] But Trieste could happily thumb its nose back: Renowned for polit-ical freedom and religious tolerance,[1] clean, safe and socially progressive, the city was a proud melting pot of Italians, Germans, English, French, Greeks, Arme-nians, Jews, and whoever else in *Mitteleuropa* yearned for better fortunes and brighter futures. Among them were Rudi and Ella Kraus.

The turn of the century was the time and Trieste was a place tailor-made for Rudi, who was willing to put in long hours: six days a week, plus Sunday morn-ings, too. Rudi soon acquired the style to accompany the substance. Even in the height of the sticky Trieste summers, Rudi was immaculately groomed; sporting the tie, jacket, and boater hat proper for a Trieste gentleman. As shrewd as he was hard working, Rudi managed to win valuable government contracts in a short, five-year span. Soon Rudi's firm, *Marittima*, was among the leaders in Trieste's shipping industry.

Rudi's family grew with his fortune. The oldest, Hans, was born in 1905, fol-lowed by Sisi in 1910. (The youngest, Franz, would be born in 1916 after the family moved to Zurich.) The children were robust, but Rudi and Ella worried about the health of their young brood all the same.

They had good cause. In this era before vaccines and antibiotics, childhood mortality was tragically common. Parents on any continent dreaded a long list of terrifying, highly contagious, often fatal diseases—spinal meningitis, rheumatic fever, scarlet fever, whooping cough, encephalitis, diphtheria, cholera, smallpox, measles, influenza, the "croup," or just plain diarrhea. Statistics from America reflect a sad, universal reality: In the year Hans was born, a baby in Chicago had a twenty-five percent chance of dying before his fifth birthday.[4] The grim odds

---

1.   While anti-Semitism was widespread throughout Europe in the nineteenth century, it was virtually non-existent in Trieste. Many prominent Trieste families were Jew-ish, who also made up an unusually high percent of the city's leaders.

affected rich and poor alike. Both children of American turn-of-the-century president, William McKinley, died by age three.

Terrified of illness, Rudi and Ella kept Hans away from other children and hired private tutors to teach him at home until he was eleven. His parents' intentions were good, but as a child, Hans felt apart, isolated, and constrained.

Earliest memories are supposed to be telling. Hans' earliest memory was when he was four, sitting between his father and mother in their two-horse carriage, their landauer, while the family was driving to a flying exhibition of the renowned French aerialist, Peugeot. Some other child might have felt snug and nurtured, nestled between his parents, listening to the clop-clop of the horses as the carriage gently swayed from side to side. Hans felt restless and restrained, as he looked outside at the open fields and longed to run free.

While Rudi was fiercely protective and controlling with his children, he was equally determined that they grow up tough and wise to life's harsh possibilities. As he saw it, even as the mountains provided relaxation and recreation, they could also teach his children a valuable moral lesson. An accomplished hiker in his own right, Rudi decided that he would take Hans for his first hike in the mountains when his son was five. After a short while, the young boy asked his father for water.

"You are not thirsty," Rudi told him. They walked some more. A little further, Hans asked Rudi for food.

"You are not hungry," Rudi told him. They continued walking. A little further, Hans said he was hot and wanted to rest.

"You are not hot, and you are not tired," Rudi informed him.

The adult Kraus appreciated his father's lessons, and would later say, "This has become my modus operandi in life and it has served me well: My father taught me that until you reach your goal, you don't complain; you don't mind discomfort or inconvenience. If you can't keep going, keep going anyway."

But it was a tough hike for the child.

Hans' world, along with the rest of the planet, was about to change. By the spring of 1914 the clouds of war were gathering, dark and grim on the horizon. Many contemporary pundits insisted there was no danger: Europe had grown too symbiotic, too sane—they explained in speeches and writing—too smart.

Rudi wasn't so sure.

Using his shipping contacts, Rudi made arrangements to move his business and family to Zurich if war were to break out. Then on June 28, Serbian and

Bosnian anarchists assassinated the heir to the Austro-Hungarian crown, Archduke Franz Ferdinand, and his wife Sophie while the royal couple was on their way to inspect troops in Sarajevo, the provincial capital of Serbia. The Great War was to start in the backyard of the Kraus family.

Amid great pomp, the nation's largest imperial battleship carried the coffins draped in black cloth back to Vienna for burial. One of the stops along the way was Trieste. Rudi and Ella, with the rest of Trieste, lined the streets to watch the funeral cortege, and hung black crepe from their windows in respectful mourning of their dead royals.

Shortly afterward, Rudi packed the family suitcases, lined them up in the hall, and insisted his family wear their travel clothes all the time, even to bed. Not incidentally, Rudi also transferred many assets—illegally—into Swiss banks. When war was officially declared on August 12, thick fighting soon enveloped Trieste. But the Kraus family was ready. They picked up their suitcases and drove to the train station.

As the train pulled away, Hans looked out the window at the Austrian flag flying in a breeze. Soldiers were standing erect at attention, singing the Austro-Hungarian anthem, "God Save our Emperor, Austria will stand forever."

Kraus later said dryly, "After World War I, 'eternal Austria' was carved up into different nationalities and the Empire existed no more. That gave me a good indication of how short a period of time 'forever' could be."

At first, Hans was upset over leaving Trieste. Soon, however, he realized that Zurich was even closer to the mountains, and he was delighted with his new home. After school, he scrambled by himself on the nearby hills, coming back bruised and scratched, to his great satisfaction.

That winter, Rudi took his family on a hiking trip to the Garmisch section of the Alps. While Ella stayed in the mountain hut with Sisi, Hans joined Rudi and two family friends on a climb of the 13,000-foot peak, Vreni Gartle.

The party left at dawn. Roped together, they traveled across a large glacier, scrambling up a small rock chimney, traversing a ridge, and hiking up to the summit. From the top of the mountain, Hans looked over the valley below, and gazed at layers of surrounding mountains fading into the horizon. "Wave after wave of mountains," the ninety-year-old Kraus recalled, smiling in utter happiness at the memory. "I knew the mountains were where I belonged."

Life for the Kraus family in Zurich continued to be comfortable and privileged, but as Hans grew older he came increasingly under Rudi's ever-critical eye. Rudi wanted to ensure that his oldest son spoke several languages. For Hans' English tutoring, Rudi hired a charming young Irishman with literary aspirations.

During the day, James Joyce taught English to Rudi, Ella, and other wealthy families. At night Joyce labored over his masterpiece, *Ulysses* (which would be published in 1922, but already, Joyce had come out with his short stories, *Dubliners*, and a volume of poetry). Without any inkling that he was keeping company with a man who would become one of the world's literary giants, Hans found James Joyce to be an inspiring teacher. A talented linguist, Joyce devised entertaining drills for learning grammar and conveyed a contagious enthusiasm for the classics. Throughout his life, Kraus would always be able to recite by heart long passages from Dante's *Inferno* that he had learned for his lessons with Joyce.

Twice a week, Hans took his lessons at Joyce's apartment on the Zurich-Berg, where Joyce lived with his common-law wife Nora, his son Giorgio, and his daughter Lucia. Joyce, who was already suffering from the eye problems that would blind him in the last decade of his life, often bathed his eyes with chamomile tea, which Lucia carried to her father in a teacup.

When Hans asked him one day about writing, the older Kraus later remembered, Joyce passed along advice. "It's like writing a chord in music, Hans. Suppose I write in Chapter One about a man who has kidney disease, and sometime later in the book I write about a person who is kicked in the kidney, and then later about someone who eats kidneys. Now I've made a chord."

Joyce also instructed the young boy in the importance of observing people around him. It was another lesson the older Kraus never forgot and would apply well. Patients and other doctors would routinely shake their heads in astonishment at how much insight Kraus gleaned by observing a patient. But it began with Joyce; the creator of Ulysses also helped write pages in the character of Kraus.

"You must observe people all the time," the adult Kraus recalled Joyce advising the young boy, "When I travel on a trolley car or walk down the street, I always carry a little notebook. I write down items like, 'Obese woman with flowered hat hugs pocketbook,' or, 'Gaunt man fiddles with cigarette but doesn't light it.' I have millions of little episodes like that which I later use in my writing."

Kraus loved recounting his days with Joyce, and inevitably, his listener would make a respectful comment, along the lines of, "Amazing! Just think, James Joyce taught you English!" This was the kind of conversational gambit that Kraus loved. He would exaggerate his accent and quip, mischievously, "Yah, but he didn't do zush a goot chob, dit he!"

When World War I ended, the Austro-Hungarian Empire broke up into several small nation states. In one fell swoop, the new geographic and political landscape knocked away Trieste's former commercial advantages and spelled an end to the city's former glory.

Rudi decided to transfer Marittima's headquarters from Zurich to Vienna, although he wisely kept his money in Swiss banks. It was yet another shrewd move on Rudi's part, which would preserve his fortune from the devastating hyperinflation of the Austrian economy in the 1920's.

During this period, as the Kraus family fortune continued to grow, Hans' life as a teenager was privileged, and in many ways, idyllic. The Kraus family lived in a mansion formerly owned by a Hapsburg, staffed by many servants, in the elite district near the Shoenbrunn Palace. There was a music room, an exercise room, a library, and a dining room so large that the table seated twenty-four. After school, Hans played in the surrounding woods and took lessons in music and sports. On weekends, the family hiked or skied.

And Hans had a secure future, which his father carefully orchestrated. Proud of building Marittima from scratch, Rudi was determined that his oldest son would follow in his footsteps. To help prepare Hans for his future business career, Rudi decided that Hans should learn to type, and that Rudi should teach him. Kraus recalled, of those times, "My father would dictate business letters to me, and invariably, I made mistakes. He used to be so rough on me. I dreaded those typing sessions so much that in all my life, I never learned to type."

Nonetheless, Rudi was not a man to be deterred. Rudi had it all set. Hans would learn typing. Then Hans would learn the shipping business from the ground up, as Rudi had done. And one day, Rudi told his son proudly, Marittima would be his.

The only problem with Rudi's grand plan was Hans.

2

Death in the Mountains

✦

Summer of 1921, The Austrian Alps

When Hans reached high school, Rudi made sure his son was enrolled mostly in business courses. But Hans was bored and his grades were poor. Not one to let details get in the way of his desire, Rudi hired various private tutors for Hans. None did much good, except one.

Dr. Schmidt, Hans' science tutor, was a recent medical school graduate and a dashing, handsome former lieutenant in the mountain troops. To Hans, it seemed there was everything about his new mentor to adore and emulate. And to Hans' surprise, he soon found he enjoyed science. Kraus said, "I started studying science much more than necessary, and began to read medical books whenever I could. I grew convinced I wanted to study medicine, but I hadn't the courage to tell my father."

It was the summer of 1921. That fall, Hans would embark on his business career with Marittima. In what Rudi and Ella intended as sixteen-year-old Hans' last carefree moment of youth, they agreed he could spend the summer hiking and climbing with his friends, at a summer camp for teenagers called the Wandervogel, in the Austrian Alps.

As an adult, late in his life, Kraus had little interest in photos. But it was different that summer. At the Wandervogel camp, Hans constantly took photos with a small Kodak camera he had received as a Christmas gift. He shot photos of the hut where the teenagers stayed; the mountains and lawns outside; and various scenes inside the hut, including hiking shoes and gear neatly lined up on shelves, and guitars and ropes hanging side by side on wooden pegs.

Hans also shot photos of his friends, posed and candid, picnicking and at play. The photos froze them in their moment of vitality, when in the sepia tones of the early 1920's, they were young and infinite possibilities stretched ahead of them. In one, there was Hans' good friend, Marcus; dark and wiry, in the fuzziness of the eighty-year-old photos, he looked older than eighteen. In another, there was Hans, handsome and confident, with thick, dark, wavy hair and muscular legs.

Even though Hans was the youngest at camp, the climbs were easy for him, and he chafed to try something harder. He suggested to Marcus, "Let's make a climb alone, something hard, just the two of us." Marcus was thrilled. The boys decided to try a peak called the Block Kogel.

The boys set off for the Block Kogel on a beautiful morning in high spirits. Typical teenagers, they started by racing each other uphill from the mountain hut. Kraus commented dryly, remembering, "Our equipment was really terrific." Hans wore espadrilles, and Marcus wore socks. The boys carried a rope, but didn't have pitons or any other way of anchoring the rope to the rock.

At the base of the mountain, Hans tied into one end of the rope, Marcus into the other. The boys agreed that if the leader fell, the other would try to catch the fall by yanking the rope tight and bracing against the rock. The problem was that neither Hans nor Marcus would be anchored to the rock.

It was an absurdly dangerous arrangement. But they were boys with a sense of immortality and a thrill of pushing limits. Looking back, Kraus said, "It was unconscionable; completely irresponsible. But you do stupid things when you're young."

It turned out not to matter. Hans, as his wont, led every pitch. The boys climbed so quickly that it wasn't even noon when they summitted and rappelled down to a ridge connecting a neighboring peak. From there, they congratulated each other, rested, and basked in the glow of a successful climb.

As they caught their breath, the boys looked across the ridge to the Pluider Kogel, higher and steeper than the Block Kogel. It looked enticingly close, and as far as they knew, it was still unclimbed. The day had barely begun. There was plenty of time.

Before packing to leave, Hans pulled his camera out of his rucksack and snapped several photos of Marcus on the ridge. Then they set off for the Pluider Kogel.

On the Pluider Kogel, as previously, Hans led every pitch. He didn't mind the extra risk that comes with leading a climb; in fact he exhilarated in it.

If a leader falls, the fall is likely to be long, and often hard. The rule of thumb is that the leader falls twice the distance to the closest point where the rope is attached to the rock, plus an additional couple of feet due to rope stretch—assuming that the crude ropes of Han's youth didn't snap.

A lead climber who falls ten feet up from a belay point could easily fall nearly thirty feet—and hit the rock hard. In contrast, when a climber following the pitch falls, it is usually short—maybe merely inches, or a foot or two—since the rope runs above his head. And often the fall is soft, with little danger of injury. However, it is the leader who is in charge of the climb, who makes virtually all the decisions, and according to the consensus in climbing, enjoys most of the emotional and psychic rewards.

With Hans leading, the boys continued to make good time. However, on the last pitch before the summit, when he reached the end of the rope, the only spot Hans could find to belay was unusually cramped. When Marcus climbed up to the spot, the boys found it awkward to switch places to recoil the rope.

Hans was tied into the rope end that lay at the bottom of the heap of rope. Marcus was tied into the rope end that lay at the top. It seemed far easier for Marcus to climb first. For the first time, Marcus started up on lead.

The rock above bulged out slightly. Hans soon lost sight of Marcus as he surmounted the bulge and climbed higher, although Hans could still hear Marcus, and could tell by the rope paying out that Marcus was making steady progress upwards.

Kraus recalled, "I leaned my head against the rock. The sun was hot. I was getting a little tired. My mouth was dry. Marcus seemed to have gotten into difficult rock, because I heard him pant. And then he called down, 'It's very hard, but I'll try it. In a few more meters, I'll be at the next ledge, and then it's easy going to the top.'"

Kraus paused before continuing. "All of a sudden I heard a scream. Then a terrific crash. A rock must have broken loose. Blocks of rock were falling down. The rock must have been overhanging, because the blocks fell far out from me. Then there was a smell I'll never forget: Nauseating, acrid, like sulfur.

"I saw a rock falling down. And then I saw Marcus falling down, too, straight over my head.

"I called out to him, 'I can hold you, Marcus; I can hold you!'

"But the rope kept pulling through my hands, pulling through until maybe ninety feet of rope was out, then 100 feet; and it kept pulling. Then the end of the rope yanked out of my hands, and fell down the mountain. Then I was alone on the mountain."

To descend a mountain without a rope is dangerous and difficult. It is always much harder to see footholds from above than below; much harder to climb down than up. But Hans tried not to let himself dwell on this, lest he move nervously and slip. One thing was clear to him: If he was to get down the mountain alive, he had to remain calm, confident, and in control. Other than that, he had no idea of what to do.

He knew his situation was terrible. He tried not to think about what might have happened to Marcus.

But even as he tried to push the thoughts out of his mind, they kept crowding in, as he stood there alone, on a narrow mountain ledge, stranded several hundred feet off the ground. [1] All he could keep thinking, again and again, was surely he wasn't meant to die today? Not him, and not on a beautiful summer day like this? Surely if he was going to die, wouldn't he know it beforehand? Wouldn't something big and momentous happen to let him know, to mark such a huge occasion taking place on the planet: He would see the skies darken, thunder crash, lightning flash, epic rain and ice storms pour down.

But as the teenager looked out from his belay ledge, high on the mountain, he felt the soothing warmth of the sun on his skin, and saw peaceful blue skies, with puffy clouds floating softly by. He couldn't help think: Death couldn't possibly come so quickly, without warning, without reason, on a day like today, for someone so young and strong as he was?

And then he remembered: Or for Marcus, for that matter? Surely Marcus was okay; surely his fall wasn't that bad. Maybe he imagined what he saw. Maybe it was a joke. Maybe it was the glare of the sun. Maybe, he thought hopefully, remembering stories he heard from his parents after they returned from a trip visiting the pyramids in Egypt—for they were avid travelers, like many wealthy Triestine—maybe, maybe it was all a mirage.

Hans remembered being a nine-year-old boy in his parent's house in Trieste, looking into a mirror in his parent's bedroom, and suddenly being struck by the knowledge that he was separate from his parents, that he was alive, and that one day, as incredible as it seemed to him, one day he would die, really die. It was a terrifying realization for the boy. For a long time, he tried to avoid that mirror.

---

1.   The boys' original plan for getting down the mountain was that after they summitted, they would either rappel, or else find an easier, less steep and technical route they would hike down.

He knew he couldn't keep thinking like this. He wouldn't get down if he did. He took a deep breath, shook out his arms, and willfully emptied his mind so it was blank of all thought.

Of the terrible day on the Pluider Kogel, Kraus said, "It was like I was under self-hypnosis. I had the strange feeling it wasn't me who was there, but someone else. It was as though I was sitting on one of the other peaks, looking down, telling this other person what to do: 'You need to throw down your rucksack, now your ice axe, now you do this, you do that, and so on.' I did these things without thinking."

Hans didn't remember much more about his descent. Somehow, he made his way down the mountain. As he drew closer to the base of the mountain, he could make out the form of his rucksack, and a little further away, the ice axe he had thrown down from his belay ledge near the summit. Then he noticed his friend. Marcus was lying nearby quietly, as though waiting for him.

"Marcus was lying on his back with his head down the slope," Kraus remembered. "Or what was left of his head. Everything was bashed in. There was blood everywhere. I called his name, and pressed my ear to his chest. There was no sound, no heartbeat, no movement. His skin was warm from the sun."

Kraus closed his eyes as he remembered, seventy-five years before. "I can still see that day like it was yesterday. The blue sky. The white clouds."

Death had come after all on that perfect summer day, but it hadn't picked Hans, but Marcus, who happened to be the leader on a section of cliff with loose rock, and who happened to be leading because his section of rope came out on top. It was almost as though the boys had unwittingly drawn lots. And nature hadn't even bothered to look up and notice.

It was growing late, and Hans knew he had to leave. The most dangerous part was behind him, but he had a long way to go to reach camp before dark. After a few hours of hiking, he reached a small lake, where he stopped to drink deeply. For the first time he noticed his hands. They were one big oozing wound. The rope had burned off the skin and cut down to bone.

It was twilight when Hans neared the mountain hut he had left that morning with Marcus. In the soft, dream-like light of the gloaming, he could make out the figures of three of his Wandervogel friends sitting outside on a bench joking. As he walked closer, they started to shout a raucous hello, then stopped, and drew silent, as they saw him alone, bloody and distraught. "They looked quizzically, then the awful question came into their eyes. They didn't even have to say anything. I had nothing to say. I just nodded," Kraus remembered.

The next day they walked down to the closest village and reported the accident to the gendarmes. Kraus recalled, "At the police station, I was questioned to make sure I hadn't killed Marcus, pushed him off the mountain or something. It was a village holiday, with lots of merry-making, but everywhere we went, people grew quiet, because they had heard something horrible had happened."

Hans had to lead his friends and the police back to the spot at the base of the Pluider Kogel. There, as he left it, was his rucksack and his camera, with the pictures he had taken of Marcus the day before. There too was Marcus' body. The older Kraus recalled sadly, "It was another perfect summer day. More blue skies and sunshine."

The gendarmes had brought a hay basket for Marcus' body, but the basket was small, and Marcus' feet dangled over the side. Whenever the cart hit a bump, Marcus' feet beat a tattoo against the side of the basket. The next day, they buried Marcus by the village church, as Kraus recalled, in a "very beautiful spot by a waterfall. The villagers brought flowers, and we strew them on his coffin."

For the rest of his life, Kraus would break his life in two parts: "Before Marcus" and "After Marcus."

3

Scars

✦

1921–1922, Trieste, Vienna and the Austrian Alps

Marcus' death was always with Kraus, although not because of physical scars. Those healed surprisingly fast.

The injuries from Marcus' death gave Hans his first opportunity to rebel against the medical establishment. After the village doctor examined Hans' torn hands, he applied heavy bandages up to the teenager's elbows, and shook his head gravely. "You need to leave these bandages on for at least several weeks. Try to move your hands as little as possible. You want them to be still so they can heal as best they can. And have your parents take you to a doctor in Vienna to remove the bandages.

"But even so, I'm sorry to tell you this, young man, but your cuts are too deep. Your hands will never heal completely and you will never regain full use of your hands."

Hans stared at the doctor in shock. Never heal? His hands useless? Both of them? He was only sixteen. How could this be happening to him? How could he do his sports? How could he climb?

He didn't want to believe the doctor. He refused to believe the doctor. Maybe he was just being a stubborn teenager, blind to reality. But the doctor had to be wrong, he had to be, he told himself. An inner voice called out: *Believe him, you fool. He's a doctor, you're just a young idiot.*

But a line-up of other inner voices quickly chimed in: *You do sports all the time,* one kept insisting, *think, think, haven't you've grown convinced that the body is meant to move...needs to move?* Another one butted in, *yeah, what about common sense? If the body needs to move, then wouldn't movement be needed for health,*

huh, doesn't that follow? Then another: *And hey, what about your athlete's intu-
ition? Isn't it telling you that if you need movement for health, then you also need
movement for healing?*

The thoughts kept pushing around in his mind as Hans returned home from
the Wandervogel camp, distraught over his bandaged, crippled hands and griev-
ing for his dead friend Marcus. He couldn't do anything about Marcus. What
about his hands? After a few days furiously crying and staring at his bandages, he
heard a new inner voice, louder than the others: *Anyway, what do you have to lose?
Think about that one! The doctor told you that your hands are permanently ruined
anyway. Why bother listening to him?*

What did he have to lose? The teenager decided to disregard the village doctor. Defiantly, in desperation, he prescribed his own treatment, not based on a
heavy cast, but on movement. He would bath his torn hands in warm salt water,
put them through gentle stretching several times a day, and undertake the unor-
thodox therapy of learning to play the guitar—an instrument he wanted to try
anyway—because of the finger and hand limbering motions.

In a few weeks Hans's hands were healed. It also turned out that the village
doctor was even more than wrong.

Not only did Hans regain full use of his hands, but for the rest of his life, he
was known for remarkable hand strength. Climbing partners continuously commented about it. One of Kraus' last patients was shocked to see the eighty-eight
year old doctor deliver his trademark "trigger point injections" with such stunning hand force that she doubted most thirty-year old doctors could duplicate.
And when *Sports Illustrated* ran Kraus' obituary in March of 1996, it titled it,
"The Hands of Hans."

When Hans returned to Vienna, for all of his difficulties with Rudi, it didn't
occur to Hans to hide the story from his parents, even if he had been able to
explain away the foot-high bandages he had come home with. His parents' loving
reception surprised him, and he was grateful that on top of his guilt he didn't
have to deal with grief and disappointment from his parents. Or from Marcus'
parents.

"In a way, I was very lucky," Kraus explained. "Marcus' mother had died years
before. When I got back to our camp, I found a telegram for Marcus telling him
that his father had died suddenly." And, it turned out that Marcus had no other
relative, except a distant uncle. A few months after the accident, Marcus' uncle
came by the Kraus house, asking for Hans. "He wanted to find out about that
day. I told him what happened. Then he went away and I never heard from him
again." Kraus said.

Even before Marcus' death, Hans had thought he wanted to be a doctor, but afterward he knew for sure. He saw it as a way to help people, and to atone for Marcus. But when Hans finally screwed up his courage to tell Rudi, he found that his father wasn't about to give up his dynastic dreams easily—especially since doctoring in that time and place was neither particularly prestigious nor well paid. Rudi insisted, "You don't even know what my work is really about. You don't even have to stay here in Vienna. It will take your mind off what happened. You can go to Trieste, work in my office, there, and see for yourself. Someday, you will take my place."

It is always hard to confront a parent, but particularly so when you are an emotionally devastated sixteen-year-old, and your father is someone as determined and imposing as Rudi Kraus. That September, Hans dutifully obeyed his father.

From the first day, Hans found the office work tedious and meaningless. In his memory, everything about that fall is bleak—the weather, the countryside, his mood, his work. Evenings in his small rented room he stayed up late writing depressing poetry and reading Otto Spengler's, *Decline of the West*, jotting in the book margins comments like, "The history of mankind does not seem more important than the history of rats."

Weekends were his salvation, when Hans hiked by himself in the countryside. One time, he found an abandoned tower on cliffs overlooking the Adriatic. Inside, stairs led up to the top, and there he found a small room. When Hans opened a window, he saw a foot-wide parapet outside below him. Edging his way slowly out onto it, he sat for some time, then cautiously stood up and pressed his back hard against the wall.

Finally, he inched forward, away from the wall. Then he took a deep breath, and inched forward again until he wasn't touching the wall, and his toes curled over the side.

He told himself his reasons were strictly practical—it would be good training, to overcome any fear of exposure he might have suffered from the accident with Marcus. He really should do this, he told himself.

But as he stood there on the parapet, he realized that he again thrilled to the height and exposure. And he realized, too; something else was going on. For the first time since the accident, he felt like his former self—confident, calm and in control. And he felt the first surge of happiness since the accident. And his first surge of hope.

He knew now he still belonged in the mountains. And that somehow, although it wasn't going to be easy, he would find a way to live with his guilt.

The fall of 1921 passed miserably for Hans in Trieste, but he dreaded returning home to Vienna for the Kraus family's annual Christmas celebration. It was a time Hans usually loved: the big house was decorated festively for the holidays; Ella and the cook turned out enormous quantities of rich Viennese pastries with chocolate, chestnuts and custards. The family sang carols and played music around the Christmas tree; everyone in the Kraus family was musical—Hans and Franz played the violin, Ella the piano, Rudi the cello, and Sisi the piano.

The problem was that Hans couldn't put off confronting his father any longer. Before the family began their celebration, Hans summoned up the courage to ask Rudi to take a walk with him. As the snow fell gently upon them, Hans told his father that he had tried working in the office, but he hated business and still wanted to be a doctor.

His father's reaction was everything Hans had feared: a mix of outrage over what he was convinced was his son's immaturity and shortsighted stubbornness, and also bitter disappointment over the dashing of his own long held, personal dream to build a prosperous business that he would pass proudly on to the next generation.

"You stupid boy, you'll see, you'll starve as a doctor!" his father had shouted, furious at Hans. "You'll get no help from me! If you want it, you do it on your own! You'll see! You'll starve!"

It was a very sad Christmas. Hans' mother cried, and his father wouldn't speak to anyone for weeks. For months, Rudi walked around tight-faced and grim.

The next year was equally bleak. Hans hadn't taken the liberal arts and science courses that he needed for entrance into the University of Vienna medical school. He could go back to night school, but this cost money, which wasn't forthcoming from Rudi. So Hans got a day job as a translator in a car export business to pay for his evening classes. That year, it seemed to Hans that he did nothing but work during the day and study at night.

But there was a bright side. Hans loved night school, and particularly any course in science.

Kraus said, "I really worked my ass off, I must say. At the end of the year, when I brought home my report card to my father, I showed him: 'A,' 'A,' 'A,' 'A.' In every course, I got an 'A.' Literature, algebra, Latin, whatever. When my father saw these examination results, he was overwhelmed. Finally, he realized that becoming a doctor was something I wanted badly. He still thought I would starve, but he relented, and accepted my decision. To this day, that is one of the things I'm proudest of."

4

Dashing Young Herr Doktor Kraus

◆

1922–1930, Vienna

Hans Kraus was now happily studying at the University of Vienna medical school: Looking at him then, you see little of a young man beset by fears or doubts. Kraus in his twenties cut a dashing figure—handsome, intense, and literally *dashing* too. It seemed that Kraus was perpetually in motion; dashing between classes and the gym—for Kraus always worked out, no matter how long his days—and dashing sometimes to a concert or the opera.

A snapshot of Kraus taken during this period might catch him dashing about on his motorcycle—his usual mode of transportation, even for house calls or getting into the mountains to ski or climb on precious weekend free time. Kraus joked that he made the first "motorcycle ascent" of many alpine roads. Climbing partners sitting behind him gripped the seat, eyes big. For all his life, Kraus was a notoriously and self-admittedly abominable driver.

Or you might occasionally catch Kraus in a street fight. He was in many when he was young—real punching, boxing, and brawling slugfests. What exactly spurred the fights was hard to say, but "I was very aggressive when I was young," Kraus admitted. "Maybe it was because I was short. A lot of short men tend to be aggressive. But who knows now what I fought over? Maybe it was something someone said. Maybe over a woman. One time after I moved to New York, I was leaving an army-navy store where I bought sneakers for climbing, and I got into a fight with a man because I didn't like the way he looked at me."

Fighting was one thing, dueling was a different story. Although illegal, dueling was fashionable among contemporary blue-blooded university fraternity boys. Kraus thought the whole thing ridiculous. "Acchh!" he protested, "There was a

20

whole traditional rigmarole about it. The guy who felt he had been 'affronted,' usually because of some trivial slight or misunderstanding, would announce his challenge to a duel to the other guy with great pomp and flourish, sending his glove to the offending party. For me, if I were angry at someone, I'd just punch the guy in the nose."

Nonetheless, Kraus took part in two duels because friends asked him to be their "second." He agreed, knowing that his medical skills would be valuable, because dueling was dangerous despite its stylized nature. Contestants carried sharp cavalry sabers capable of delivering fatal blows, and fought bare-chested without protection, only a black silk scarf wrapped so-chicly around their necks. Injuries were common, and small ones actively desired—dueling scars were considered sexy and boosted machismo.

In both of Kraus' duels, his friends were soon cut. Relieved, Kraus had grounds to stop the duels with honor on both sides. But when he took the duelists to the hospital, he made sure to report that their injuries were "cuts from glass" so no one, including Kraus, got into trouble with the police.

At medical school, Kraus was a good, but not outstanding student. Medical school was too theoretical for his taste. As much as Kraus loved medicine, there was nothing of the scientist in his personality, no yen to study knowledge for knowledge's own sake, no concern about adding to collective understanding or helping the human race in generations to come. His drive was *now*, to heal a specific person, *here, immediately*. Kraus was impatient to get into the real world and *do*, not just discuss it, or read about it.

The highlight of Kraus' medical school experience was summer vacation. Away from the city and Rudi's disapproving eyes, Kraus mixed his love of medicine with his love of mountains. Over the course of time he spent in the Alps, Kraus had befriended a farmer who offered him free room and board in return for Kraus' help with the farm chores. Kraus was in his element—haying, birthing calves, and herding cattle. The work was hard and physical, and Kraus loved it: Every morning, he ran up 2,000 vertical feet to herd the cattle to higher meadows, and in the evenings he drove them back down. In his spare time, Kraus hiked, picked edelweiss, and studied his medical texts.

Life during those summers was spare and simple. 'Simple,' when Kraus used the word, was high praise; as in, 'good, *simple* cooking' and '*simple*, plain accommodations.' Dinner etiquette was simple, too: Kraus took his meals with the other farmhands and the farmer's family. After the farmer's wife placed a big wooden bowl filled with stew in the middle of the table, everyone dipped his spoon into the bowl, family style.

Perhaps some other son of a wealthy businessman would flinch, but Kraus ate with gusto; just as he slept soundly at night in the same hut where the farmer housed his cattle in the winter.

When Kraus graduated from medical school in 1930, he was thrilled. From the beginning, he loved practicing medicine. "It was exactly everything I hoped for. There was action, the chance to heal, the chance to make a difference in a way that was important to people's lives," Kraus said.

Kraus shook his head with wonder at how far medicine progressed since that time. Medicine in Vienna was considered state of the art, and the hospital attached to the University of Vienna was the largest in Austria, and one of the largest in Europe. Kraus easily recalled the hospital layout: four rooms, one for x-rays, one for operating, and separate wards for men and women.

Kraus' first assignment was as an intern in the hospital's emergency department. The doctors had to be prepared to handle whatever came their way. As was customary, Kraus was first entrusted with the simplest tasks, like pulling teeth and suturing lacerations. Once he had proved himself, he moved on to more complex tasks. One time when Kraus was on duty in the emergency room, a man in critical condition was brought in with a pair of nail scissors embedded into his heart. It was clear that he needed open-heart surgery immediately if he were to have any chance of survival. As the most junior person on duty—nurse or doctor—Kraus knew he would be responsible for giving the anesthesia. The problem was that Kraus had never given anesthesia before.

The senior doctor gave Kraus on-the-spot training meant to reassure him. His instructions consisted of the following: "Don't worry, Kraus. It's very simple. Just remember: Chloroform, you drop. Ether, you pour."

Kraus watched as the chief surgeon cut open the patient's ribs, exposing the heart and an inch-long gash in the left ventricle. At one point during the operation, the chief surgeon told Kraus to slip his hand inside the chest cavity and hold the beating heart. Kraus was struck by the wonder and power of being a doctor. "Amazingly, the patient recovered within a short time, and did very well. He used to come back to visit us at the hospital at regular intervals," Kraus said.

Kraus remembered his first time on overnight call at the hospital. A new case had been admitted the night before, and Kraus was eager to impress the eminent Herr Professor Doktor. The next morning, Kraus proudly handed his mentor the battery of x-rays he had taken of the new patient, and launched into his diagnosis based on the x-rays. But instead of the glowing praise Kraus expected, Herr Professor Doktor stopped him short with a stern rebuke.

"Young man," he said sharply, "Don't you know that you take x-rays to *support* a diagnosis, not to make one?"

"But if you don't take x-rays to make a diagnosis, what do you use instead?" Kraus had asked.

"Ah! You must look at the symptoms! Yah, that's right, the symptoms. First, you must observe, and listen to the patient." Herr Professor Doktor explained.

It was a lesson Kraus would never forget.

When the time came for Kraus to choose a specialty, the choice for him was easy: Fracture surgery, or what today is called orthopedic surgery.

Medicine in the 1920's was primitive compared to modern standards. Internal medicine was by and large a field devoted to diagnosis—figuring out what was wrong with the patient. After a diagnosis was made, there was startlingly little the doctor could do to treat the patient and make him better. There was no molecular medicine, no genetic science; nor were there antibiotics, prescription drugs or rigorous screening procedures with double blind crossover studies. But, as Kraus explained, orthopedic medicine was different.

"In those days, there were few areas where a doctor could actually cure a patient. Mostly we determined what was wrong, but then couldn't do anything to treat him. But orthopedics was an exception. There you could set a broken leg, and make the patient well."

Kraus didn't have to think twice: He had gone into medicine to become a healer. He would become an orthopedic surgeon.

5

Slide into Chaos

◆

1922–1930, Austria

On the outside, Kraus had the world in his palm. Inside was a different matter. There were stretches when he didn't care whether he lived or died.

A certain amount of angst would be expected in Kraus. He grew up knowing he was disappointing the father he desperately longed to impress. First with school, and then his chosen path in life—Kraus knew that Rudi's acceptance of his decision to become a doctor was grudging, in his formidable father's eyes, he was a disappointment.

Rudi could be harsh and exacting. But in defense of Rudi, his was a harsh, exacting world. Rudi's exasperation was fueled by what he saw as his older son's foolishly naïve, dangerous choice of idealism over pragmatism. Rudi knew that money might not buy happiness in times of peace, but in times of danger, it could buy safety and survival. Money was what got the family safely out of Trieste, let them live comfortably in Zurich, and afterwards enabled their move to Vienna.

If Vienna were to become dangerous, Rudi was convinced it would be money that would save his family again. And Rudi had good reason to be concerned. As the 1920's unfolded, Rudi again watched the country around him slide into political and economic chaos.

Unlike Germany, Austria never enjoyed even a short lived, illusionary recovery after losing World War I. The rest of the world was strutting through the Roaring Twenties, but Austria suffered a shaky economy, fragile consumer confidence, and weak government. As the decade progressed, conditions in Austria slid from bad to worse.

The turning point for the Kraus family and other Austrians was 1928, when unemployment and inflation soared and Austrians pretty much gave up. The Austrian national bank suffered enormous losses—it would go bankrupt in 1932—and businesses and wealthy individuals began moving their assets abroad. Among them was Rudi.

Meanwhile, the nominally democratic Austrian government grew even weaker, violence grew more common, and Rudi and other Austrians braced for a possible coup. The political situation was a total mess—both the right and the left posed threats to the middle, with extremist factions within the right and left fighting each other. Bloody demonstrations were so common, that the Kraus family often ate breakfast accompanied by the sound of gunshots reverberating from downtown. For good reason, historians characterized Vienna in this period as exuding "an atmosphere of perpetual fear and lawlessness."[5]

Making it worse, Rudi also knew that the fear and lawlessness weren't spread by typical street thugs, but by members of established political parties openly espousing violence, authoritarianism, and militarism. The message was clear to the Austrian middle class: their political system had failed them and was in shreds. Increasingly, of the range of terrible political choices, many felt the right wing was "safest." When the Nazis first appeared on the Austrian ballot, they managed to capture eight per cent of the vote. Eight percent. A figure almost three times than that in Germany.

That gave Rudi a lot to think about. Being Rudi, he wasn't just going to sit, wonder and worry. By 1934, he was doing something about it, for his business and his family.

6

Through a Glass Darkly

✦

1922–1933, the Austrian Alps

Having a father like Rudi would likely create a complex stew of emotions in any son. But particularly a son such as Kraus, particularly at the time he was entering manhood. Father and son were much like, with one big, glaring difference, as Rudi regularly intoned to him: When *Rudi* was his son's age, *Rudi* was settled in his path in life, well on his way to a happy marriage and prosperous business career.

That wasn't what the young man wanted to hear. To normal father-son push-pull coming of age dynamics, Kraus already could add tormenting guilt over a friend's death. Now on top of that, he faced the extra whammy of failure in the eyes of his revered and resented father. The result wasn't surprising: Emotional turmoil, psychological angst, and black moods, at times so bleak, that Kraus turned to the mountains for his own form of medicine.

There in the Alps, Kraus climbed alone, no partner, no rope, no pitons, no protection, no margin for error. It is what today in climbing is called "soloing." In soloing, the stakes are absolute. Any slip, even slight, is usually fatal.[1] To most people, it seems crazy that anyone would solo; and to most people, it is. But to Kraus at this point in his life, it provided the kind of startling clarity that you get with the knowledge that you live with a fatal disease.

By reducing the world to the inches of rock making up the next foothold and handhold, soloing boils down issues to their essence—win, you live; lose, you die.

---

1.   It is not uncommon for soloists, no matter how accomplished or experienced, to die while soloing. The most obvious and sad example is the legendary soloist, Derek Hersey, who died in the 1990's while soloing, on what was for him, an easy climb in Yosemite. The theory is that he was caught on the rock during an unexpected rainstorm.

Several years later, Kraus would find some catharsis from his guilt in another close call in the mountains. But until then, Kraus had discovered that when he soloed and had to fight for survival, he came away with a renewed upsurge of appreciation for the sweetness of life.

Soloing to Kraus wasn't a sport, but a spiritual purging, an artistic endeavor even, in the way that a writer or painter confronts and expresses his inner demons through playing them out on paper or canvas. In Kraus' case, his creative medium happened to be rock. When, in the 1980's, the climbing magazines reported on extreme solos as if they were a competitive sport like the 100-meter dash, Kraus was appalled.

Kraus' soloing was more understandable considering the times. For the climbing leader, climbing in the 1920's was a lot like controlled soloing anyway.

Gear was makeshift: Climbers wore sneakers and knotted heavy clothesline around their waist—no comfortable climbing harnesses, high performance climbing shoes, reliable lightweight rope, or nylon climbing "slings" to clip onto the rope to reduce potentially dangerous rope drag on meandering pitches. Climbing protection was equally crude: Pitons were often hand made, heavy, expensive, precious, and tiring to place. The leader carried only a small handful, unlike today's climbing rack, which features a wide assortment of different sizes, shapes and types of protection. Sometimes whole pitches—fifty, seventy-five feet, or more—went by without the leader able to hammer in a single piton; so in essence, he was soloing.

Climbing lore is full of stories of ascents made under conditions today considered outrageously daring and foolhardy. But climbers in the 1920's had no choice if they wanted to climb. Key to a lead climber's survival was bluntly assessing his physical and mental abilities, considering objective dangers like bad weather or bad rock, and then choosing routes well within his limits to cut down the possibility of falling.

But when Kraus' moods were blackest, he didn't bother to consider objective dangers nor stay well within his limits. And in the mountains, if you look for close calls, you will find them.

Once in the thralls of depression, Kraus started soloing a hard route on sight, without any idea of what lay ahead. When he stopped to rest at a small ledge near the top, he saw that the climbing above was much harder than he expected, and that the rock formation was a dreaded slab: relatively low angled rock, but without sharply defined rock features, climbed by pressing hands down on nearly indiscernible holds and balancing feet carefully on sloping, inclining edges.

Slab technique requires patience, finesse, subtle footwork, and delicate weight shifts. Little about Kraus was subtle or delicate, on or off the cliffs. Not surprisingly, Kraus never liked slab climbing. "I knew I was at the limit of my abilities. I couldn't climb down it. I really didn't know if I could climb up it without falling," he said.

But that was precisely the kind of naked, clawing, all-consuming challenge that the guilt-ridden Kraus craved. Kraus explained, "Such was the blackness of my despair that I approached the pitch calmly. I rested on the ledge for a minute before I started up. I was prepared to die. When I reached the top, having barely survived, I found my depression had gone. It's when you come close to death, you really appreciate life."

As a youth, even though Kraus was an atheist, he had carried a small copy of the New Testament in his climbing rucksack. At night, camping in the mountain huts, he found comfort reading his favorite passages, over and over. Kraus' most beloved never changed: *Corinthians*, chapter 13, verse 12–13. "For now we look through a glass, darkly; but then face to face: now I know in part; but then shall I know even as also I am known. And now abideth faith, hope, charity, these three; but the greatest of these is charity."

Kraus insisted that the Bible really meant the word, "love," instead of "charity." Whenever Kraus quoted the passage, he "corrected" the wording.

7

The Big Fall

✦

Spring of 1933, the Oetzal Mountains, Austria

By the time that Kraus graduated medical school and began work as an orthopedic surgeon at the University of Vienna Hospital, despite occasional respite, his guilt over Marcus had become dangerous. Like an alcoholic, Kraus sought temporary blessed forgetfulness, except that his intoxicant was soloing up mountains instead of slugging down martinis.

Kraus had grown convinced that ten years before, on the Pluider Kogel, the mountains had capriciously let him live. By continuing to solo, Kraus kept offering himself back to the mountains and give them a chance to rethink their decision and make amends, if they wished. When Kraus found himself still alive after a day of soloing, he took it as a sign that the mountain had decided to grant him a reprieve, and he was filled with renewed appreciation for the sweetness of life.

But inevitably, Kraus needed to solo again. Kraus was caught in a trajectory of self-destruction as sure as that of any addict. Either he would crash and burn, or survive and climb painfully back to life. Either way, matters were bound to come to a head. They finally did in the spring of 1933.

When Kraus was working as a surgeon at the Fracture Emergency Clinic, among his close friends was a fellow doctor, Ernest Dehne. Sometimes they went into the Alps for ski weekends, joined by their girlfriends of the moment or Kraus' younger brother, Franz. That year, Dehne came up with what he thought was a terrific idea for their Easter holiday. "Let's go to the Oetzal Mountains, Kraus. We've never been there before."

Kraus froze. The ski area in the Oetzal Mountains was across from the Block Kogel. To get there, they would have to pass through the town where the Wandervogel camp had stayed. Kraus had not been back since Marcus died.

At first he refused. He was sure if he went back he would die; the symmetry was undeniable, the appropriateness overwhelming. Kraus didn't want to tell Dehne his reasons, so his colleague kept pressing him. "C'mon, Kraus, why not? The skiing will be great. I hear the food's great, and the inns are wonderful. You can bring your girlfriend. You've never been there before, and we'll have a great time. You'll see."

Finally, Kraus changed his mind. "I realized it was my duty to obey my fate. I knew I wouldn't be coming back. For the first time, I made out a will."

The trip began ominously. The first day they hiked a popular 3,400-meter peak, the Gubernokogel, which lay across a valley from the Block Kogel. On the summit were several parties. A guide pointed to the Block Kogel, "See that peak there?" he asked his client. "Two teenaged boys from Vienna tried climbing it many years ago. One of them, a fellow named Kraus, fell off and died."

Kraus listened, horrified. He walked over to the guide and his client. "You're wrong," Kraus said, "I was one of the boys you were talking about it, but my name is Kraus, and I was the one who didn't die. The one who died was named Marcus." To Kraus, this was further proof he was about to die.

A few more days passed. No close calls, no accidents. Kraus waited, tensed. The last night, Kraus went by the front desk to settle the bill. When the innkeeper saw him, she greeted him pleasantly, "Yes, right away, Mr. Marcus. I'll have your bill ready for you in a moment."

Later, Kraus realized there was a rational, straightforward explanation for the innkeeper's words. "I thought about it," he said, "and it could have been that the guide I met on the top of the Gubernokogel was also staying at the inn, which was popular with climbers. The guide might have repeated the story to the innkeeper. When the innkeeper saw me that night, the explanation was probably something simple, like she thought of the guide's story, but confused the names."

But at the time, the innkeeper's words felt like doom. Kraus took them as an omen that he had no hope of reprieve, that he would be foolish to harbor any hope. Kraus knew he deserved to die. Now he knew it would happen the next day.

In the morning, Kraus and Franz set out together for a day of skiing, leaving Dehne back at the inn. Franz idolized his older brother, who was like a second father to him. But Franz was also constantly trying to prove himself to him. When Franz spotted a beautiful slope for skiing, it didn't bother him it was below a steep, heavily snowed, avalanche-prone slope. When Kraus pointed this out, Franz shrugged.

"Oh, you're just old and scared." Franz said.

"Actually, I was young and scared," Kraus recalled, "But I wasn't going to let Franz show me up."

Franz had already started across the slope, so Kraus let him cross completely before he himself started—that way, only one brother would die in an avalanche. And when his brother had made it safely to the other side, against his better judgment, Kraus started across.

Midway, where Kraus was too far to reach either side, he heard a rumbling noise from the slope above him. Then creaking. Heaving. Then he heard a noise like a sigh…like snow and ice shifting…like the warning signs of an avalanche.

Kraus tensed, waiting for retribution. There was nothing else he could do. He had been waiting for over ten years.

The snow settled. There was no avalanche.

Kraus continued to the other side, and the brothers began climbing the slope for their run.

In those days, there were no ski lifts. To ski a slope, first you had to climb it. Skiers would get in at most two runs per day, but the climb up was part of the experience. Skiers carried rucksacks, eating lunch at the top before skiing down. To Kraus, this was always part of the sport's appeal—not like contemporary "yo-yo" skiing.

Kraus started down first. Conditions were nearly perfect, a deep layer of powder-soft snow beneath a thin coating of breakable crust. He recalled, "I was swooping down the slope in deep powder, picking up speed. I felt like I was flying. It was exactly what I loved most about skiing. Then suddenly I found myself in air. I had skied off the edge of a cliff."

He continued. "I looked up at the sky. It was just a beautiful day—blue sky, white clouds. It struck me—it looked just like the day when Marcus died. Right then I *knew* I was going to die."

The cliff hung like a ski jump, its edge probably no higher than twenty feet off the ground at any point. Like a ski jumper, once Kraus launched off the lip, momentum took over, and he continued falling through air. Not given to exaggeration, Kraus estimated probably quite precisely that he fell one hundred to two hundred feet.

Moments of danger are often remembered in sparkling clarity years later, even though they lasted mere seconds. Of this fall, Kraus said, "I thought to myself, 'Well now, this is my just reward, my absolution if you will. I'm paying for coming back alone when Marcus died.' I felt no fear, none, but was filled with a tremendous sense of peace. Then I blacked out."

When Kraus came to, he thought he was dead. He remembered he had toes, and wiggled them. He remembered he had legs and hands, and cautiously moved them. He looked around, and saw he was lying on the ground, in a deep pile of soft snow.

He looked further, and saw skis attached to his feet, lying crossed, and ski poles on each side. He realized he was alive. He remembered what had happened, and looked himself over. Except for a few scratches, he was completely unhurt.

Franz was watching from the slope above. He made his way to his brother, and the two continued to the bottom. The next day, they returned to Vienna.

"The big fall," as Kraus called it, was another turning point in his life. His survival excised much of his anguish over Marcus. Kraus explained, "I had offered myself to the mountain, but the mountain decided it didn't want me. I had paid my debt, and from that point on, I was absolved of much of my guilt."

The wounds inside from Marcus finally began healing, and the pain grew more bearable. Kraus still soloed, but no longer with the same neediness or recklessness. He also never returned to the Oetzal Mountains.

8

Emilio

✦

1933–1938, the Austrian Alps

Yet in between Kraus' binge and purge soloing, he had plenty of happy, even lighthearted moments in the mountains. He loved to stay overnight in the mountain huts run by the alpine clubs. Accommodations were simple. For sleep, there was one big wooden room with bunk beds and cubbyholes to stash clothing and gear. For the communal dinners, there were the soups, risottos, stews, peasant breads, salamis, and chocolates that Kraus loved. After dinner, Kraus would pull out his guitar, strumming and singing doleful Italian love songs to his climbing partners, who might be Franz, friends from the hospital, a never-ending succession of girlfriends, or Emilio.

Emilio Comici was an Italian mountain guide who became one of the greatest climbers of the pre–World War II era. Kraus and Emilio first met because of Kraus' motorcycle. When Kraus heard that a climber broke his foot in a fall and was stranded in a mountain hut, Kraus drove up on his motorcycle and brought the climber down. The climber turned out to be a good friend of Emilio, who then introduced them.

"Emilio was the most beautiful climber I ever saw," Kraus recalled, "graceful and flowing on the rock, moving like a dancer." A natural climbing talent, Emilio, who also grew up in Trieste, began climbing relatively late. He already had the taste for adventure, and had established himself as one of the leading cavers in the world. But as a teenager, working as a railroad clerk, Emilio contracted a common lung disease like tuberculosis.

Doctors recommended the mountain cure. It worked, and Emilio never left the mountains. A man of simple tastes, Emilio lived for two things—climbing and women. He was happiest when he combined both, which evidently, was easy and often. Handsome, charming, and with a sunny personality, Emilio attracted women like the proverbial bees to honey. Emilio also had his vanities. One time he couldn't help boasting, "Hans, we did it six times last night. *Six times.*"

Equally short, Emilio and Kraus would argue good naturedly over who was taller. Eventually, Emilio settled the matter in his favor. They were on a climb Emilio had led in his usual effortless manner, but seconding his friend on the rope, Kraus struggled at one spot, unable to reach a handhold Emilio easily grasped.

There were several *other* possible explanations—greater flexibility, longer arm span, better body position—but Emilio was delighted to seize on the one he liked best. Afterwards, he periodically tweaked Kraus gleefully, "You see, I *am* taller than you are."

Sometimes Kraus joined Emilio as the third on the rope when Emilio was guiding. Kraus particularly enjoyed a client named the Conte Dal Torso. Kraus never figured out what the Conte did. "I don't think he had a regular job. He was a professional Count," Kraus explained. When Kraus returned to the Dolomites after a ten-year hiatus brought about by WW II, he met up again with the Conte, then sixty-five, no longer climbing, but now a serious amateur painter.

The Conte's specialty was mountains scenes, and he carefully left out modern features he considered unaesthetic, such as roads or hotels. The Conte gave Kraus a painting of Lake Misurina—modern hotel missing conspicuously—which Kraus hung in his bedroom. It remained there until Kraus' death.

As a self-described "free loader" on these climbs with the Conte, Kraus pitched in by carrying Emilio's rucksack. On the Cima Grande di Lavaredo, a difficult route with overhangs, Kraus found the pack unusually heavy, and he grew hot and sweaty as he muscled his way up through the roofs. He was very happy when they topped out. On the summit, Kraus handed the pack to Emilio, who mischievously pulled from it a roast chicken, two bottles of wine, and other picnic delicacies. Breaking into a big smile as he recalled the moment, Kraus declared, "I was so angry, I could have killed him."

When Kraus and Emilio climbed together without the Conte, they tackled extreme routes, including, in the fall of 1937, the second ascent of the North Face of the Cima Grande. Emilio had made its first ascent after several other guides had failed and promptly declared it "impossible."

The route was a serious undertaking, whether leading or seconding, steep, overhanging, terrifically exposed—everything Kraus loved. Its crux involves a long traverse, then moving straight up until the climber again traverses left. On the Cima Grande, if the lead climber doesn't hammer pitons into the rock at key spots on the traverses (thereby attaching the rope to the rock) and if the second falls, the weight of the ropes will pull the climber off the rock and yank him out into space.

Emilio managed to surmount the first traverse by aid climbing (pulling on the rope clipped into pitons in the rock). But the rest of the pitch, including the scary second traverse, Emilio "free climbed"[1] without hammering in a single piton. Kraus knew it wouldn't be so effortless for him. He remembered, "Emilio didn't understand I couldn't free climb what he could. He was so many grades above me in climbing ability, that he hadn't realized it would be hard for me."

When it was Kraus' turn on the first traverse, he found it hard to climb, even by pulling on the rope. As he unclipped the rope from the last piton, he had an awful sense of dread as he felt one foot start to slip. He tried to fight it. His heart beat fast, and he tried to press his fingers hard against the rock. But his heart kept beating faster, and even faster. He knew exactly what would happen if he fell. He could feel the weight of the heavy rope starting to pull him off the rock even as he tried to press harder against it. Now his heart was beating even faster, and his other foot was starting to slip. He couldn't help himself, his fingers were slipping, sliding, greasing off the rock.

And the heavy hemp ropes were pulling him out and off the rock. And he found himself falling.

He launched into space, hundreds of feet up, plunging out into a prodigious arc, until finally, he start to slow, almost stop, and then momentum took over and he swung back violently toward the rock. Even over the beating of his heart, he could hear the sound of the hemp ropes, an ominous creaking, scraping and fraying against the rock. Just as he swung in close to the cliff, he thrust out his hands, hard, to try to grab the rock. And then he swung back, out into space again, the rope hurtling him outward in another huge arc. And then it plunged him back again toward the cliff.

Kraus kept swinging back and forth, back and forth, all the time hearing the creaking of the ropes above, as he dangled in thin air. He explained, "I faced a lot of scary moments in my life, and they weren't nearly as scary as on the Cima Grande. When something happens fast, you don't really have time to get scared, like during my big fall. But on the Cima Grande, I knew what was going to happen, and I had time to think about it and get scared silly."

---

1. "Free climbing" is when the climber moves upward without using the rope, although, unlike "soloing," he is tied into the rope. In free climbing, the rope is there only for protection, in case the climber falls.

Finally, the momentum died and the swinging stopped. Kraus was left suspended in space, stranded far out from the rock, dangling. His predicament was serious. Emilio could not haul him up the rope; Kraus' only hope was to build enough momentum so that he could swing in close enough to grab a protruding rock horn or jam his fingers into a crack.

After several tries, Kraus finally managed. Fortunately, he carried a hammer and a few pitons, which he planned to use when it was his turn to lead. He quickly hammered in a piton as an anchor, clipped himself to it, and leaned back, secure on the cliff wall. Shouting up to Emilio, who could barely hear him because of the rock[2], Kraus finally made Emilio understand his predicament.

They had been climbing with double ropes; Emilio untied from one so that Kraus could pull it down and use it to rappel from his stance; which was itself a dangerous maneuver, given his single anchor point. Emilio managed to descend by rappelling from his belay stance above. They made it safely to the ground, and undeterred, returned to the Cima Grande the following weekend. This time, Emilio was well equipped with pitons.

Kraus rappelled when he had to, particularly enjoying the airiness of a long, free rappel through space. Generally, though, he disliked rappelling. He had good reasons: Rappelling in the 1930's was uncomfortable and dangerous.

Without modern waist harnesses or rappel devices—such as a figure-of-eight or sticht plate—that generate crucial friction and slow rope speed, a climber slung the rope around his shoulders and hip, in an awkward configuration known as the Dulfersitz rappel. For protection against chafing and rope burns, on long rappels, a climber stuffed newspaper in his shirt and trousers. It was easy for the rope to unwrap and for the climber to fall out, as Kraus witnessed firsthand, when he watched a girlfriend of the Conte trying her first rappel. Somehow, she managed to hang on and get down safely.

Danger even came from the rope itself: Unlike nylon modern ropes, hemp ropes could rot from inside, invisibly, without leaving visible telltale traces on the outside.

Kraus considered climbing risks warranted, since they were integral to the grand experience. But risks from rappelling he considered foolish, since to him

---

2.   Rock can absorb sound, leading to seemingly illogical situations. A climber underneath a five-foot rock overhang might be unable to hear his partner right above the overhang, while a climber on a smooth rock face might clearly hear a partner fifty feet away.

rappelling was a mechanical experience, without athletic challenge or soul. Kraus' concerns were reasonable. In 1940, Emilio died while rappelling.

Kraus heard the details after the war. By this time, Emilio had become a national hero in Italy for his climbing exploits, and mayor of the small mountain village where he lived. It was an off-day of climbing for Emilio; he had strolled to some nearby practice cliffs with his girlfriend, intending to picnic and serenade her on his guitar with love songs, for Emilio, like Kraus, loved music.

However, at the cliffs, his girlfriend said she would like to climb, and Emilio borrowed a thin rappel rope from another climber and soloed up a crack. After one pitch, he realized the climbing was too difficult for his girlfriend, and decided to descend. Kraus commented, "It was a route Emilio easily could have down climbed. But he was feeling lazy, I guess, and decided just to rappel."

Emilio placed the hemp rope around a rock spur serving as his anchor, looped it around his shoulder and hip, and swung around to get in position to rappel. He weighted the rope and began rappelling. After a few feet, it snapped and Emilio fell to his death. He was thirty-nine.

Emilio's friendship touched Kraus deeply. A kind of yin to Kraus' yang, Emilio was a kindred spirit in reverse. Whereas Kraus was driven, angst-ridden, and multi-dimensional, Emilio was simple and happy, brimming with a childlike joyousness, devoid of ambition or complexity. His presence to Kraus had been a soothing balm, a reminder that life did not have to be a series of painful, gritty challenges; sometimes, it could simply be straightforward and fun. When Kraus talked about Emilio, he invariably broke into a big smile.

9

The Circus Strongman

✦

1932–1936, Vienna

From the beginning when Kraus first started practicing medicine, his approach changed little over the years. He would continue to refine and expand it. But his basic philosophy didn't change at all.[6] It began with his self–prescribed treatments for the hand injuries he suffered in the accident with Marcus. And it grew into a deeply held conviction that movement, exercise, and fitness are the most important ingredients to getting and keeping emotional and physical health.

By the time Kraus graduated medical school in 1929, he was determined to build those beliefs into his practice. He just wasn't sure exactly how. But soon, he would stumble across two clues.

The first clue came to Kraus in a traditional way: At the hospital.

Kraus was preparing a paper on wrist fractures based on the results of several hundred patients he had treated in the hospital's clinic. All of the patients had their wrists in casts. Half were given simple exercises to perform—movements like shrugging their shoulders and rolling their wrists—and half were not. Kraus noticed something curious. The patients who had exercised healed better and faster than the ones who had not exercised, even if their injuries were worse.

The second clue came to Kraus in a decidedly non-traditional way: From a circus strongman.

Even as a busy young doctor, Kraus always made time to work out. The building across the street from the hospital, where he conveniently kept his office on the second floor, housed a gym. The gym's owner was Heinz Kowalski, whom Kraus called Ko.

Ko had grown up in a circus family; in fact, for his first job he had been the circus strong man. Later, the powerfully built Ko became a boxing coach and president of the Austrian Sports Teacher Federation. Ko was close to Kraus in age, outlook and physique—both men were short, muscular, extremely physical. Both also appreciated mental and physical toughness. The two started working out together, relished each other's company, traded jokes, and soon formed a close friendship.

One time, Kraus had sparred some rounds of boxing with Ko, and the two were chatting as usual. Kraus wondered about some puzzling wrist fracture findings at the hospital.

"You know, it just occurred to me," Kraus mused aloud to Ko. "You refer injured athletes from your gym to me all the time, but none with fractures or sprains. Why is that?"

"Oh, you doctors don't know how to treat those injuries," Ko said.

Kraus was taken aback. "What do you mean? Of course we do. We learn all about it in medical school. After all, this is what I do. I'm a fracture surgeon," Kraus said.

"You might have been to medical school and you might be a surgeon, but that doesn't mean you know how to treat fractures or sprains," Ko replied. "I'll show you what I mean. Okay, how do you treat a sprain, for instance?"

"You immobilize a sprain in a cast," Kraus replied, surprised by the obviousness of the question. But Ko's face took on a look of exasperation; kind of a *humph, yup, exactly as I feared.*

Kraus explained, "You have to, otherwise it won't heal."

"I'm not a doctor, so I don't know about that," Ko said, "But *immobilize*! In a *cast*! Pshsh!"

"Okay, then what do *you* do?" Kraus retorted.

"Look, I grew up in a circus family," Ko said, "We didn't know about fancy, expensive doctor treatments. What we knew was that if we didn't perform, we didn't eat."

Ko continued, "We got sprains and fractures all the time, but we couldn't afford to immobilize them in casts. Instead, when we twisted a knee or sprained a shoulder, we wrapped the injury in a towel soaked in alcohol, then held the whole thing close to steam from a boiling kettle."

As Kraus looked dubious, Ko explained further, "Doing this numbs the injured area, which allows you to start moving it gently. We would do this several times a day, the steam treatment followed by the gentle movements. Pretty soon, the whole injured area loosens up, and stops hurting. After a few days of treatments, we would find the injury healed, and we could go back to work at the circus."

"After a few days?" Kraus repeated.

Not only did this seem preposterous, but it also contradicted what Kraus learned in medical school and had practiced in the hospital. On the other hand, by now Kraus knew Ko well, and he knew that Ko was the type of person who didn't talk about something unless he knew what he was talking about. Kraus decided to try his friend's method at the first opportunity. And a few days later, Kraus had his chance.

Kraus was on duty at the hospital clinic when two teenaged boys hobbled in. They had sprained their ankles while skiing—a common injury in the 1930's, when ski boots were made of soft leather and offered little support. When Kraus told the boys that he needed to apply heavy casts, their faces grew long—even longer, when Kraus explained the casts would keep them from skiing for two months.

"Two months! Hey Doc, isn't there something else you could do?"

Kraus thought of Ko's circus treatment. "I explained to them I heard about this new type of treatment, and that maybe it would work, but maybe it wouldn't. Could you imagine?" He was thinking of medicine in the 1990's. "In those days, we didn't have consent forms. If I tried to do something like that today, I'd be scared silly about malpractice suits. Someone would end up suing the pants off me."

The boys were game. Anything sounded better to them than being stuck in a cast for two months. So in his office, Kraus gave each of the boys one of Ko's circus treatments, showed them how to do the treatments at home, and told them to return the next day. When they did, to Kraus' surprise and their delight, they were already much better. He gave each boy another treatment, and sent them off with instructions to do the treatments on their own several times a day and return one week later.

To Kraus' greater surprise and their total joy, when they returned, they were each completely healed. Kraus remembered, "I thought to myself, this is great! But I didn't understand why the boys were better. However, for me, the important thing was that they were better and that the treatment worked. I always felt that if I could understand why something worked that was great. But if it worked and I didn't understand why, that was okay, too."

He continued, "I didn't understand why the alcohol was needed, but the fact that it worked was the important thing. When I tried the treatment on myself with the alcohol, I nearly burned myself. I wanted to find something better, so at that point, I set about experimenting with alternatives."

On one of the shelves in his office he had lined up various substances: acetone, ether, and other topical anesthetics. Kraus began on one side of the shelf and made his way down. One day he tried ethyl chloride.

The first patient to whom Kraus administered Ko's circus treatment, with the substitution of ethyl chloride instead of alcohol, happened to be a veterinarian. He had limped into Kraus' office with a badly sprained ankle. Kraus sprayed the vet's ankle with the ethyl chloride, and followed it up with Ko's circus treatment. As soon as the ankle numbed, Kraus began limbering it gently.

The vet was able to stand, and soon even walked out of Kraus' office without limping. Like the two teenaged skiers, after a week of daily treatments that he gave himself at home, the vet returned to Kraus' office for a check-up to find that he was completely healed. "Now I knew I had something!" Kraus recalled.

After one month, the vet returned for a routine follow-up visit. He turned to Kraus, "I don't know if you realize it, but you have a very good thing here in this ethyl chloride. I've started using it myself on my injured horses and dogs, and it works just as well on them as it does on people. After I spray their injuries with this stuff, they get up and run away, good as new."

After the experience with the vet, Kraus tried ethyl chloride on anything that he felt might respond to it—painful backs, sprained joints, strained muscles, even appendicitis. "I found all of these responded well, except for the appendicitis," he said.

Since his approach was based on movement, in contrast to the traditional "immobilization" treatments based on bed rest and casts, Kraus decided to name his approach, "immediate mobilization."

10

Susie

◆

1936–1938, Vienna

Sometime during the late 1930's, Kraus got married. It was a time that he didn't like to talk about—the marriage came apart on a bitter note—and it was a topic that the surviving friends of Kraus from that era demurred talking about as well.

Kraus had met Susanne Simon in Austria before 1938, and they were married by 1941, then lived together in New York, and climbed in the Shawangunks in the early 1940's. After 1944 they separated, and divorced in the 1950's.

Part of Susie's appeal was easy to see. She taught aerobics and was, well, drop dead gorgeous. One Shawangunks old timer recalled, "She looked like a dancer and had an allure which many Viennese women had, like a ballet dancer."

Another added, "Wow, what a superb body! What a knock out!"

Susie was lively, entertaining, and cultured, but some remembered she could also be superficial and dissembling. Like many women with stunning looks, Susie had relied more on skin-deep appearance than depth of personality. She was used to easy attention, which had discouraged sustained effort while producing a sense of entitlement.

The climber, Betty Woolsey, took a climbing trip to the Wind River with Kraus, Susie, and several other friends from the Shawangunks in the summer of 1941. In her memoir, Woolsey recalled both Susie's charm and indolence "(Susie) was Viennese and shared my enthusiasm for opera in general and Mozart in particular. Hans and Harry [Harry Snyder, another Shawangunks climber] made many first ascents; among them the southeast ridge of the Sphinx, the northeast ridge of Warren and the south face of Woodrow Wilson…I was able to join them infrequently, to my disappointment, due to a pulled muscle in my back. This kept me close to camp where Susie kept me company as she was feeling lazy."[7]

Kraus had an old photo album from the 1930's. Many of the photos showed him in a group of friends, many of who were attractive women. He shrugged as he looked at the pictures.

"You might call her an old friend," he would say.

Then, "Oh, she was also an old friend...yes, yes, another old friend..." He made a pushing away gesture with his hand. "You could call her an old friend, too."

There were quite a lot of "old friends," often in quite affectionate stances with the young Kraus. Were these old *girl*friends?

"Yes, you could say that," Kraus conceded.

Among all of the photographs in the album, there was one blurry picture of Kraus and Susie. They stood side-by-side, without touching, staring in different directions. It was hard to tell exactly, but they looked like they were frowning, possibly bored. There was no physical connection, and seemingly no emotional connection.

Kraus looked closely at the photo, the first time in half a century, and didn't say anything. Then he picked up the album slowly, like it was heavy, or a burden, and sighed. "That was Susie. God, I haven't looked at this in I don't know how long."

Kraus looked more closely at the photo. "Things weren't good between us from the start," he said. You didn't need Kraus to tell you that. That was one of those times when the picture told a thousand words.

11

The Missing Link

✦

1936–1938, Vienna

Excited by his new approach of "immediate mobilization," Kraus submitted a paper on his work to the Chairman of the hospital's Surgery Department at the University of Vienna. The Chairman in turn recommended Kraus' paper to the Academy of Physicians—a great honor for a young doctor.

Kraus recalled how excited and nervous he was when it was time for him to present the paper. "I had a real case of stage fright." He said.

To relax, Kraus went to Ko's gym to work out. Noticing that his friend was unusually tense, Ko pulled him aside. "Let's spar a couple of rounds before your big evening tonight," he suggested.

Ko was the much superior boxer, and as he chased Kraus around the ring, Kraus soon forgot his nervousness. It was only when leaving the ring, happy and relaxed, that Kraus noticed he had picked up a large black eye.

The presentation was a great success. Not only were there no comments about his shiner, but Kraus managed to impress "The Czar" of fracture surgery in Vienna. Dr. Bohlen shook his hand afterwards, and made an appointment to meet him over coffee at a Viennese coffee house.

These were exciting times for Kraus professionally. His practice was off to an extremely promising start and his new fitness message was ready for responsive ears. The Viennese loved their chocolates, schnitzels, and strudels *mit schlag*. But they also exercised and stayed active. Calisthenics classes and gym workouts were popular, as well as outdoor activities like skiing, skating, biking and hiking. Kraus recalled how shocked he was when he moved to New York and saw how sedentary most Americans were.

Athletes flocked to Kraus' office in Vienna—figure skaters, runners and skiers. (Later on, he would mistakenly be described as the trainer for the Austrian Olympic ski team. That was never the case, although he had treated many members of that team, and in 1934, was named the surgeon to the Austrian Sports Teacher Association.) Athletes were Kraus' favorite patients. Partly it was the bond they shared; partly too because he found they dealt better with pain, understood the importance of working out, and followed the treatments.

Kraus was blunt and outspoken even then. A few months after his successful talk before the Viennese physicians, he was at a popular ski area where he ran into a junior doctor training under Dr. Bohlen. After they exchanged greetings, the other doctor, who will be called Dr. Mueller, turned to him, "So, Kraus, tell me; are you still playing around with that immediate mobilization approach of yours?"

Kraus replied that of course he was. Mueller shrugged his shoulders and made a face. He was clearly not a convert. They chatted a few minutes further when Kraus spotted a woman finishing up a run. Pointing to her, Kraus asked Mueller, "What do you think of that woman's skiing?"

Mueller replied, "Great, she's a beautiful skier! A real pleasure to watch!"

"Yes, she is," Kraus said, "Funny you should say that. She's [Liesl Schmidt]."

When Mueller looked blank, Kraus explained, "She used to be one of your patients. When she came to me, she had her leg in a big cast you had put on. If she had stayed with you, she would still be in that big cast for several more months, and you wouldn't be watching her skiing today."

Mueller mumbled something and left.

Kraus' most amusing patients were the motorcycle racers. Motor racing clubs were very popular in Austria. Kraus found that motorcycle racers were very different from the other athletes he treated. For one thing, they begged Kraus for casts, even when their injuries were small. For another, they wanted their casts to be as big and heavy as possible. And, they wanted their casts to stay on as long as possible.

Kraus soon figured out why. Motorcycle racing attracted heavy betting, and it wasn't yet illegal for the racers themselves to place bets—or to race with casts. The racers who had casts—the bigger and the thicker, the better—had an unfair advantage braking around turns and curves.

After a year of adopting the immediate mobilization approach into his practice, Kraus observed a puzzling pattern: Patients seemed to fall into two groups. Those who had more recent injuries were often cured completely. But those whose injuries were long standing at best found only partial relief. Kraus was convinced he was missing something in his understanding of muscles. There was a crucial missing link he had yet to discover.

As he tried making sense of this, Kraus came across a book called *Muskelhaerten*, written in 1931 by a Viennese orthopedic surgeon named Max Lange, which describes a muscle condition characterized by hard, localized spots forming mostly in the hips, buttocks, lower back, shoulders, and neck.

Patients had complained to Lange that these spots felt raw and sore, and extremely painful when pressed. He found he could identify these spots by touch. Healthy muscles felt like silky, well-kneaded bread dough; in contrast, these spots appeared in the dough like clumps that required kneading and breaking down.

Lange found that no conventional methods could get rid of these painful spots. Eventually, through trial and error, he found that the only way to get rid of them was by extremely forceful injection with glucose.

Lange also noticed that these spots produced funny pain patterns. Patients complained the spots triggered pain in surrounding muscles, radiating down the sides of the legs if the spots were in the buttock or hips, or radiating down the arms if the spots were in the neck. Lange decided to call these spots "trigger points."

Max Lange's findings got Kraus thinking. Perhaps there was a connection between the pattern he observed with his patients and Lange's work. Perhaps trigger points were the reason why his ethyl chloride and immediate mobilization treatments cured patients with acute muscle pain, but not patients with chronic pain.

Kraus followed this line of thinking: If that was the case, then perhaps with his chronic pain patients, he needed to get rid of their trigger points first, before he tried restoring muscle strength and flexibility. Kraus had discovered the key missing link.

By 1938, Kraus had his circle of loyal patients, and his practice was growing. Away from medicine, he had an established life in the mountains that provided both an important emotional outlet and a deep source of pleasure. He was finally coping more constructively with his guilt over the death of Marcus. He was living in a city he loved, and had created a life filled with friends and family, even if it included the formidable Rudi and the ravishing but exasperating Susie.

It would take a lot to give up a comfortable, rewarding niche in Austria to venture into the unknown in America. A person would need a strongly compelling reason. By 1938, Kraus had it: Hitler.

12

Flunking the Hitler Test

✦

1938, Vienna

Hitler first became known in Germany and Austria in 1923 when he tried unsuccessfully to overthrow the German government. But throughout the 1920's, when the German economy stayed strong, his Nazi party stayed weak. In fact, throughout the 1920's, the Nazis didn't seem particularly threatening; not that different from previous, fringe, anti Semitic parties that plagued German politics for centuries.[1] When the Nazis first appeared on the German ballot—in 1928, before the Great Depression—they won less than three percent of the vote.

Most Jews in Germany and Austria, like many Kraus family friends, laughed when they talked about Hitler. "That buffoon!" they'd guffaw, "Hitler couldn't make it in Austria, so he had to move to Germany! A homeless street person! A watercolor artist before he entered politics. Not even a good artist at that!"

Rudi, though, would shake his head, not convinced.

---

1.   The Nazis were not the first rabidly anti-Semitic party to gain a toehold in German politics. When in 1873 hard times hit Germany, many blamed the Jews. In 1878, the Austrian Socialist Workers Party was founded on a Nazi-type platform of hatred, and in 1893, a quarter of a million German voters elected sixteen deputies running on Anti-Semitic platforms (out of 397) to the Reichstag. In 1894, the Dreyfus Affair revealed the virulent and deeply rooted nature of Anti-Semitism throughout Europe. A French Army Captain and the first Jewish member of the General Staff, Alfred Dreyfus was found guilty of selling state secrets to Germany and sentenced to hard labor at Devil's Island based on obviously faked documents. Although Dreyfus was later exonerated in 1906, it didn't diminish the shocking zest with which French and other Europeans were quick to blame Dreyfus and Jews. (On an ironic note, during World War II, Dreyfus' granddaughter, Madeleine, was deported from France and murdered in Auschwitz.)

"C'mon, Rudi," they'd say, "How could you take someone like that seriously?"

The Great Depression changed everything, fomenting a ripe environment for bitterness and hatred. Germans were now much more open-minded to reassurances of their superiority and that all their problems was someone else's doing. In 1930, eighteen percent of Germans voted for the Nazis. In 1932, it was up to thirty-seven percent.

Rudi had been right not to laugh.

But Jews in Germany and Austria could still take comfort in the fact that the Nazis didn't rule Germany. At least, not yet. That took the ineptitude of the moderate German government.

Terrified of the Communists, German President Paul von Hindenburg and Chancellor Franz Von Papen aligned with the Nazis to create a moderate-right coalition intended to hold off a leftist coup. Thus, through legal methods, in January of 1933, Hitler became the German Chancellor.

Then Hitler turned around and outfoxed his former moderate allies: In 1934, he established himself as absolute dictator. In 1935, he solidified his power by eliminating all opposition through murder and other criminal methods, proceeded on a program of robbery, brutality and murder against the Jews, and passed the Nuremburg Laws, stripping German Jews of citizenship, all legal rights, and any protection.

Like millions in Germany and Austria, the Kraus family watched the unfolding nightmare with special horror. According to *Mein Kampf*, descent from a single Jewish great-grandfather or great-grandmother "tainted" a person as Jewish. Rudi and Ella each had a Jewish parent. Although Rudi was baptized Protestant and Ella baptized Catholic, they knew that to the Nazis they had, as Kraus put it, "flunked the Hitler test."

For now, though, the Kraus family and Austrian Jews were safe. Austria was still an independent country—that had been mandated by the treaty ending World War I—and Hitler couldn't yet rob, brutalize or murder Jews in Austria as he did in Germany.

The next year, some Austrian Jews even breathed a cautious sigh of relief. In 1936, Hitler eased off his anti-Semitic reign of terror, hoping to present a nominally civilized front to the world at the German Summer Olympics in Berlin and the Winter Olympics in Garmisch-Pattenkirchen. "Maybe things won't be so bad after all," some Jews rationalized, "After all, how bad could things get? C'mon, how could they possibly get *any* worse?"

Rudi, though, wasn't fooled. He wasn't shocked to see, that after the Olympic Games ended, Hitler picked up where he had left off. In 1937, Hitler was ready to proceed with his plans. His next step: Austria.

But if Austrian Jews were safe throughout the 1930's, they still had plenty of reason to worry. In 1934, Austrian Nazis had assassinated the Austrian chancellor and tried to take over the government. The Nazi coup was unsuccessful, and the moderate, anti-Nazi Austrian government remained in power, but it was weak. And it was clear that many Austrians were sympathetic to Hitler and his idea of re-uniting Austria with Germany as one country.

Hitler stepped up pressure to "re-unify" with Austria in January of 1938. He threatened to invade unless Austria handed over control of its economic and foreign policy to Nazi Germany. Austria did so, but two months later, Hitler again threatened to invade Austria, unless Austria handed itself over completely to Nazi Germany. This time, the moderate Austrian government paused, and decided to hold an election, a "plebiscite," so that Austrians could vote on whether to join Nazi Germany or remain independent and take their chances.

Hitler decided not to take his chances. The plebiscite was scheduled for March 13. Two days earlier, Hitler invaded.

That night at dinnertime, the Kraus family heard a special broadcast abruptly interrupt their usual radio program. It was the Austrian chancellor announcing his resignation. "German troops are invading our country," he said wearily, "The world is not willing to help us to defend ourselves, and alone we are not strong enough. We will not fight, not spill the blood of our German brothers. May God protect Austria." Afterward, the Austrian national anthem played: "Austria will last forever."

The next day, Austria came to an end. Rudi watched Nazi troops march into Austria and Nazi planes fly overhead dropping leaflets announcing, "Germany greets his brotherland." The following day, Hitler rode into Vienna and declared the two countries "unified."

Despite the Austrian Chancellor's brave words on the radio, Austrians were thrilled. Rudi saw thick crowds in Vienna line the streets to cheer and throw flowers at invading Nazi troops. It was a scene replayed again and again throughout Austrian cities and towns. Betty Woolsey, an American Olympic ski team member who in March of 1938 was training in the Austrian town of St. Anton, recalled celebrations with candlelight processions and delighted shouts of, "Heil Hitler."[8] Film footage captures the Austrians screaming deliriously, crying with happiness, "One Reich, One People, One Fuehrer!"[9]

Equally terrifying to the Kraus family was to see how quickly their neighbors embraced Nazism: The day after the invasion, Jewish businesses were "Christian-ized," Jewish possessions were destroyed or stolen without restitution or redress, and Austrian Jews were beaten and robbed. In Vienna, crowds forced Jews to scrub streets on their hands and knees and beat elderly Jews for fun; parents lifted children onto their shoulders so that they could see better.[10] By April, signs appeared in parks, restaurants, stores, and movie theaters: "Jews not permitted to sit here."

The window for the Kraus family to flee to safety was shutting fast. In Sep-tember of 1939, Hitler invaded the Sudentenland part of Czechoslovakia, and five months later, invaded the rest of the country. Six months later, the window shut tight, with no chance of escape, when Hitler invaded Poland. Britain and France declared war against Germany. World War II began.

Luckily for the Kraus family, Rudi had been ready.

13

Escape Plans

♦

1934–1938, Vienna

Maybe it was Rudi's experiences twenty years before in Trieste when World War
I threatened his family's safety. Maybe it was his connections into the Austrian
government, just like twenty years before in Trieste. Maybe it was information
that Kraus had gleaned from observing senior level Austrian officials he treated as
patients.

Whatever the reason, as early as 1934—when Hitler first became dictator, first
consolidated Nazi power, and first attempted to take over Austria—Rudi again
recognized his family was in danger. And again, he took action.

On the surface, a sightseeing vacation Kraus took in 1934 to New York and
Chicago seems unrelated. In interviews for magazines and books, and conversations with friends, Kraus simply explained that he took the trip because he
wanted to visit the U.S. Sometimes, Kraus cited American medical advances as
the motivation, sometimes curiosity about America inspired by his friendship
with expatriate Americans like track and field coach, Harold Anson Bruce, who
was living in Vienna to train the Austrian Olympic running team.[11]

Chicago made little impression on Kraus, other than the twenty-five-passenger
prop plane in which he flew from New York to Chicago: It was Kraus' first time
in an airplane, and he found the ride exciting despite the noise, constant lurch-
ing, and uncomfortable wooden seats.

New York was different. Kraus visited some of the leading hospitals and came
away impressed with the level of sophistication of the medicine. Plus, he fell in
love with the city. Kraus recalled, "The Depression was recently over. People
were optimistic and eager to return to work. New York was very exciting then.
There were no traffic jams and not much crime. You could walk through Central

Park in the middle of the night without any fear. People were friendly to strangers. You could go anywhere you wanted, in clean subway cars, for a nickel."

Kraus would say that he decided on the spot he wanted to move to New York.

Yet this was curious: This was a man who didn't like big cities, who fled them at the first chance, throughout his life, whenever he could, for the mountains. Nor did Kraus like sightseeing, which was wildly out of character for him. Before and after this trip, he showed no interest in museums, historical monuments, grand restaurants, or cultural events like theatre and dance.

Yet he must have badly wanted to take this trip. This was no casual junket. Travel in the 1930's was time consuming: Cumulative round-trip travel time from Vienna to Chicago took nearly a month. And the trip was expensive; particularly flying between Chicago and New York, which was exotic and only within the realm of the wealthy. All in all, this trip was a serious commitment for any young doctor with limited funds and time.

Kraus' suggestion, frequently reported, that he emigrated to advance his career is ludicrous. His practice in Vienna was taking off; starting over as a doctor in the U.S., under any circumstances, would be hard and discouraging. It would require retaking medical boards, getting re-certified, and rebuilding a practice from scratch. Under the best of circumstances, immigration would set any doctor back several years. It was so disheartening a prospect, that even openly Jewish doctors living in Hitler's Germany put it off as long as possible.[12]

However, from a different perspective, Kraus' 1934 trip makes a great deal of sense. If, for instance, it was part of early stage emergency plans to escape Austria. Although Kraus only confided this to a very close friend, the trip was the brainchild of Rudi, who also provided the funding and picked the itinerary. (It was probably no coincidence that New York and Chicago were both cities with significant expatriate Jewish German and Austrian communities.) Acting under instructions from Rudi, Kraus scouted places for the family to live, transferred funds, and executed various financial arrangements. This explained the Kraus family's unusual and extremely fortunate situation after moving to the U.S.

Up through 1939, the Nazis openly let Jews leave Austria and Germany, but insured that the process was arduous, painful, and prohibitively expensive. In order to emigrate, Jews needed money for precious passports, visas, and bribes. Then they needed money in the new country during the long, painful transition period while they found housing and jobs. But the Nazis let Jews leave the country with only 10 marks per person—about $2.50.

Even putting money into a Swiss bank account wasn't a solution. If the Nazis suspected someone held a foreign bank account, they threatened to put him in a concentration camp until he revealed its whereabouts and transferred the monies back. Sometimes, the Swiss banks even colluded with the Nazis to steal money from Jewish accounts. This was what happened to all of the assets of two prominent Jewish Viennese families, the Bloch-Bauers and the Picks, who owned one of Austria's largest sugar refineries. "Having marketed themselves to the Jews of Europe as a safe haven for their property, Swiss banks repeatedly turned Jewish-owned property over to Nazis in order to curry favor with them," a U.S. federal judge concluded in 2005 during landmark Holocaust legislation.[13]

Even for the lucky Austrian and German Jews who got out of Germany and Austria, life afterwards was grim: Typically, they lived in poverty, underemployed, gratefully taking menial entry level jobs regardless of former professional training or status. In the U.S., Stella Hershan, who in Vienna employed a maid and cook, sold socks at Macy's in New York. Hertha Nathorff, who in Germany was a doctor, became a housekeeper. The mother of former Secretary of State Henry Kissinger found work as a cook. The Austrian artist, Oscar Kokoschka, wrote about his experience with the Nazis from Zurich in 1941: "They took away everything from me. I am totally impoverished, and probably will have to live very modestly for a few years, if you can call this vegetation living."[14]

In this light, what Rudi pulled off is truly remarkable. Presumably, he made extensive use of his Marittima connections, just as he had done during World War I. But this time around, Rudi accomplished much more than even twenty-four years before.

For starters, not only did Rudi get his family out of Austria, but he also managed to save the family furniture, including the grand piano and the dining table which seated twenty-four. Rudi left with so much money, after he and Ella moved to the U.S., that he never had to work again. For the rest of their lives, they lived off savings and investments in a huge, handsome Victorian house overlooking the Long Island Sound in the affluent New York suburb of Larchmont.

Rudi even managed to engineer it so that Marittima was never "Aryanized"—sold for a fraction of its value to a Nazi sympathizer. Somehow, amazingly, Marittima survived Nazism with Rudi's ownership intact. He chose to sell it after the war, on his own terms, when it was clear that none of his children wanted to carry it on.

Most impressive, though, was what Rudi accomplished in human terms. Somehow, he was also able to offer the precious visas and passports to his entire extended family and circle of close friends. His actions must have cost him a small fortune. And they resulted in his saving close to twenty-five lives.

Only Rudi's brother, sister-in-law, and niece turned down his help and chose to stay in Austria. After the war, the family found out from his niece that she was the only left alive. Rudi's brother and his wife were murdered in the gas ovens of Auschwitz.

14

Escape

✦

March 1938, Europe and the Atlantic Ocean

Kraus was the first in the family to leave Austria. The same day that Hitler's army marched into Vienna, Kraus boarded a train in Vienna bound for Trieste. Before he was allowed onto the train, along with the other passengers, Kraus had to undergo questioning by the SS. He was escorted to a chapel near the train station, converted into a makeshift Gestapo interrogation center, where a large portrait of Hitler already hung above the altar.

Perhaps the timing of the invasion caused Kraus' departure to be moved up. For reasons not clear, he did not have all the required emigration papers. Kraus knew this was extremely dangerous. Everyone had heard the stories: If the SS caught you trying to leave without all the proper papers, they would pull you off the train and send you to a concentration camp.

While he waited, Kraus could hear the interrogation of each person before him. "Why are you leaving now, before such a glorious chapter in Austria's history is about to begin?" the SS officer asked. Recalling that the Nazis had scheduled a "vote" to "confirm" that Austria chose to become part of Nazi Germany, Kraus had rehearsed his answer carefully. When it was his turn, he replied to the Gestapo, "I need to travel to Trieste to obtain my ancestors' documents so that when I return I can vote for Hitler."

The soldier liked the answer and waved him on.

Remembering the incident, Kraus said dryly, "I refrained from adding that these documents would have had exactly the opposite effect, since they would have prevented me from voting entirely."

It was a rare, if oblique reference Kraus made to his Jewish ancestry. In fact, in hours and hours of interviews, and in the notes Hans made for his autobiography, it was the *only* mention of his Jewish background that he volunteered. Listening to Kraus literally, you could conclude he never gave much thought for Hitler, during the 1930's or afterwards.

Kraus' feelings about his Jewish roots were tangled. He didn't like to talk about them or acknowledge them openly. Admittedly, he was only one-quarter Jewish and wasn't raised Jewish. Once in the U.S. Kraus found little to challenge his feelings.

Upper crust social circles were openly anti-Semitic. Senior State Department member Breckenridge Long wrote the State Department policy which rejected pleas of asylum from Jews in Nazi Germany or Austria—while offering asylum to Christians in countries Nazis overran. American national hero, Charles Lindbergh, accepted an award from Nazi leader, Joseph Goebbels, and worked vociferously to keep America out of the war.[15] A year after Hitler enacted the Nuremburg Laws, Lindbergh's wife, Ann Morrow Lindbergh, wrote to her wealthy mother: "Hitler I am beginning to feel, is a very great man, like an inspired religious leader—and as such rather fanatical—but not scheming, not selfish, not greedy for power, but a mystic, a visionary who really wants the best for his country and *on the whole* has rather a broad view."[16]

Meanwhile, through the 1950's, Ivy League universities openly had Jewish quotas;[17] many "nice" restaurants quietly reassured patrons they did not serve Jews, and a leading Shawangunks climber of the era, Bonnie Prudden, recalled being approached by some Appalachian Mountain Club members trying to enlist her support to expel Jewish members from the club. [18]

Yet, Kraus had a Jewish sensibility that shaded his outlook. When Kraus discussed politics—like many in the 1930's, he briefly was sympathetic to the Communists, but grew disillusioned and increasingly conservative—at one point he mentioned Roosevelt. "FDR did a lot of good things, but don't forget, he had some sad sides to him too," Kraus said. "There was that boatload of Jews."

Kraus was referring to the tragic story of the German liner, the *St. Louis*, which left Hamburg, Germany, in May of 1939 for Havana with 937 Jews aboard. Everyone on board held valid immigration permits. But while the ship was at sea, Cuba changed its immigration laws. The passengers' visas became worthless. When the passengers reached Cuba, they were refused permission to land. The *St. Louis* then sought asylum in the United States.

Letting nearly a thousand poor Jews into the U.S. was controversial and politically sensitive. America might be the land of freedom and opportunity, but not, as many Americans were resolved, for so many poor Jews. Many Americans would have agreed with Charles Lindbergh, when he wrote in his journal in 1939, while crossing the Atlantic from France to New York in choppy waters: "The steward tells me that most of the Jewish passengers are sick. Imagine the United States taking these Jews in addition to those we already have. There are too many in places like New York already. A few Jews add strength and character to a country, but too many create chaos. And we are getting too many."[19]

FDR refused to let the *St. Louis* land in the U.S., and eventually the boat ran out of food, fuel and options. It had no alternative but to return to Europe, where most of the passengers ended up in the concentration camps. Kraus said, "Roosevelt wouldn't let that boatload of Jews into the U.S. He could have, but he didn't. He did what was best for himself politically, not for those poor people." And he shook his head at the thought.

After a few days in Trieste, Kraus entered Switzerland where he withdrew money Rudi had deposited, and then went on to France, and London. Crossing into France, he was stopped by a border guard who examined his passport. "Your Austrian passport is no good," the soldier announced to Kraus, "Austria doesn't exist anymore."

Kraus drew himself up to his full height and looked at the soldier squarely. "For me, Austria will always exist." He declared it with as much dignity as he could summon.

"Passez," the guard grunted, waving him through. Kraus smiled at the memory. "God, I had nerve in those days," he said.

In London, Kraus stayed with cousins while his immigration papers were processed. One cousin, who ran a girls school and was very proper herself, invited Kraus to a tea attended by other proper cousins and proper friends. Kraus recalled, "It was a painful experience, because I found it hard to balance sandwiches and a cup of tea on my lap while being polite."

Even more painful was the isolationist attitudes he encountered. At one tea, he described what was going on in Austria. His shocked listeners shook their heads, made clucking noises with their tongues. "This is a terrible situation, of course. But it's not our problem."

Kraus didn't recall which one of his proper cousins announced this, but she managed to do so while balancing her finger sandwiches and cup of tea quite properly. The others in the room shook their heads again in sympathy.

"After all," she continued, "There's really nothing we can do about it."

"Your inability to act is regrettable, because soon you'll have German planes flying over your heads. But this time you'll see: they won't scatter leaflets but bombs," Kraus bluntly announced.

"Well, really, that's enough, young man!" his cousin broke in, turning to another lady at her side. The conversation steered toward safer ground, like weather.

A few months later, after the blitz had started and Kraus was living in New York, he received a letter from his cousin, telling him that, unfortunately, he had been right. "It gave me no pleasure," he said.

After Kraus' immigration papers were ready, instead of boarding a steamer for New York as would be expected, Kraus added considerable miles, expense, time and risk by returning to the Continent, and traveling back to Trieste. Undoubtedly, Kraus was carrying instructions from Rudi to the Marittima staff, and making additional arrangements involving visas and funding for the rest of the Kraus family, who followed him to New York later in 1938 and 1939.

On the Continent, Kraus found the atmosphere "paralyzed with tension." Everyone was waiting with awful anticipation for Hitler's next move and wondering whether there would be war. But for Kraus, the hardest part of his escape was over. For him, now, there was more tedium from waiting—the refugee's bane—than from actual danger.

From Trieste, Kraus traveled across Italy to Naples on the western coast, where he finally boarded a ship for New York, the Conte *Biancamano*. Ironically, given the masses of Jews trying desperately to flee Nazism, the boat was nearly empty. The Atlantic crossing was one of the smoothest he ever experienced. After a pleasant one-week's passage, Kraus reached New York.

Kraus had made it safely at last, but not without enormous help from his father. Once in America, Kraus's relationship with Rudi became even more tangled by their Nazi experiences. With his resolute independence, Kraus hated being beholden to anyone, especially to Rudi, who was still reminding him he made a dumb choice by foregoing the family business and choosing medicine. Yet without Rudi, it is doubtful Kraus would have gotten out of Austria.

To escape Nazism required a repertoire of business skills that Kraus completely lacked—patience to deal with bureaucratic inanities and navigate red tape, ability to negotiate on the black market, and possession of considerable savings and assets. Without Rudi's planning and financial help, Kraus almost certainly would have perished under Hitler along with his aunt and uncle. The knowledge that Kraus bore such a huge debt to his father carried a huge price.

Just as Kraus was growing into his own as a man—becoming established professionally and making peace with his guilt over Marcus—there emerged an entirely fresh set of emotionally charged issues to rekindle the flames of his volatile relationship with Rudi.

Perhaps this was partly what Kraus was thinking when he commented, "I was glad that I had daughters. If I had had a son, he either would have been meek, which I wouldn't have liked; or he would have stood up to me and we would have fought, like I did with my father. Up until the day before my father died, we fought bitterly."

PART II
NEW YORK 1938–1949

15

New American

✦

1938, New York

Once in New York, "the very first thing I did," Kraus recalled, was call Bill Darrach, head of the Fracture Surgery Department, at Manhattan's renowned Columbia Presbyterian Hospital.

Then, as today, Columbia Presbyterian—since renamed New York-Presbyterian Hospital—is one of the leading university hospitals in the world. It is incredibly prestigious to be associated with it,[1] and no easy feat to be hired there, even for an Ivy League-trained doctor. It is even more difficult for a completely unknown doctor, without a U.S. medical license or references. Such was the situation of Kraus in 1938.

Kraus had met Darrach briefly five years earlier, during Kraus' trip to New York. Immediately Kraus was impressed. Darrach, like Kraus, was a medical maverick who believed in the importance of movement. As Kraus listened to Darrach talk, Kraus could barely contain his excitement: Here was a senior doctor criticizing immobilization in large, heavy casts for fractures and other injuries! Expounding the importance of gentle exercises for fractures, started as soon as possible! For the first of many times, Kraus heard Darrach say, 'The best way to treat a fracture is to wish the bones back in place, keep them there with a wish, and exercise them immediately."

Then too, Kraus admired Darrach as a thoughtful and caring doctor, with an open, easy accessible way about him. "A prince of a man," as Kraus put it. "Uncle Bill," as everyone called him, was adored by his colleagues and his staff. He was

---

1. In 2004 *U.S. News & World Report* ranked New York Presbyterian higher in more specialties than any other New York area hospital. The hospital also had more physicians named to "America's Top Doctors" than any other hospital in the country.

also known for his devotion to his patients, and for treating people he met even only casually with courtesy and respect. These included a young Austrian doctor with whom Darrach briefly chatted in 1934.

Kraus said, "The Clinic must have had hundreds of visitors passing through there between my visit in 1934 and when I went back in 1938. I'm not sure if they remembered me. But when I called to make an appointment to see 'Uncle Bill' it was easy. After we spoke for a few minutes, he suggested I give a talk to the staff of the Fracture Service. The talk went well, and a few days later, he asked me to join the hospital's staff as an assistant surgeon."

Kraus paused, smiling as he thought of Darrach. "You know, it was really an extraordinary thing," he said, "Here I was, no immigration papers, no medical license, no professional recommendations, nothing. But 'Uncle Bill' wanted me, so he made sure that the hospital hired me."

Reflecting the less litigious age, Kraus worked part time three days a week while he studied for his New York State medical licensing exam. He passed on his first try, but he feared it might be close. During the exam, he became so engrossed in answering a question on back injuries that he barely left enough time for the other questions.

Living in a small rooming house on 73rd Street near Madison Avenue, license in hand, Kraus' next task was to rebuild his practice. At first, it was slow going. Despite Rudi's wealth, Kraus didn't want to take money from his father. Kraus couldn't afford rent for his own office space, so he sub-let space in another doctor's office. Even then, Kraus could only afford one hour, three times a week. He had a few patients from the hospital, but mostly, it seemed to him, he spent his days waiting for patients to show up and his nights drinking.

Eventually, through word of mouth, a trickle, then a small stream of patients found their way to Kraus' sublet office space. There were enough that Kraus figured out he could afford renting an office for himself—if he didn't also have to pay rent. His solution was straightforward: he gave up his room in the boarding house, slept in his office, and ate a lot of oatmeal.

In most ways, Kraus immersed himself in Americana. He wrote a steady stream of medical articles, laboriously, in English, and to develop colloquial English speech—"which I hadn't learned from Joyce," he joked—Kraus read popular tabloid newspapers and mass magazines like *Readers Digest*. "It still took me a full year before I could understand New Yorkers' strange sense of humor," he added.

But there was one sensibility about him that he could not shake and which seemed more Austrian than it did American. Austria between the wars was far lustier than America. In this regard, Kraus, who embraced America and thought of himself proudly as an American rather than, in his words, a "hyphenated Austrian-American," never shook off the influence of his native land when it came to Susie and other women.

It's not clear at exactly what point the ravishing Susie joined her husband in New York. If Susie had not yet arrived, Kraus was likely relieving émigré stresses by enjoying the company of other women, undoubtedly also striking and athletic. But that might have been true even if had Susie arrived. To both husband and wife, it was becoming increasingly clear that the problem in their relationship wasn't how to work out their many problems; their problem was that they didn't have much of a relationship.

It may seem as though having escaped Nazism, Kraus would happily spend the war safely in the U.S., but really the opposite was true. Kraus yearned desperately to return to Europe. Kraus wanted to fight Hitler.

And once the U.S. entered the war in December of 1940, Kraus felt he should defend his new country. The most natural place, he felt for him to be was as a doctor with the U.S. Mountain Troops while they fought in Europe. Kraus explained, "After all, I intimately knew the area of combat in the Italian and German mountains, I was one of the better skiers and climbers, spoke all the necessary languages—Italian, German, and in those days my French wasn't bad—and I was a surgeon."

But here Kraus ran into a wall that even his persistence couldn't surmount. It wasn't his age—the thirty-five year old wouldn't see much fighting as a doctor, so that was not an issue; and anyway, Kraus was in superb shape for a man of twenty-one; he wouldn't even put up many of his hardest climbs until he was fifty. Instead, the problem was State Department red tape.

Although Kraus was legally living and working in the U.S., he was still classified by the State Department as German. And therefore Kraus, who fled the concentration camps, was labeled an enemy alien.

This curious classification was because of Kraus' place of birth in Trieste. The State Department didn't care that Kraus had lived over two-thirds of his life in Austria, entered the U.S. on an Austrian passport, and had been an Austrian citizen since he was a teenager. To the U.S. State Department, the defining factor was that Trieste at the time of Kraus' birth in 1905 belonged to the Hapsburg Empire. To the State Department, that made Trieste officially German—even though the Hapsburg Empire was disbanded in 1918, and Trieste afterwards became Italian.

To the State Department, all Germans—even Jews—were tarred with the same brush and considered enemies. Ironically, the State Department considered all Austrians to be political refugees, entitling them to expedited citizenship; Germany "invaded" Austria, as they saw it, despite the delirious Austrian reception to Nazism.

The State Department's Byzantine rules often separated Eastern European parents from their children with different citizenship and refugee status. For instance, at the time they entered the U.S., both Rudi and Ella, born in the Sudentenland—which Hitler invaded—were labeled political refugees; Franz, born in Zurich, was a Swiss citizen, able to enlist in the U.S. military (which he did, serving in an infantry unit in Europe); while Sisi was British through marriage. The exception was Hans, the "enemy alien."

Every time Kraus saw a notice about a shortage of doctors in the U.S. military, he tried enlisting. Always, he was turned down. (Kraus would later become an American citizen at the earliest opportunity, as soon as his five years of mandated residency expired in 1945.) He even tried enlisting as a private in the army, but the recruiting officer pulled him aside.

"As a private you won't be in the Mountain Troops, but assigned randomly to mundane tasks, like driving trucks in motor convoys. America needs doctors at home as well," the officer reminded him sympathetically. "I'm sorry, but I refuse to take you, Dr. Kraus."

Finally, this persuaded Kraus, who gave up after thirteen attempts. "That made sense to me, since I was always a poor driver," he said, "but it was one of the biggest regrets of my life and I always felt I missed out on something big. Maybe I would have gotten killed or injured or god knows what. But I've always felt I belonged in the action and should have been part of the experience."

16

Cookie

✦

1939, New York

The Austrian émigré community in New York in the late 1930's was closely knit, like members in an unofficial club. They socialized among themselves, and those who could afford such entertainment ran into each other at the opera and concerts at Carnegie Hall. Many former Austrians settled in towns such as Stowe, Vermont—including the von Trapps of *Sound of Music* Fame—and in the winters they gravitated to the ski slopes in the Catskills and New England, which reminded them of their native Alps.

In those days, few people skied in the Northeast, but virtually everyone who did ski—ex-Austrian or not—knew each other. At the heart of the skiing community was Hannes Schneider, an ex-Austrian ski instructor.

Before the Nazis, Schneider, nicknamed the "King of St. Anton," had been an Austrian national hero. Foreign ski team members, including Americans, often trained in his hometown of St. Anton to learn his state-of-the-art techniques. It is not clear whether these methods included "eight hours of sleep, a limit of seven cigarettes a day and not more than two glasses of wine or beer," as U.S. Olympic skier Betty Woolsey recalled, when she trained in St. Anton with Schneider.[20]

The Nazis arrested Schneider, an ardent anti-Nazi, soon after they took over Austria. But Schneider was incredibly lucky. The American women's ski team happened to be training in St. Anton at that time. Its manager, Alice Damrosch Wolfe, came from a wealthy and politically well connected family. Outraged by Schneider's arrest, Alice pulled strings to pressure the Nazis for Schneider's release. Afterwards, Schneider fled to the U.S. where he started a ski school in North Conway, New Hampshire. Schneider's systematic teaching approach became widely adopted throughout the U.S. Later, he was dubbed the "father of American recreational skiing."

Kraus met Schneider in 1939 while skiing in New England and the two men became lifelong close friends. Most of Kraus' early patients came to him at Schneider's urging. Then Schneider recommended that Cookie, a prominent amateur ski racer who had injured his knee, should go see his friend.

Cookie hobbled into Kraus' office with his leg in a thick plaster cast from hip to toe—the handiwork of a local surgeon, Cookie reported to Kraus, who had told Cookie that he would be disabled for months while his knee healed. Kraus made a sound of disgust, removed the cast, and gave Cookie several immediate mobilization treatments. After a few days, Cookie was healed.

A few days after this, Kraus was treating a patient who knew Cookie. The patient remarked, "It's amazing what you did for Cookie. After just a few days, too! Here he thought he was going to be stuck in that cast for months, and with you, it's off after several days and he's walking around fine. Not only that, he's skiing this weekend at Sun Valley, racing no less."

It was one thing to walk around, maybe do some easy skiing; it was quite another matter to race, which Cookie well knew he was not supposed to be doing! As soon as Kraus finished treating the patient, he shot off a telegram to Cookie.

DO NOT RACE. KRAUS.

Kraus quickly got back a reply from Cookie.

GOT YOUR TELEGRAM.
TOO LATE.
RACED.
KNEE FINE.
HURT SHOULDER.
WANT TO SEE YOU FRIDAY SO CAN SKI ON WEEKEND.
—COOKIE

Cookie played a pivotal role in Kraus' life. All the Northeast skiers soon learned of Cookie's stunning recovery. It was a real start for Kraus' practice in the U.S. Kraus could at least afford to move back into his boarding house. And he earned the nickname "The Ski Doctor."

Not longer after the episode with Cookie, Alice gave a cocktail party in her Manhattan apartment. She invited Cookie who, like so many of Kraus' patients, had also become a personal friend as well as a patient. And so Cookie, in turn, invited Kraus.

By this point, Alice was a widow. Dudley Wolfe had died the summer before during the 1939 K2 expedition. An amateur sportsman—skier, climber, yachtsman—Wolfe's main contribution to the expedition had been the expedition's funding. Nonetheless, although completely inexperienced in big mountains and glaringly untalented in climbing—photographs show a stocky and ungainly looking man—somehow, amazingly, Wolfe managed to get up to Camp 7 at 25,300 feet.

Wolfe's feat isn't even easy today. And, weakened by altitude, he died at Camp 7, becoming the first American climbing fatality in the Himalayas. Three sherpas also died trying to rescue him—in all, four deaths among twelve climbers who set foot on the mountain.

The American Alpine Club, which sponsored the expedition, was appalled. The AAC blamed the expedition's leader, an expatriate German climber named Fritz Wiessner. The ensuing hostilities and controversy were bitter. Wiessner resigned from the Club, and never attempted another big mountain in the Himalayas—or anywhere else—so that, as he saw it, he wouldn't be dependent on other people's resources or abilities.

Alice, now remarried and known as Alice Kaier, didn't blame Wiessner for her former husband's death, and in fact, the two remained friendly. When Cookie introduced Kraus to Alice, they chatted amicably for a bit. Alice would also become a patient of Kraus, and a friend.

That night, she asked Kraus, "How do you like living in New York?"

"Very much so," Kraus replied enthusiastically. "The only problem is that I miss climbing."

Alice said, "Oh, I can help you with that." Then she called Fritz Wiessner.

17

The Partnership

◆

1940–1944, New York and the Shawangunks

Kraus and Wiessner, Wiessner and Kraus: the founding fathers of the Shawangunks; the patriarchs of the Gunks. In the vertical world, their names are as indelibly connected as Joe Montana and Jerry Rice in football, or Magic Johnson and Kareem Abdul Jabbar in basketball.

Like Kraus, Fritz Wiessner, who was born in 1900, had been introduced to climbing by his father. Wiessner showed his extraordinary talent early. At the age of twelve, Wiessner climbed the highest peak in Germany, the Zugspitze; as a teenager, he established extremely difficult climbs on the nearby 300-foot-high Elbe cliffs; and at age twenty-five, he made the first ascent of the southeast face of the Fleichsbank in the Tyrol, which was proclaimed the hardest rock climb ever done at that time. For an encore, Wiessner followed it up with the equally impressive first ascent of the North Face of the Grosse Furchetta.

When the Depression hit Germany hard in 1928, Wiessner immigrated to New York. A chemist by trade, he applied his discipline and hard work to the pharmaceutical import-export business, and began working with large U.S. companies, such as Squibb. Eventually, Wiessner started his own successful ski wax manufacturing business, "Wiessner's Wonder Waxes."

If Wiessner wasn't working, he was climbing. In 1932, he attempted the Himalayan giant, Nanga Parbat, the world's ninth highest peak, and made first ascents throughout North America; including New England, upstate New York, British Columbia, as well as three of the four highest summits in the Canadian Rockies. Not surprisingly, Wiessner thoroughly explored the cliffs around New York City for rock climbing potential. But most of the terrain he found—on cliffs such as Arden, Storm King and Breakneck Ridge—was buggy, crumbly, easy, and generally unappealing.

Then one unusually clear afternoon in 1935 while hiking at Breakneck Ridge, Wiessner spotted a tantalizing line of shining, white cliffs somewhere northwest across the Hudson River. The next weekend, Wiessner determined to find them. They turned out to be the Shawangunk Mountains, in Ulster County, New York State.

Despite its proximity to New York City—less than two hours from midtown Manhattan—Ulster County, even today, is still largely countryside. The soul of Ulster County is the college town of New Paltz.

First settled by the Huguenots in the eighteenth century, New Paltz had become a haven for aging hippies and alternative lifestyles by the 1970's. Even during the conservative Reagan years, the town existed in a flower-powered time capsule; one of the few places left on earth where shops still sold tie-dyed t-shirts and peace signs for daily ordinary wear, not costume party dress-up. By the late 1990's, the town evolved into a weekend hotspot for affluent Manhattanites, but exuded its own uniquely weird and wonderful aura of historical, cultural and new age funk.

Throughout the town's evolutionary twists and turns, one thing remained rock solid: Dominating the New Paltz vista, eight miles west of its Main Street, is a seven-and-a-half mile long ridge of sparkling white cliff. The Shawangunks.

By international climbing standards, the Shawangunks are not high; up to only 300 feet—a stark contrast to the imposing 1,000-foot–plus cliffs in Yosemite in California or the Dolomites in Italy. But the Shawangunks offer a charming setting overlooking the Walkill Valley, excellent, firm rock, a steep 90-degree pitch catering to strenuous upper body maneuvers, and most of all: exposure.

Exposure is a sense of airiness and openness, which is more than a matter of height. While the Shawangunks are not extremely high, they are extremely exposed. A 100-foot pitch in the Shawangunks has more exposure than many routes on cliffs many times higher. Several reasons account for this. The Shawangunks themselves perch on a hillside, several hundred feet off the deck, while the rock is typically overhanging and full of outward features—overhangs, roofs, buttresses, dihedrals and jutting corners—that require the climber to lean back and look out.

And while it is no more dangerous to climb exposed rock than, say, a lower angled "slab" that might not feel as high as it really is, exposed rock is titillating, and often terrifying. When a lead climber looks down, he sees his rope falling between his legs, literally into thin air.

In typical Wiessner fashion, the first time he ventured to the Shawangunks, even though his climbing partners were beginners, he was drawn to the highest section of cliff—a seemingly wild, remote setting that feels more like 1,000 than 100 miles from midtown Manhattan.[21] Undaunted, Wiessner scaled to the top despite difficult route finding, heavy vegetation, and loose rock,[22] thus becoming the first person to rock climb at the Shawangunks.[1]

The next weekend, when Wiessner returned to the cliffs and made his way to the other end of the Shawangunks, it was as though he stepped into a different world. There the cliffs are situated on the grounds of a nineteenth-century grand hotel, Mohonk House, overlooking a bucolic lake, near trails where wealthy hotel guests take leisurely weekend strolls. More importantly to Wiessner, the rock by Mohonk House was firm and of superb quality, and the cliff angle so steep that a rope dangled from the summit might swing freely in air to the ground.[2]

Wiessner was elated by his find. However, for the rest of the decade, Wiessner returned to the Shawangunks only a few more times. Wiessner's energy and time were consumed both by business pressures and bigger peaks. Wiessner made the first ascent of the remote Mt. Waddington in British Columbia in 1936, of the imposing Twin Towers in 1938, and in 1939, led the tragic but nearly successful American K2 expedition.

Often forgotten amid the ensuing K2 controversy was Wiessner's magnificent climbing. K2 would not be summitted until 1954, but fifteen years before, Wiessner nearly made it to the top, in the most purist and exemplary climbing style. Wiessner led and broke trail the whole way—an impressive feat even today, for those who attempt it with modern gear and without the psychological burden of venturing into the unknown. At one point, Wiessner opted to solo hard rock instead of hiking a gentle, but avalanche prone, snow slope—a portion of K2 still unrepeated by 1992.[23]

Accompanied by the sherpa, Pasang Dawa Lama, Wiessner made it up to 27,450 feet, just 800 feet below the summit, and above all technical difficulties. From there, Wiessner would have likely summitted easily, since, it looked like

---

1. Amusingly, the best-selling murder mystery, *The Alienist,* posits a fictional murderer who supposedly learned technical rock climbing in the Shawangunks some fifty years before Wiessner.
2. Wiessner named this route, Gargoyle, after a slug of rock on the route reminded him of a statue.

there would be no storms for at least several hours, and unlike Everest, the top several hundred feet of K2 is a stroll for world-class mountaineers.

But it was already dusk, and sherpa Pasang Dawa Lama, who believed that ghosts roamed the mountain at night, refused to continue climbing. Wiessner faced a choice: He could leave Pasang alone and go for the summit himself in precious, favorable weather, and likely make it. Or else he could stay with Pasang, but given the notoriously swift and unpredictable K2 storms, risk bad weather moving in overnight and preventing a summit attempt the next morning.

Wiessner realized this could be his only shot for the top. And he chose to stay.

The next morning, Wiessner awoke to high winds and heavy snow. A summit bid was too dangerous, and he and Pasang retreated safely down the mountain.

Kraus said, "I always think it should be brought out that Fritz could have gone for the summit, and he would have made it. But he chose not to because he wouldn't abandon his sherpa, who wouldn't climb higher at night. If you look at climbing nowadays, you'd see that many people, maybe most, would not have done what Fritz did. They would have left the sherpa and gone back for him the next day after the summit. But Fritz wouldn't leave him. That was just a terrific thing."

And back in New York, throughout the 1930's, no other climber in the area besides Wiessner was capable of leading a rock climb at the Shawangunks. The cliffs remained untouched until Kraus and Wiessner started climbing together.

By 1940, Wiessner owned a car—a considerable luxury in that era—and arranged to pick Kraus up at his boarding house. The first time they would climb together, Wiessner took Kraus to Breakneck Ridge, and as was his way, insisted on doing all the leading. (The one criticism sometimes made of Wiessner as a climber was that he hogged the position of leader.)

The next weekend, the two men climbed together in the Shawangunks for the first time. Again, Wiessner insisted on doing all the leading.[3] Those few pitches were enough: Wiessner realized that Kraus was different from his previous partners. From that point on, the two men swapped all leads and climbed as equals.

Immediately, Kraus felt at home in the Shawangunks, which strikingly resemble a smaller version of his native Dolomites. The next weekend, he too was making first ascents on the Shawangunks cliffs. Kraus' motivation was partly love of adventure, partly practicality. He explained, "Almost nothing had been climbed.

---

3.   Wiessner led a variation of Gargoyle, and put up another steep, new climb, Overhanging Overhang.

If you saw a line up the rocks that looked appealing to you and you wanted to climb it, by necessity, you had to put up a new route and make a first ascent. Almost everything you climbed was a first ascent."

Soon Wiessner and Kraus were going to the Shawangunks every weekend and established a routine. Whoever first pointed out a line up the cliffs had the privilege of leading its first ascent. The next weekend they returned for the other to lead its second ascent.

There was no doubt they spurred each other on. But Kraus quickly dismissed the suggestion they competed with each other in quantity or difficulty of first ascents. "Competition? There was no competition," he insisted. Kraus couldn't believe his luck, to find such beautiful rock, fairly close, along with such an outstanding partner like Wiessner.

On one of Kraus' first weekends at the Shawangunks, he took a walk after dinner. It was a clear night, the sky full of stars, a full moon hung over the cliffs, and not a light could be seen in the valley below. Kraus looked out at the beauty of the countryside and was filled with a sense of serenity he found only in the mountains. He said, "I knew then I could survive New York."

Kraus loved New York, but keenly felt the absence of nearby mountains—a loss as aching as that of a religious person deprived of his house of worship. He would later say, "When I say the 'Gunks saved my life, I mean it, literally. They were necessary for my emotional and spiritual health.

"I never expected to live to ninety. My father was in his early seventies when he died; my mother was in her early eighties. If it were not for the 'Gunks, I would have died much sooner—of a stroke, heart attack, or some other stress-related condition."

Under Kraus' and Wiessner' leadership, the ranks of Shawangunks climbers soon swelled to ten regulars who migrated to the cliffs each weekend from New York. They were a closely-knit fraternity. In those days, climbing was less a sport than a club, whose admissions standards were democratic but stringent: good cheer, love of the outdoors, and willingness on weekends to be renegades outside of mainstream society. During the week, most had professional mainstream jobs, like Wiessner and Kraus, often in business or science.

Jim McCarthy, a former American Alpine Club president and one of Kraus' closest friends, recalled, "People nowadays forget, in this day when 'extreme' has become chic and you find climbers featured in mainstream advertising campaigns or manufactured extreme experiences watched on TV shows like *Fear Factor* and

Survivor. But in those days, climbing was considered really strange, and climbers were truly outsiders.

"It was still like that when I started climbing in the Shawangunks in the 1950's. God, you couldn't tell anyone you climbed. They'd look at you like you were really crazy, really nuts, like you told them you were a circus performer or something."

Most of the climbers knew each other previously from skiing. They all slept and took their meals at "Schlueters," a boarding house run by two Austrian émigrés. Located on the road under the base of the cliffs, the inn later closed, in the early 1950's, replaced by a liquor store. The original stone house exists, deserted, still bearing the sign, "Liquors."

On Saturday nights, the climbers went dancing at a nearby bar where a band played polkas and waltzes. Or else Kraus played his guitar and they sang the doleful Italian ballads of lost love, suffering, and death that Kraus had taught them. "It was so funny to see these people who had mostly never been out of the country, singing these Italian songs in Italian," Kraus said.

By the end of the 1940's, the Shawangunks had fifty-eight routes, twenty-six of which were first ascents by Kraus, twenty-three by Wiessner. The first several routes Kraus put up are very easy by contemporary technical standards, but at the time were serious undertakings, particularly in the style he did them.

Kraus' routes reflect the man. It would be common for later Shawangunks climbers to stop and pause on a Kraus route, thinking of Kraus making his way up the same piece of rock so many years before—touching the same holds, placing his feet on the same edges, looking up to the same next moves. Because Kraus' climbs are both so strenuous and so exposed, they offer a strangely compelling mix of the physical and spiritual. Many contemporary climbers have commented that they feel Kraus' spirit in the Shawangunks rock. As one modern day Shawangunks regular, Arthur Sulzberger, Jr. said, "Even though I never met Hans, when I climb his routes, I feel like I know him."

Without being a climber, it is hard to fully appreciate the enormity of Kraus' gutsiness on the cliffs—the sheer size of those *cojones.* Even his "easy" routes, the ones with moderate climbing grades, can still be scary, even with modern, safer, comfortable climbing gear. Arthur Sulzberger, Jr., continued, "I know full well the many benefits I enjoy that Hans didn't. I have climbing shoes with sticky rubber where Hans had boots. I have modern camming devices and chocks where Hans had pitons. Where his ropes were hemp tied at his waist, mine stretch to ease a fall and are attached to a waist harness. Most of all, I know the rating of climbs that, to him, were first ascents."[4]

Looking back, Kraus and Wiessner's equipment in the 1940's was downright laughable. They wore street sneakers bought at Army-Navy stores in contrast to the over fifty brands of specialized climbing shoes available today. Kraus reserved a "special pair" with thin soles for the cliffs. "I was very particular choosing my sneakers," Kraus said.

For the rest of his attire, Kraus simply wore army pants, a denim shirt, and a bandana tied around his brow. Ropes were still hemp and always used in pairs, at least one of which was a heavy twelve millimeter, since a single rope could snap from the force of a leader fall or even simple body weight while rappelling, as Emilio had sadly demonstrated.

When later in the decade far superior nylon ropes appeared, Kraus, like many, was initially dubious. "They were so much thinner and lighter than what we were used to. When you went to the Alps, all the guides there were distrustful of these new nylon ropes. But that was because they couldn't afford any for themselves," Kraus said.

In all, Kraus made over sixty first ascents in the Shawangunks. His greatest, and most characteristic, was High Exposure, in 1941.

In so many sports, as years go by, it's increasingly hard to capture the sense of awe aroused by a milestone sporting achievement. To modern eyes, the ice skating jumps of 1936 Olympic gold medalist, Sonja Henie look clunky and novice-like, the downhill skiing turns of 1936 Olympic gold medalist Franz Pfnur would look casual and quaint.

Yet in 2005, the climbing magazine, *Rock and Ice* wrote about High Exposure: "The first ascent of this Gunks uberline marked a quantum leap in American climbing. Dead vertical and at the time covered in lichen and moss, this imposing line was led by Kraus with the occasional soft-iron pin for protection. Wiessner [was] awed by Kraus' display of commitment."[24]

---

4.   Particularly since when Kraus climbed, the cliffs were thickly covered with lichen—now worn off—which hid many key climbing features, such as edges, holds and cracks.

18

High Exposure

◆

1941–1944, New York and the Shawangunks

Late one Sunday afternoon, when the sun was already low in the sky, Kraus was walking with Wiessner along the dirt trail at the base of the cliffs, built originally for horse drawn carriages. Looking up, Kraus spotted a huge rock buttress. He recalled, "I saw this big overhang and I wondered what it would be like to experience being there. I said to Fritz, 'That ought to make a beautiful climb.'

Wiessner replied, 'Well, let's try it.'"

It was too late that day. But the next weekend they returned.

Standing at the base of the huge buttress, Kraus could see that the bottom 150 feet would be straightforward and easy climbing—a heavily veined rock face led up to a wide ledge wedged under the buttress. Kraus, in fact, soloed the bottom portion, without bothering to hammer in a single piton. Now at the ledge, the real challenge began: After belaying Wiessner up to his stance, Kraus explored his options for the remaining seventy-five feet.

Kraus still couldn't see what lay above on the buttress. And he could see only one way he might even reach the buttress: On the ledge's right side, was a roof with a notch. Conceivably, Kraus could climb up the notch, up over the roof, and on up to the buttress. However, the first move would be blind.

Kraus would have to inch out from the ledge, look down 150 feet, lean back into space, awkwardly reach his right hand back, out, up, over the roof, and then feel around for a hold. Even if he managed to climb up the roof, Kraus didn't think he had the ability to down-climb it. He also didn't think he could survive a fall from it.

It was a one-way trip. Once up, he could not turn back.

Like Kraus on the Block Kogel with Marcus above him, Wiessner, on the ledge below, wouldn't be able to hear or offer help to his partner. The decision for Kraus, though, was easy. Kraus said, "I was scared silly. My tongue was stuck to my throat, my throat was dry. But I wanted it badly. So I did it."

Kraus leaned out from the ledge, reached his right hand out and into the notch, found a good rock edge, and climbed up.

There he gazed on the scene before him. The rock buttress was so steep and so much wider than the ledge below had been that from his stance, it looked to Kraus as though he and the buttress were floating in air.

Air—when Kraus looked below, air—when he looked to his left, air—straight ahead, air—above. The north facing buttress, "the wall of high exposure," as Kraus called it, seemed so much colder, windier, and wilder than anyplace else in the Shawangunks. Wiessner might have been less than fifty feet away, but Kraus felt completely alone, completely cut off. And completely at peace.

It was on exposed rock, on soaring spaces, feeling closer to air than earth, that Kraus found order and harmony lacking in a dislocated world, a spiritual framework absent in his daily existence. Even as a child in Trieste, he had wondered to himself, as he surely did then, *What is it all about? Why are we here? What does it all mean?*

While he realized he would never find answers to these questions, he found solace in the beauty of nature and the concrete challenges of the rock and mountains, where issues are clear and answers are absolute. Kraus might have been disdainful about organized religion, yet he was deeply spiritual. For him, the cliffs became a place of worship, the act of climbing a form of prayer. "I don't know what I believe," he would often say, "yet I believe it very strongly."

Kraus still had to make it to the top. The climbing was hard, but he could see a trail of well-defined edges leading upwards. But would they continue to the top? Or would they stop abruptly, stranding him on his wall of high exposure? Climbing down was never an option—he knew couldn't make it without falling, and he wouldn't be able to fall without killing or hurting himself badly. He had no choice: He had to keep moving up, following the holds, hoping they would continue and that he could soon hammer in a piton for his protection.

Kraus climbed higher. And higher. The climbing was still hard, and though the holds were still good he still found no spot for a piton. Aware of the precariousness of his position, he tried to hammer in a piton anyway, choosing a flat, horizontal-shaped piton. He called it a morale booster, but he also immediately knew it was no good, and that if he fell, it would pull out.

Finally, twenty-five feet up from the bottom of the buttress, Kraus found the spot. As soon as he banged in the ring piton, he heard the telltale *twang*, and knew it was good and secure. Now he could relax, thoroughly savoring the exposure to the sky and the breeze against his skin. There on the wall of High Exposure, he felt very far from the ground, very far from the worries and cares of daily existence.

Kraus followed holds out to the edge of the buttress—now air to the left and right, above and below. His heart beat fast and he thrilled to the beauty of his situation. The climbing remained hard, but further up, he found another spot for another good, secure piton, and more good holds. Finally, he pulled over the top.

What would have happened if the holds on the "high exposure wall" were too small or stopped abruptly? "I don't know. I guess I would have prayed," Kraus always replied to this sort of speculation, "Or cursed."

After Kraus belayed Wiessner up, they sat on the top looking contentedly over the countryside below as the sun lowered in the sky. In German, the language they spoke when the two were alone, Wiessner said, "That was quite a beautiful climb, Hans."

To celebrate, Wiessner pulled a package of cigarettes from a pants pocket, took one and passed the pack to Kraus. At that time, both men smoked. Kraus would continue until 1951, when he woke up one morning and decided, "Smoking is a dirty, disgusting habit." He threw away the cigarette he was holding and never smoked again.

The top pitch was so exposed and committing, that breaking with their routine, Wiessner demurred from returning the next week to lead the climb. It was two years before even Wiessner would lead High Exposure.

Knowing Wiessner was on the other end of the rope gave Kraus a good feeling. Kraus was always very particular with whom he climbed; if he didn't like the person, he didn't climb with him. Nonetheless, Wiessner was not someone with whom Kraus could share clever quips or passionately debate his favorite topics of love, sex, women, and death. Although good-natured, Wiessner was as utterly devoid of humor as though humor was a genetic trait and he was born lacking the necessary DNA sequence. Jim McCarthy recalled, "It was funny, in a way, because Fritz married one of the funniest women you could imagine."

"Fritz had a strange outlook," Kraus allowed. He recounted a story Wiessner told him about a climbing trip Wiessner took to his native Dresden in 1973.

Wiessner was standing at the base of the cliff when a large rock fell next to him. Without irony, humor, fear, or any other emotion, Wiessner said to Kraus, "So I'm standing there, Hans, and the rock went, '*pshhhh, thud.*' So I told myself, '*Humph.*'"

"Fritz said it just look that," Kraus recalled, "'*Hmmmph,*' so I told to myself.' And that was it! Fritz was not someone you got into a deeply charged emotional discussion with."

Kraus and Wiessner soon began developing their own circle of climbing protégés. By 1943, many of their hardest climbs were with other partners. When that year Kraus led what many considered his second greatest climb, Madam Grunnebaum's Wulst, his belayer was Harry Snyder, a pediatrician at Columbia Presbyterian Hospital whom Kraus had taught to climb.

On Kraus' first attempt to lead the second pitch of that climb, a rock hold broke. Kraus fell to the ledge where Snyder was belaying. After Snyder realized Kraus was unharmed, Snyder broke into laughter and deadpanned, "So what are *you* doing here?"

Kraus, who enjoyed Snyder's wry humor and unflappability, returned to finish another steep, exposed, and strenuous first ascent. The route remains among the most popular in the Shawangunks, although the origins of its name are almost forgotten.

With the name Madam Grunnebaum's Wulst, most assume Kraus was honoring either a French female climbing partner or a sandwich from a local German restaurant—this second explanation was not so farfetched, since that was the origin of the name of another Shawangunks climb, Raubenheimer's Special. Few realize, instead, that the name is an insider joke, inspired by the common practice of naming a route after a prominent rock feature, leavened with Kraus' love of wordplay and bawdy humor.

On the ledge where Kraus had first landed used to be a green tree—thus Grunnebaum, or "green tree" in German. The technical climbing crux consists of two rounded bulges near the top, which Kraus likened to women's breasts—thus the *wulst*, a common slang term in German. Kraus' route ascends the cliffs by weaving up through the bulges—like tracing a line through cleavage.

The route's name in English: Mrs. Greentree's Boobs.

19

Cojones So Big...

✦

1941–1944, New York and the Shawangunks

As Kraus showed on his first ascents of climbs such as High Exposure and Madam Grunnebaum's Wulst, he was willing to take leader falls under certain conditions. In this, Kraus, already an outsider to mainstream U.S. society by virtue of being a climber, was even an outsider to mainstream U.S. climbing circles.

Prevalent U.S. climbing philosophy of the era was that leaders must not fall. Most prominent American climbers went their entire climbing career without taking a leader fall. Climbing leaders who fell, it was generally held, shouldn't be leading; it was a sign of gross irresponsibility and poor judgment. Contemporary climber John Case summed it up, "If I ever take a fall, then I'll quit."[25]

It made sense for the time. The unreliable gear meant any leader fall could snap the rope and endanger the life of the leader and everyone roped to him. But the philosophy also provided insight into the prevailing American attitude about climbing: as an extension of hiking and a way to enjoy camaraderie in nature, rather than a competitive activity, as it was in Europe.

During the 1930's, leader falls in the Dolomites were common. Kraus caught several of Emilio's and took several himself. Not coincidentally, climbing standards in Europe were also much higher than in the U.S. In the 1940's, the hardest climbing grade in America was 5.7, and even that was rare. (When technical rock climbing started in the 1920's, each route received a climbing grade describing its difficulty.) Yet in 1933, Emilio Comici made the first ascent of a Dolomites climb, Gelbe Kante on the Cima Piccola, graded 5.10—a standard not reached in the Gunks until 1961.[26]

But sometimes a climbing grade doesn't fully capture the climb's challenge. Climbers gave High Exposure a technical climbing grade of 5.6—extremely difficult for 1941—but laughingly added a psychological climbing grade of 5.9. For good reason, Jim McCarthy joked about Kraus, "His *cojones* were so big, he needed a bag to carry them in." Certainly, Kraus was climbing as boldly in the Shawangunks as he had climbed in the Dolomites.

But on closer examination, there was a key difference. Kraus' boldness was now tempered by new found maturity and judgment. Having survived twenty years of close calls—by luck as much as skill—Kraus was in a position to know and understand his mental and physical capabilities, and also to know when to limit himself. He was willing to push himself to the edge, but not hover there precariously. Climbing partner, Howard Friedman, a former member of the renowned 10th Mountain Division and a photographer for *Life Magazine* and *Sports Illustrated*, recalled, "I never saw Hans looking harried or out of control. He never let a situation get out of hand, but stayed the master of the situation."

Even Kraus' ascent of High Exposure was more thoughtful and measured than might appear. By then, too, Kraus appreciated a distinctive and unusual characteristic of the Shawangunks cliffs: Sections of sheer-looking cliff often lay close to sections with big holds. Unlike at most climbing areas, a difficult route at the Shawangunks might lie immediately next to an easy one. When Kraus led High Exposure, he knew that if the section of rock immediately above was too difficult or didn't offer enough exposure for his liking, he could eventually find a path of bigger holds on the cliff wall.

To do that safely, "all" this required for a climber was inordinate physical strength to hang out indefinitely on the steep cliffs, inordinate mental strength to stay cool, calm, and in control, and vision and ability to figure out complex rock route finding to lead to the safety of the summit or next belay—which in the Shawangunks could involve long sections of moving sideways across the rock or diagonal traversing.

Not to mention dealing with the occasional loose block, periodic rock fall, and encounters with snakes, lizards, hornets and wasps. (Not for nothing, there are climbs in the Gunks named Wasp, Hornet Rocks, Snake, Bee Bite, Black Fly, and Gelsa—German for mosquito.)

That's all. In other words, no problem for Kraus.

For the first time, Kraus was now willing to back off climbs. On the rare occasions he started up a section of cliff and decided that his desired route seemed too hard, too dangerous, or he didn't feel up to it that day, Kraus would climb down and simply announce to his astounded partner, "The rock doesn't like me today."

Kraus only refused to listen to his inner voice once, on the first ascent of a Shawangunks climb he called, Asphodel. As he started up the first pitch, he got an uneasy feeling, which he ignored and continued upwards. Nothing happened, but Kraus swore he would never do that again.

Kraus believed strongly in his premonitions, which was funny enough for an atheist, but to him was completely reasonable. But he wasn't going to chance fate. Now that, to Kraus, was reckless.

20

Bad Posture

✦

1940–1945, New York

Despite his disappointment over not fighting in the war, Kraus, at thirty-five, threw himself into the task of rebuilding his life with the energy, optimism, and determination of a young man. In this, Kraus was fortunate to have work that he loved and colleagues whom he respected.

At Columbia Presbyterian Hospital, in addition to his adored "Uncle Bill" Darrach, Kraus worked closely with fellow Austrian émigré, Dr. Sonja Weber. When in 1940 she founded the hospital's Posture Clinic, she recruited Kraus to join her.

Growing numbers of parents noticed their children had poor posture and brought them to the hospital for treatment. At first, Kraus and Weber assumed these must be sick children; those with injuries, birth defects, or diseases such as polio. How else to account for such swayed backs, rounded shoulders, protruded stomachs, or pronounced slumping or hunching over? But they were surprised after they put the children through physical exams and x-rays: Very few of the 200 children at the clinic, less than twenty percent of the total, had anything physically wrong with them.

The doctors were left scratching their heads in bafflement. It was a group of perfectly healthy, normal children. So why couldn't they stand up straight?

Kraus and Weber noticed something else: The children managed to stand with good posture for short periods of time when they wanted to; for instance, when the children thought they were being examined they had no trouble doing so. Afterwards, though, they went back to their poor posture. Kraus said, "It occurred to us that perhaps the children's poor posture was due to muscle problems which prevented them from holding their bodies erect."

Could the answer simply be that the children didn't stand up straight because they couldn't? That they simply weren't strong enough?

To test their theory, for the next several years, Kraus and Weber used calipers, protractors, and water rulers to conduct laborious and time consuming experiments. They took body measurements from different angles and positions. They made line drawings. They measured chest expansion, leg length, and pelvic tilt. They tested relationships between different kinds of muscle contraction to muscle length, varying muscle groups, and the nervous system. Then they went back, and did it all again.[27]

After four years, Kraus and Weber had some answers: First, they identified the key muscle areas responsible for holding a child's body erect. They called them the *postural muscles*, which consisted of six muscle areas around the hips, stomach, hips and stomach combined, upper back, lower back, and hamstrings. Then they defined fitness for these muscles, concluding it was the *minimal amount* of strength and flexibility needed to support and move the child's body in routine, daily activities, so that the body could work properly. This was an important—and it turned out, highly controversial—discovery. It blatantly contradicted two established tenets of medical wisdom then, and it is still little understood today.

When looking at muscles, even today, most doctors and health officials look broadly at multiple muscle areas (most of which are arguably irrelevant to the particular problem), define muscle fitness by comparing a child to his or her peers (based on fixed averages, medians, norms, and other fixed mathematical standards for size, gender, and age), and test muscle fitness based on extraordinary, unusual physical activities (such as maximum weight lifted, most number of sit-ups completed in a given time, and speed-running short distances in a given time).

To Kraus and Weber, this didn't make sense: No one would argue that the muscles of a five-year-old, forty-pound girl face the same demands as those of a sixteen-year-old, 160-pound boy; why would they even face the same demands as those of another five-year-old girl, who might be more or less active, weigh a lot more or a lot less? Why compare one child's muscles to another child's muscles? Why test the child on rarely performed—arguably contrived—physical skills that have little to do with how a child needs to move his or her body in daily life?

The two doctors realized they needed to develop a brand new set of tests for their new definition of muscle fitness. Here they could take advantage of Kraus' keen knowledge of muscles. Their resulting tests would focus solely on the postural muscles, and would focus solely on measuring strength and flexibility against the child's body; not against, as they saw it, irrelevant norms or meaningless averages.

When Kraus and Weber tried their tests—the Kraus-Weber tests, also known as the K-W tests—on the children at the Posture Clinic they found, to their initial expectation and later delight, that the K-W tests worked on *all* the children, regardless of age, weight, physical condition, socio-economic backgrounds, or gender. The doctors then felt they were on to something. If poor posture came from poor muscles, and if they corrected the muscles, then the children should be able to stand correctly.

How to do this? The answer seemed obvious, but also exciting.

Exercise.

Through years of trial and error, Kraus and Weber next developed a series of strengthening and loosening therapeutic exercises. But the tricky part still wasn't over; now they had to make sure each child at the Posture Clinic did the right exercise for his or her particular muscle problem. Kraus explained, "Prescribing therapeutic exercises is an art, and exercises are like medicine. You wouldn't go to a drugstore with a prescription that simply read 'medicine.' You'd of course expect your prescription to be fully described and specific about what you're going to take, how much, and when. It's the same with therapeutic exercise."

Kraus explained further, "You must get the right type, in the right amount, and take it in the right way, which is [for example] everyday, for up to twenty or thirty minutes, slowly, relaxed, and consistently, for several months. It's crucial to prescribe the right exercise, in the right amount, for a particular problem. I wouldn't give everyone the same exercises any more than another doctor would give all his patients the same medicine, whether their problem was a cold, broken leg, or heart condition."

By 1944, the pattern was clear: Regardless of the original problem, children who did their K-W exercises were cured of their poor posture. Children who initially did their K-W exercises, but stopped, showed improvement at the beginning of the study, but regressed to where they were before by the end. Children who didn't do their K-W exercises didn't improve at all.

The resulting data from the Posture Clinic supported Kraus and Weber's theory: poor posture was caused mostly by "poor" postural muscles, either because these key muscles were too weak or too tight. And if you "fix" the poor muscles, then you "fix" the poor posture.

Although Kraus' work with the children at the Posture Clinic was gratifying, he started to wonder whether weak or tight muscles might cause other types of problems for children or adults. Then, a more serious and widespread medical challenge caught his interest.

Just at the time that World War II was ending, a new epidemic was striking America for the first time. Few ever heard of it before the war. Now it struck seemingly out of the blue, hitting indiscriminately across all demographic lines. No one knew where it came from, what caused it, or how to stop it. Finding its causes, prevention and cure would occupy the rest of Kraus' life. The epidemic was back pain.

21

The Epidemic

✦

1946–1949, New York

Inspired by the success of its Posture Clinic, Columbia Presbyterian Hospital organized a similar type of specialized clinic for back pain in 1946. It was such a new problem that no one knew how to treat it. "Before the war, in Europe," Kraus recalled, "No one had back pain. No one had heard of it. Suddenly after the war, all these Americans had back pain."[1]

To head the Back Clinic, Columbia Presbyterian picked another remarkable, strong-willed woman: Dr. Barbara Stimson. Kraus said, admiringly, "If Barbara had been born a man, they would have made her head of the hospital." Stimson came from a prominent family long devoted to public service. Her uncle was Henry L. Stimson, a Republican who from 1911 to 1945 served in the administrations of five U.S. Presidents, and was Secretary of War under Roosevelt and Truman. Gutsy and civic minded, during World War II Barbara Stimson volunteered for the Red Cross to serve in Great Britain.

Nowadays, multi-disciplinary approaches in medicine are common, but Barbara Stimson was a pioneer. And, when she became head of the Back Clinic, she was determined to apply this broad perspective. Stimson recruited a range of specialists from within Columbia Presbyterian to join her clinic, including orthopedic surgeons, psychiatrists, physical therapists, internists, radiologists and neurosurgeons. Among the group were Kraus and Sonja Weber, who Stimson

---

1. No one also knew that the epidemic was just beginning. By the late 1990's, eighty percent of U.S. adults were estimated to suffer back pain at some point in their lives, [Source: Robertson Stephens & Company Health Case Research, 6/16/97, p.4.] with five million Americans disabled by back pain. [Source: Journal of Back and Muscular Rehabilitation, vol. 8, no. 2, p. 95].

asked to explore possible links among poor posture, poor postural muscles, and back pain.

Kraus and Weber started, just as they had done at the Posture Clinic, by taking standard x-rays and physical exams of the 3,000 patients at the Back Clinic. The results were virtually identical to those at the Posture Clinic.[28]

Just like at the Posture Clinic, Kraus and Weber found, to their surprise, very few patients (eighteen percent) had a physical or physiological reason for their condition. The remaining, overwhelming majority (eighty-two percent) of the back pain patients had no apparent reason for their back pain, although they also failed at least one failed the K-W tests.

Was this a coincidence? Or did it suggest that the cause of most back pain was the same as that of most poor posture—weak or tight postural muscles? If true, Kraus and Weber mused, then the K-W exercises developed for children at the Posture Clinic should also work for adults with back pain. Indeed, when they tried the exercises at the Back Clinic, they got the same resounding results: after several months, eighty percent of patients were cured and pain-free.

The results continued to be encouragingly similar to those at the Posture Clinic. When Kraus and Weber conducted follow up studies on the Back Clinic patients eight years later, they found the same link among exercise, fit muscles, and health: patients who continued to do the K-W exercises remained pain-free, but patients who stopped or substituted other exercises found that their back pain had returned or had grown worse.

Kraus and Weber also discovered something extremely important. When they tried the K-W tests on people who didn't have back pain, they found that if someone failed any of the K-W tests—even just one test—the person was likely to develop back trouble. In other words, they found a kind of medical crystal ball for back pain. They realized that the K-W tests, by identifying which muscles were too weak or tight for a person's body, could predict, with extremely high certainty, who would develop back pain in the future—even if a person seemed fine at the time.

But this raised a new set of questions: Why should people, like many men, develop back pain if their muscles were extremely strong, but tight, for their bodies?

It was intuitive to Kraus and Weber that weak muscles could cause back pain, because muscles needed to be sufficiently strong for daily activities. But why tight muscles? Why would flexibility matter? And what role would it play in back pain?

The reason, they decided, was stress. And to explain their finding, Kraus and Weber thought of the work of the great Harvard physiologist, Walter Cannon, who discovered the "flight or fight syndrome."

Cannon had found that lab animals subjected to unreleased stress tensed their muscles, setting off a barrage of physical responses: faster heartbeat, faster breathing, higher blood pressure, more adrenalin released into the bloodstream, and higher blood sugar levels in the urine. Once the animal sensed that the danger had passed, it resumed its previous state—relaxed muscles, lower blood pressure, slower heartbeat and normal breathing.

Cannon theorized that muscle tensing and the resulting physiological responses were crucial for animals to be able to survive in the wilderness, by physically preparing them to fight or flee danger.

What about people? Did the same physiological response also apply to us? After conducting follow up studies on humans, Cannon concluded the answer was indeed yes.

Cannon theorized that million of years ago, when human beings were cavemen, they were genetically programmed, like other animals, for "fight or flight." Cannon concluded this was a physiological response that helped the cavemen survive, under the environment of millions of years ago. The problem came with civilization and more fortunate lifestyles.

Modern men and women no longer lived in caves, led lives like animals, or physically fought for survival. But modern men and women were still equipped with the same physical structures as the ancestor cavemen. When faced with stress—more likely from being chewed out by wearisome bosses than chewed by wild beasts—modern men and women couldn't fight or flee.[2] But their muscles "thought" they needed to, and prepared their bodies accordingly. Then instead, modern men and women were forced to sit and seethe.

---

2.   See *New York Times*, "Always on the Job, Employees Pay with Health." www.nytimes.com/2004/health/05stress.html. "'The physiological changes associated with stress are part of a complex system that once saved the lives of human ancestors, warning them of danger,' said Dr. Bruce S. McEwen, director of the neuroendocrinology laboratory at Rockefeller University. The quick flood of hormones like adrenaline and cortisol pump up the body for fight or flight…But human physiology was not intended to handle the chronic stress that is an inescapable accompaniment of modern life. The wear and tear of long hours, ringing phones, uncertain working conditions and family demands lead to what he calls 'allostatic load,' a stress switch struck in the half-on position."

There is a good reason why expressions come about, such as these to describe annoying, stress-provoking people: "He's a pain in the neck," and "She's a pain in the butt." In the case of back pain, it's literal.

During the early 1940's, Kraus still practiced as an orthopedic surgeon, although he rarely operated. Increasingly, he found he could cure most of his patients with exercise. When in 1946, Columbia Presbyterian formed a brand new department specializing in Rehabilitation Medicine, Kraus was invited to join it. Kraus faced a major career decision: He could stay in orthopedic surgery—the safer and likely more lucrative path—or he could jump into this new, unproven field.

Kraus said, "There were many good orthopedic surgeons. If I had stayed in orthopedics, I would have been one among many. But," he continued, "there was virtually no one who was doing what I was with exercises. In Physical Rehab, I felt I could do more good for the patients."

For Kraus, the decision was easy. He transferred into Physical Rehab.

22

A New Partner

✦

1946–1949, New York and the Shawangunks

Meanwhile, of course, Kraus continued exercising and climbing. He still enjoyed climbing with Wiessner, but increasingly the approaches of the two men differed. Wiessner relished challenging sections of cliff that required him to use his extraordinary climbing technique, while Kraus delighted in exposed sections of cliff enabling him to experience exhilaration and feel closer to nature. Wiessner only wanted to free climb, while Kraus was equally happy to free climb or aid climb. Wiessner cared about *how* he got up the cliff. Kraus cared about *being* on the cliff.

At first, the distinction didn't seem important. Since before Wiessner and Kraus, nothing at the Shawangunks had been climbed, there were plenty of exposed, gorgeous routes within Kraus' free climbing ability.[1] That had changed by 1946, however. Afterwards, to reach new and exhilarating positions on the cliffs, Kraus had to aid climb his first ascents.[2]

Meanwhile, that year Wiessner made the first ascent of perhaps the hardest climb in the country. Wiessner's Minnie Belle was a short, wide crack demanding impeccable "jamming" technique. At the grade of 5.8, it would be several years before anyone, including Kraus, could free climb it. Kraus didn't even care to try. For him, there was no point. There was no exposure.

---

1. Kraus made an exception in 1941, when he "aid climbed" a new route he called, *Emilio*, after his friend.
2. Good example from 1946 was a Kraus' first ascent in the Skytop section of the Sha-wangunks, the Hardware Route, an exposed face with several intimidating roofs.

After 1946, Kraus and Wiessner turned to other partners for their first ascents. For Kraus, that increasingly meant Bonnie Prudden. At a glance, Prudden seemed an unlikely candidate.

An affluent Westchester County mother of thirty-three, she had two young daughters and began climbing with her husband, Dick Hirschland. During the week, Prudden led the life of a well-to-do matron: raising children, doing volunteer charity work, and attending fashionable soirees. But on weekends, she and Hirschland escaped into the mountains and eased into different personas. "I'm living life to the hilt; you have to be in good shape for that," Prudden had commented.[29]

As an adult, Prudden remained the competitive tomboy and hell raiser she had been since a child. She developed toughness while young. Her father had lost the family money in the Depression and her mother was an alcoholic who would leave her family to go on weekend binges. Growing up, her escape was physical adventure.

Delighting in family lore that Davy Crockett was an ancestor, Prudden soon found she was a natural climber and tried to clamber her way up anything: trees, cliffs, houses. A favorite childhood nighttime activity was to climb out her second story bedroom window and traverse a six-inch ledge. Her father sent her to dance lessons, hoping she would be too tired at night for such escapades, and at her parochial school, Prudden was the despair of the nuns, who thought strenuous physical exercise and muscles inappropriate for a young lady. It didn't bother Prudden, who soon established herself as the star of the sports teams.

When she grew older, Prudden declared she wouldn't date any boy who couldn't follow her up a tree. A school friend introduced her to Dick Hirschland, who worked in his prosperous family business. Presumably, Dick was an adept tree climber, for they married in 1935.

The Hirschlands loved the mountains even before they knew about the Shawangunks. When they honeymooned in Austria, in addition to visiting the Hirschland ancestral palace—which Prudden remembered filled with Renoirs, Matisses, and "fifteen foot high doorways"—they summitted the Matterhorn in a snowstorm. It was Prudden's first time climbing.

But in 1937, Prudden, an avid skier, broke her pelvis on the slopes in Vermont. A prominent orthopedist put her in traction for three months; afterwards she had to wear a full leg brace of steel and leather. For several years, she was in constant pain and had to cut back on the active life that she loved.

Prudden and Dick Hirschland had met Fritz Wiessner in the 1930's through skiing, and with his encouragement, tried climbing in the Shawangunks in the early 1940's. Despite her leg injury, Prudden started leading, because before the invention of belay plates, when climbers simply wrapped the rope around their hips, Bonnie worried she couldn't hold her much heavier husband in a leader fall. But the pain in her leg from her ski injury grew worse. Finally, she had to stop climbing and skiing altogether.

Like so many of Kraus' patients, in desperation, Prudden made her way to the "Ski Doctor." When she hobbled into Kraus' office wearing her cumbersome brace, he exclaimed, "Gut got, vat is zat?" Then Kraus proceeded to another of his routine miracle cures. After examining her, he threw away the brace and prescribed some K-W exercises. Within weeks, Prudden felt better. A few weeks later, she was completely healed.

Now the Hirschands took up climbing in the Shawangunks with zest. But differences between husband and wife were immediately apparent. Hirschland was clunky, clumsy and without talent. Prudden was compact, muscular, bold, and a natural. Unlike her husband, Prudden was quickly able to second the hardest climbs and yearned to lead.

Casting about for new climbing partners, Kraus settled his glance on the Hirschlands. Like many of Kraus' climbing partners, the Hirschlands became friends off the cliffs as well, joining him on August climbing trips, as well as winter ski trips to Vermont and the Catskill Mountains of New York State. Sometimes Kraus climbed with Bonnie and Dick Hirschland as a three-some (including a short, stubby climb Kraus led, belayed by Dick Hirschland, called Dick's Prick).

But it was only Prudden who could second Kraus on his hardest routes. Under Kraus' tutelage, she blossomed. Soon, Kraus and Prudden were a steady climbing team. Not long afterwards, they were swapping hard leads, and Prudden herself was putting up hard first ascents, including one of the area's great classic routes, Bonnie's Roof.

Prudden played an even more important role in Kraus' medical career. It came about because of a lazy, casual conversation after a morning of climbing. Kraus and Prudden had just topped out on an easy but extremely exposed climb, and as climbers often do, were sitting on the summit relishing the experience.[30] The sun was hot and the views were stunning. They sat on the top chatting, looking out over the countryside, hawks and turkey vultures swooping below them. For some reason, Kraus thought of his puzzling findings from the Posture Clinic, where most of the children flunked the K-W tests. When he mentioned this aloud, it made Prudden think of the small neighborhood exercise school she ran.

Although the Hirschlands lived in Mamaroneck, one of the country's most affluent communities, Prudden was unhappy with her daughter's gym program in the supposedly much vaunted public schools. To compensate, on her own, twice a week, she led her daughters through exercises: simple calisthenics, a little running, and a little stretching. Over time, friends of her daughters dropped by and joined in. Eventually, Prudden found herself running an informal gym class for neighborhood children. After a couple of months, though, she noticed a troubling pattern. Some of the children had trouble with the calisthenics and stretching. When it came to run, they simply shuffled along.

Prudden didn't know what this might mean, but when Kraus described the K-W tests, she grew curious. She wondered how her little exercise class would do on them, and asked Kraus whether she could try them out on her class.

"Sure you can, but why would you want to?" Kraus said, "The K-W tests are for children in poor shape, with poor posture. Not for healthy, normal children."

Still, Kraus was happy to oblige. Later in the weekend, he gave his climbing partner descriptions of the K-W tests, and directions for giving them. A few weekends later, after they had topped out on another route at the Shawangunks, Prudden reported her findings.

"Something must be wrong with the tests," she said, "Over half the kids in my exercise class failed at least one test. And these are healthy kids."

"You must be giving the tests wrong." Kraus said.

"I followed your instructions exactly," Prudden retorted, "If you think that's the case, why don't you come out and test them yourself?"

Kraus' curiosity was piqued. He decided to do just that.

23

More Exposure

✦

1946–49, New York and the Shawangunks

But when Kraus himself gave the K-W tests to the children in Bonnie Prudden's exercise class, it made no difference. He got exactly the same disturbingly high rates of failure. It was one thing to find those high failure rates among children in a hospital clinic, quite another in a group of supposedly normal children. Kraus considered the possibilities: Something was wrong with the K-W tests, which appeared unlikely, since they had been used by the Posture Clinic and Back Clinic for several years. Or else something was wrong with the children.

Kraus thought more about this: Maybe the problem was the kind of children at Prudden's exercise school. After all, these children were from extremely affluent households; maybe they were more privileged, more pampered and softer than most children. To get answers, Kraus would need to put more children—from average, middle class backgrounds—through the K-W tests.

Armed with his credentials from Columbia Presbyterian, Kraus met with the head of Children's Health for the New York City public schools to ask permission to administer the K-W tests to children in the New York City public school system. Kraus assumed that after he explained the situation, he would have little difficulty: the official for the New York City public schools would be alarmed there might be a problem, and anxious to figure out a solution.

To Kraus' shock, though, the head of Children's Health listened politely and shook his head regretfully. He itemized several reasons why this would be impossible: complex logistics, lack of scientific validation, etc. For each point, Kraus had a ready answer. Finally, the head of Children's Health got down to his real reason.

"I can't let you test the children, Dr. Kraus. What if you find the children don't do well on the tests? It will look bad for me and what do you think that will do to my career? No good, I can tell you. I can't take the chance. I'm sorry, but that's that."

This was an objection for which Kraus had no reply. It was the first time he had encountered that kind of blatantly self-serving attitude in his children's fitness campaign. It would not be the last.

Luckily, Barbara Stimson could help. She used her connections in two different types of Westchester County communities—the affluent town of Rye and the middle-class city of Poughkeepsie—both of which agreed to let Kraus put their public school children through the K-W tests. Results in both cities were the same. Regardless of age or sex, over half the children flunked the K-W tests.

Instead of an answer, Kraus was left with more questions. He had the feeling he had stumbled onto something important. He just wasn't sure what it was. He would figure it out in the next decade.

Depending on one's viewpoint, it is possible to think either that Kraus's medical practice hobbled his climbing or highlighted his perspective. Even though Kraus had the necessary ingredients to make a superb Himalayan climber—drive for adventure, strength, stamina, technical skills, tolerance for risk, tolerance for suffering—he wasn't sufficiently tempted. He always turned down offers to climb the really big mountains.

Medicine to Kraus, always, came before the mountains. "Medicine I did for other people," he would say, "the mountains were for myself." Expeditions to the Himalayas simply would take him away from his patients for too long—Wiessner, for instance, had to be away six months while attempting K2. To Kraus, that was a personal indulgence he couldn't justify while people needed his help.

Kraus had absorbed his father's work ethic. Kraus liked to say, "A good office runs itself; you simply have to be there all the time." Kraus practiced what he preached; his standard 8-hour workday often extended into nights and weekends.

The exception was August. In European fashion, Kraus shut his office for the entire month to take off for a climbing trip into a wilderness area. He started the tradition right after he moved to the U.S. "It was easy for me to get away then, since I had no patients anyway," Kraus said.

Kraus' first August climbing trip was to the Tetons in Wyoming, with which he immediately fell in love and returned to several years in a row. His companion was his old friend from Vienna, Anstel Dehne, then living in Chicago, who had accompanied him on the Easter ski vacation when Kraus took his big fall. For other trips, Kraus chose Estes Park in Colorado and the Wind River in Wyoming.

Regardless of destination, these trips were not for the dainty or faint hearted. Kraus sought out remote areas with difficult access, no supplies, no baths (although he somehow managed to shave daily) no communication with the outside, no chance of rescue. Accompanying him on these trips were various Shawangunks protégés, such as Betty Woolsey, who found Kraus a "witty and delightful companion," and recalled some of the Tetons' remote beauty.

> On a previous visit to the Tetons, Hans had made the second ascents of the North Face of the Grand with Paul and Bernice Petzoldt. His objective this trip was the steep north face of Owen, unclimbed at this time. Although I would not join them on this attempt, I agreed to help pack in their gear, setup a camp on Cascade Creek, and establish a bivouac site at the base of the Owen Face. We made a comfortable camp the first night, near the creek and next to a great boulder that reflected the heat from our campfire nicely into our tents. The following day we had a rough, steep bushwhack carrying sleeping bags, climbing equipment and food to the foot of the face, where it took a long time to find a spot level enough to lay out the two bags.
>
> Hans and I then made the first ascent of the most interesting looking of the group of pinnacles that form the west side of Valhalla Canyon. The approach involves crossing icy Cascade Creek, then scrambling straight up for over 2,000 feet, fighting through a tangle of bushes and down timber...The canyon is well worth the struggle as it is one of the most remote and beautiful spots in the Tetons. Enclosed on three sides by the cliffs of the Grand, Owen and the pinnacles, there is a crystal-clear stream running through the many wildflowers on the canyon floor.[31]

The trips were filled with plenty of first and early ascents, of which Kraus didn't bother keeping track. More appealing to him was the adventure, physical challenge, and chance to be close to nature.

If Kraus had his way, every weekend, all year round, he would have climbed. Cold, snow—it didn't matter; if anything, it made him feel he was back in the Dolomites. His Gunks route, Three Pines, with its very easy but exposed traverse, was a particular wintertime favorite. But even for Kraus, at some point, it grew too cold and snowy to rock climb safely or enjoyably. And then it was time to ski.

Yet someone who knew Kraus from the cliffs and then watched him on the slopes would be tremendously bemused. It was as though a different persona took over. Just as on the rock Kraus was fast, bold, and powerful, on the ski slopes he was slow, cautious, and awkward. He had no illusions about his skiing ability, and didn't care, often joking about it at his own expense.

"One time skiing with friends, I was so slow, they grew roots waiting for me," Kraus said.

"God, he was terrible, just an awful skier," close friend, Jim McCarthy, agreed, laughing.

Once you understood Kraus, you realized this made perfect sense. The skiing that he really loved was mountaineering skiing—no amenities, no chairlifts, no groomed trails, no lift lines, no other people. The "yo-yo" skiing of the U.S. resorts was less physical, less committing and therefore less appealing to him; he always felt skiing lost much of its essential nature when skiers no longer had to hike up the slope.

The main draw of skiing for Kraus was that it got him back into the mountains. Except for that, he cared little about skiing as an activity. He didn't try hard, and didn't want to. He didn't want to chance a ski injury like a broken leg. Considering the risks Kraus took in climbing this would seem strange, but that was precisely the point. He explained, "I didn't want to do anything skiing that might cause an injury where I wouldn't be able to climb."

Also late in the 1940's, Kraus began an affair with a married woman. This in itself was nothing new or notable. Until his second marriage, he had many affairs, with single and married women. At that time, the rule of thumb for Kraus with women was similar to climbing: If there was a woman he wanted, he went after her; and as several people attested, the woman didn't stand a chance. This affair, though, was different.

While it didn't keep Kraus from sleeping with other women, it lasted over ten years and meant more to him than any other relationship up to that point, including his first marriage. As the affair wound down, it became clear to both there were basic, irreconcilable differences. They discussed marriage. Kraus and the woman agreed it wouldn't work. They went separate ways, but with great bitterness which endured for decades.

In medicine, there was still so much Kraus wanted to do and accomplish. His work at the Posture and Back Clinics was just the beginning, he felt. His K-W tests on children hinted at something big and alarming going on, but he didn't yet know what it was. Then there was his tumultuous, love-hate relationship with his intimidating father.

Kraus dearly wanted Rudi's respect, which he felt he didn't yet have. Rudi, who still begrudged him his "childish" and idealistic choice of medicine over a practical and lucrative business career, could be crudely blunt. It hurt when Rudi would remark, "You know you're really not a doctor, you're just an exercise teacher."

For all these reasons, Kraus in 1949 could not be called a contented man. But nor was he unhappy. For one thing, he was too busy to dwell on that. For another, he was too philosophical. A poem he wrote while in his 'twenties still summed up his belief nearly twenty years later, "Life is fleet…a mere whisper."

For now, though, Kraus had his patients, his climbs, and his women. For now, that was enough.

PART III
NEW YORK 1950–1961

24

King Kraus

◆

1950–1954, New York and Europe

As the new decade dawned, Kraus, nearly fifty, was basking in his prime. The definitive climbing history, *Yankee Rock & Ice*, wrote, "For the next ten years the diminutive Austrian bestrode the towering cliffs like a colossus…Rarely has one man so dominated a major climbing area."[32]

There was one noticeable change, though, between the younger and older Kraus. After a climbing trip to Europe in 1951, his climbing attire underwent a shift. Gone were the worn work pants and bedraggled $.39 sneakers bought in Army-Navy stores. In their place was a dapper new wardrobe, inspired by the latest in European climbing fashions, including the state-of-the-art climbing shoe—the *klettershoe*, with suede leather uppers and rubber-cleated soles.

To a modern rock climber, now used to sleek and skin-tight rock climbing "slippers," the klettershoe looks as clunky as a rubber rain overshoe. But its engineering was actually a huge improvement over the sneakers climbers previously wore. Ted Church, a Shawangunks climber from this period, recalled, "You could now stand on narrow footholds that your sneakers used to just roll right off." Church estimated that the klettershoe might have boosted ability on some Shawangunks climbs by as much as fifty percent.

To go with his klettershoes, Kraus adopted the climbing attire that was now a virtual uniform among his European climbing guide friends—matching corduroy vest and knickers, custom-cut for climbing with extra-wide vents to accommodate high steps, overhead reaches and wide stemming. Topping off the ensemble, Kraus added a snug fitting Italian motorcyclist cap.

Shawangunks climbers took note of everything about Kraus: what he did, what he said, even what he wore. Just as during the 1940's, when Kraus unintentionally popularized a proletariat look for Shawangunks climbers, now he also inadvertently spearheaded a cliff-side fashion revolution. Following his example, tailored ensembles now became the rage—climbers even sported the Italian motorcyclist cap, although few had climbed in Europe.

Kraus' leadership in the Shawangunks continued beyond his status as fashion icon. After Wiessner married and moved to Stowe, Vermont, in 1952, Kraus was left alone at the top of the Shawangunks social strata. Throughout the decade, it was Kraus, and Kraus alone, who dominated the Shawangunks, to a degree unusual at any time, in any climbing area.

Yankee Rock & Ice reported that Kraus was nicknamed "King Kraus," and he was indeed a figure of awe to some and of authority and intimidation to others.[33] Kraus insisted he never heard that nickname, but one moniker that he heard a lot, used out of endearment and respect, was "Papa." The reference wasn't to his age or parental status, but to Ernest Hemingway, who ruled the American literary scene with his powerful writing output and was revered as an American icon for his adventurous and macho personal style. To the Gunks climbers, in culture there was Hemingway; on the cliffs there was Kraus.

By 1950, climbing in the Shawangunks had become a popular activity. Then, about twenty-five climbers visited the cliffs on weekends; three years later, the number was nearly quadruple that figure. Kraus saw this as a mixed blessing. He was delighted to serve as mentor to many, but more climbers also meant more potential for accidents. Even in that less litigious era, that could mean law-suits—and the cliffs might then become closed to climbing.

Kraus had started taking action to prevent accidents through education and instruction in the 1940's. From the beginning, when just a handful of enthusiasts attempted Gunks climbs, both Kraus and Wiessner climbed at least once with everyone at the cliffs. Afterwards, they gave a critique and shared cautionary personal experiences. Kraus would tell the story of Marcus, and Wiessner told the harrowing tale of Otto, his cousin and climbing partner, who died soloing when Wiessner was a teenager. (Otto's death led Wiessner to declare, "If I ever fall climbing, I'll die." Wiessner, despite all his derring-do feats in the mountains, never did fall.)

Kraus and Wiessner felt responsibility to the new climbers, but were also "scared silly that if a serious accident happened," Kraus recalled, "the Shawan-gunks would be closed to climbing." Their fears were reasonable. The 5,000 acres of the Shawangunks were privately owned by a single family, the Smileys. None of the Smileys climbed. And there wasn't any logical reason for the Smileys to allow climbing; from it they received no financial windfall, no tax incentive, no prestige or conceivable social benefit. The safest, easiest, and most expected and sanest course, would be, in fact, for the Smileys to close their land to climbing.

However, the Shawangunks climbers were extraordinarily lucky in the remarkable Smiley family. As Quakers, the Smileys felt more like stewards than owners of their land, valuing its wilderness atmosphere over potential profits, taking great satisfaction knowing their land brought pleasure to other people. As the number of climbers grew steadily, Kraus and Wiessner met with the Smileys.

"What can we do to ensure that you'll keep the cliffs open to climbing?" they asked. "What if we make sure there are no accidents?"

"If there are no accidents," the Smileys replied, "We'll be happy to keep the cliffs open to climbing."

"That's more than fair and reasonable," Kraus and Wiessner replied. "Leave it to us."

Kraus and Wiessner's informal mentoring climbs evolved into a formal training program for all Gunks climbers. By the end of the decade, Kraus and Wiessner taught all brand new climbers to "second" the leader and experienced climbers to lead safely. (Before anyone could lead, Kraus or Wiessner had to put him through a check out climb and grant formal approval.)

This was an extraordinary effort on many levels: The time commitment for Kraus and Wiessner was enormous—for ten years, it consumed half of their precious weekend climbing time. And they ran it as volunteers, without any official means of enforcement, other than their personal reputation and authority.

Undoubtedly some climbers grumbled; it was true that Kraus and Wiessner brooked no discussion or debate over their decisions. But no Shawangunks climber dreamed of disobeying them. At the Shawangunks, Kraus and Wiessner were gods, rigid and controlling to some, benevolent and gracious to most, absolute and awe-inspiring to all.

And no one would argue with the results. Kraus and Wiessner taught well; their training worked. Despite the mix of bold climbing and crude gear, during the 1940's, there was not a single serious climbing accident in the Gunks.

By the early 1950's, though, change was afoot at the cliffs. With Wiessner away in northern New England, responsibility for the training program fell to Kraus alone. Meanwhile, a new force in northeast American climbing emerged—the Appalachian Mountain Club.

Founded in 1876, the AMC is the oldest conservation and recreation organization in the country, dedicated to protecting the environment and promoting appreciation of mountains, rivers, and nature trails in the northeastern United

States. It might seem as though Kraus would be one of the organization's biggest supporters, but it had different ways of doing things. Kraus didn't dispute the values of the AMC mission. He just got into disputes with certain AMC officials.

Partly, this was to be expected. Lacking finesse, patience, or politicking skills, as Kraus himself pointed out, he didn't work well in organized settings, whether the arena was business, medicine, or climbing. (A rare exception was Columbia Presbyterian Hospital.) Kraus found the AMC officials bureaucratic, but as long as their procedures didn't interfere with his training program, he didn't care.

For its part, the AMC found Kraus authoritarian and dictatorial. But, similarly, as long as Kraus didn't interfere with AMC authority, the organization didn't care to challenge the all-powerful Kraus, and it even bestowed on him the official title of "Head of the Safety Committee."

Still, neither party was satisfied. A run-in seemed likely. It came over a scientist.

Lester Germer was a physicist with Bell Labs whose work in the 1920's demonstrating the wavelength characteristics of electrons was Nobel Prize material. Brilliant, amicable and eccentric, Germer was also an extremely enthusiastic climber, and popular with the AMC board. But, at least, for the first couple of years after he started climbing, he was also fairly inept.

On a personal level, Kraus and Germer were like oil and water: To Germer, Kraus was stiff and intimidating. To Kraus, Germer was an absent-minded, head-in-the-clouds, theoretical scientist. Kraus couldn't care less that Germer had almost won a Nobel. Kraus dismissed the scientist as someone who dealt well with theory, but less so with real world issues that needed judgment and common sense. When Kraus took Germer out on a climb to see if he was strong enough to be certified to lead, the experience reinforced Kraus' opinion.

Obviously nervous even before they started, as Germer climbed, he grew flustered and made several small but potentially dangerous mistakes. At the crux—the hardest part the climb—Germer stopped, peered at the rock and then peered back at Kraus.

This went on for some time. It was clear to Kraus that Germer didn't want to admit that he was scared to go ahead, but didn't want to say so either. Finally, to Germer's obvious relief, Kraus said he was taking over and would lead the rest of the climb. When they reached the top, Kraus told Germer that he had flunked. Kraus thought that was the end of the matter.

But the next night, the head of the AMC called Kraus at home. The AMC Head explained that Germer was extremely upset, that he had stopped by his apartment in Manhattan and that they had walked around the block for several hours talking about what had happened. He was now calling to persuade Kraus to reverse his decision.

Kraus was outraged, and if anything, that type of pressure on Kraus was bound to produce the opposite effect. Anyone who knew Kraus well could imagine he pulled himself up stiffly as he declared, "This call is one more reason why I won't change my mind. As head of the Safety Committee, I'm supposed to have responsibility for everyone's safety at the cliffs. If that's the case, I must have the authority to do what I see best. If not, then the position is meaningless."

They talked some more. Kraus added, "To show I am fair, let me remind you of another climber I recently checked out. He had led very well until we reached the crux, where he stopped and said, 'I can't do this. You need to take over.'

"So I did and led the rest of the climb. When we got to the top, I said to him, 'Okay, you pass.'

"He was very surprised. He said to me, 'But I couldn't lead the crux.'

"I had said to him, 'Yes, but you knew it, and showed good judgment when you asked me to take over.'"

But the head of the AMC continued to speak on Germer's behalf, and insisted that he be passed. Disgusted, Kraus resigned from the Safety Committee and refused to have anything more to do with the AMC.

But there was a bright side: Without the training program, Kraus had all weekend to climb for himself, and though he continued to feel responsibility to climbers on the cliffs, he no longer felt constrained to set an example when not climbing.

Now, after a sweaty day of climbing, Kraus and his climbing partners cooled off with sprightly co-ed skinny-dipping in one of various ponds and swimming holes in the Shawangunks. (Their favorite was the "Crystal Pond.") They unwound with their trademark cocktail, which inspired the route name, "Dry Martini," although, as with so many Kraus route names, there is a double entendre, as "drei" in German means three.[1] And, as climbing partner Bonnie Prudden made clear to *Sports Illustrated* in a 1956 interview, in Kraus' milieu, there was always much laughter and liveliness. "'People think you shouldn't drink if you want to set a good example of fitness,' she said, tossing her cropped head of curls, 'I say, the main reason for having a good body is to get the most out of life—and that means having fun, and it may mean having a drink now and then.'"[34]

---

1. First climbed in 1955, receiving the technical climbing grade of 5.7.

Kraus also continued to push himself on the rock. His route, Bitchy Virgin,[2] received the first "R" rating in the Shawangunks for danger—designated an extremely serious undertaking for the leader, meaning a fall would likely be long, and entail serious injury or death.[3] Kraus explained his inspiration for the route's name: "'Virgin,' because it had never been climbed before." He shrugged, as he continued, "'Bitchy,' because she wouldn't let me in."

There was no double entendre, though, intended by the name of the first ascent of his 1951 route: Never Again. In the wildest section of the Shawangunks, Kraus made his way up a poorly protected portion of cliff face below a huge, exposed roof. To figure out how to climb up and above the roof, he went through several hours of huge, scary falls and swings into space; caught by his rope, he was secured to the cliff wall only by a single, although well-placed piton.

The experience was so scary and exhilarating, that Bonnie Prudden recalled thirty-odd years later, "There was lots of laughter [throughout the climb]. We finally got through; we didn't know how. We were so hysterical with the fact that we weren't dead we just rolled down the mountain to the bar." Employing selective memory—considering she was on the first ascent party of Dry Martini and her *Sports Illustrated* quotes—Prudden added, "Neither of us were drinkers but we had five vodkas each and they didn't touch us. We were so adrenalized we stayed perfectly sober."[35]

During the early 1950's, Kraus climbed outside of the Shawangunks as well, particularly in the Adirondacks of upper New York State and in the Dolomites, where he had one of his closest calls on the Campanile Basso, in August of 1953.

He and Bonnie Prudden had just topped out on the summit when an unexpected hailstorm hit. The only way down was from a series of long rappels, requiring two ropes tied together. But they had only one rope. The other rope was supposed to be carried up by the climbing party behind them, led by Kraus' good friend, the great big wall climber, Gino Solda.

When the hailstorm grounded Solda, Kraus and Prudden were stranded on the summit without a second rope. They couldn't rappel. But they couldn't stay on the summit either. Dressed in light cotton, Kraus realized that he and Prudden were growing hypothermic. They needed to descend immediately, or else they could die.

---

2.   First climbed in 1954, receiving the technical climbing grade of 5.6.

3.   In technical rock climbing, in addition to grades describing climbing difficulty, there are also four ratings describing danger to the climbing leader: "G" for good protection, "PG" for pretty good, "R" for dangerous, and "X" for death fall potential.

They had no choice. Kraus untied himself from the rope, using the full length to lower his partner to the rappel anchor. He took a deep breath and started down climbing without any rope or protection for himself. If he slipped, he and Prudden would both die.

All around them the wind howled, the snow blew thickly, and the ice coated the rock slab below with a fantastic, if dangerous, beauty.

Kraus expected to die in the mountains: a slip, storm, avalanche, rock fall, broken rock hold. All were possibilities; these were terrible odds. He thought likely this was it.

Yet Prudden recalled how cool and calm Kraus was: one part of him rationally assessed their survival options, another part comforted her, and a third kept sufficiently detached to thrill to nature's spectacular show around them. When Kraus finally reached Prudden at the rappel anchor, his reward was that he had to repeat the dangerous maneuver, again and again, until finally they reached the ground.

In journals Kraus kept for his August European trips of 1951 to 1953, he mainly jotted down unadorned information: telephone numbers, routes, hotels, American Express traveler check serial numbers. And in the entry for the day he climbed the Campanile Basso, Kraus simply added, "Memorable. Rain, hail, snow."

25

Rudi's Last Lesson

✦

1952, New York and the Shawangunks

Death had been much on Kraus' mind during the early 1950's. In 1952, Rudi died. Even though Hans and his father had fought bitterly, Rudi's death created a watershed in Hans' life, and afterwards, an ache in his heart.

Right until the end, Rudi had disapproved of Kraus' life: the precarious living he made from medicine, his unsettled personal life, and even his climbing; this last was ironic, since it had been Rudi who introduced Hans to the mountains. But as Rudi made clear to his son, it was one thing for Rudi and his circle of wealthy friends to climb with a professional guide in the European mountains; it was an entirely different matter for his son to spend all of his free time playing on the cliffs, without a guide, as though he couldn't afford to hire one.

"Probably because he wanted to discourage me, but my father always kidded me that I was childish to climb," Kraus explained. "So I was surprised when one day, he and my mother came up to the Shawangunks to visit me. At the end of the day, he escorted me to the car, an open Chevy. And he said to me, in Italian, 'You have all my respect.'"

Rudi's comments were balm to Kraus, after so many years of friction between them and the dangers they had faced together. Knowing he had finally earned his father's respect made all the difference to Kraus. In one fell swoop, so much of the pain and angst fell away. Father and son were left looking at each other clearly eye to eye, man to man. Rudi put out his hand and placed it on his son's shoulder. And father and son embraced.

It was one of the happiest moments Kraus knew. He said, "I had been fighting with my father ever since I was a little child, but for the first time that day I felt I had finally earned his respect and acceptance, and finally made peace with him."

The very day after Rudi's visit, Kraus was sitting at breakfast when the telephone rang. It was his mother, calling from their home in Larchmont. "Come quickly, your father is dying," she said. When Kraus got there, though, Rudi was already dead.

Kraus and his brother Franz arranged for Rudi's body to be cremated. About the occasion, Kraus said, "The next morning when I woke it was a beautiful day, but everything to me was black. My grief was abysmal.

"I felt like doing a difficult climb because that always helped me. I took along two climbers for instruction purposes. [Here Kraus mentioned their names, one of whom was a prominent Gunks climber.] I led up, and went over the crux, and then a few more meters was up to the ledge. There was loose rock there, which I carefully avoided, but when I stood on the ledge, the whole damn ledge came right off. I pushed off and fell down to the bushes right above the start of the climb, maybe thirty feet above the ground.

"I blacked out, and when I came to, I was lying head down in the bushes. It was very quiet. My two partners had left, in a panic, scared silly. They said later they went to 'get help.' But they left me alone, without even tying off the rope." Kraus shook his head in a mixture of disgust, amazement and exasperation at supposedly experienced climbers panicking and behaving so atrociously.

"I opened my eyes, moved my fingers and toes, and everything felt okay. I righted myself and climbed over to the corner. There was a little crack, which I was able to climb down to the ground, which wasn't very far at that point.

"I pulled down the rope, coiled it, and walked out. On the way, I ran into my two supposed 'rescuers.' When I went to bed, I thought, 'This is terrible, even the rock doesn't like me anymore.'

"Yet death makes you appreciate life. In the morning when I woke up, the sun was shining, and I was filled again with a sense of purpose and awe. And I found that this terrible grief over my father's death was gone. The rock actually saved me weeks and months of grief. You see how the rock, the mountain, did so much for me in every way. At crucial points, it helped me."

Here Kraus had paused, before adding, "I still miss my father; I miss him even today." And Rudi had one last lesson for his sons. After his body was cremated, his ashes were delivered to his family. But instead of the customary urn, Rudi's ashes had been placed in an ordinary tin can, like the kind used for canned fruit.

The brothers read the label on the outside of the can: "Sample, without value."

26

Pieces of the Puzzle

◆

1950–1954, New York and Europe

During this period, Kraus transferred his affiliation from Columbia Presbyterian Hospital to New York University's Rusk Institute of Rehabilitation Medicine, and continued to ponder the meaning of the children's K-W test results from Poughkeepsie and Rye. When in 1951, while Kraus had spent his annual August vacation climbing in Austria, Italy and Switzerland, the thought came to him: "Why not return the next August, and on rest days in between climbing put children there through the K-W tests?"

The more Kraus considered this, the more excited he grew about it. He had been planning to return to Europe the following August anyway. (He would also return in 1953 as well). He spoke the languages and still had enough medical contacts to make the necessary arrangements. Plus, testing in Europe would help keep costs low; a significant consideration, since Kraus paid for all the K-W children's testing out of his own pocket.

In Europe Kraus found the officials much more open to his research than those he had approached in the U.S. This was true even among those who were initially distrustful, such as Dr. Bauer, the Chief of Children's Health in Zurich.

Bauer grudgingly conceded to meet Kraus and Prudden, who by now had become Kraus' research assistant as well as climbing partner, but granted them only five minutes before Bauer had to catch a train. Soon after Kraus started talking, however, Bauer perched forward in his seat and began listening intently. After the five minutes was up, Kraus paused to remind Bauer of his train, but the doctor waved his hand aside.

"Don't worry about my train. What you're saying is important and I can't be certain that our children are physically fit. Please continue."

One half hour later, Kraus finished. Bauer said, "I'll let you test the children, Dr. Kraus, but on one condition."

Kraus stiffened, remembering the reaction from the health official in New York. But Bauer took him by surprise. "Dr. Kraus, I want to know the results *personally*," he stressed. "If they're not good, I intend to do something about them."

Bauer pulled out a map of Zurich, identified a good demographic cross sampling of schools, and as Kraus and Prudden still sat comfortably in his office, he made calls to arrange for their school principals to help them.

In all, Kraus and Prudden had tested 4,400 American children between the ages of six and sixteen, and found that over half (fifty-six percent) flunked the K-W tests. But when they tested 3,000 children of the same ages in Europe—2,000 in Italy and Austria, with another 1,156 in Switzerland—they found only eight percent flunked.[36]

The results were consistent across all categories: Regardless of gender, age, or particular test, European children scored dramatically better than the American children. Even more telling, unlike the K-W test results of American children, the results of European children didn't get worse as the children grew older.

What could explain this? What could it mean? Kraus dismissed the possibility that European children were born in better condition or had superior genes. He thought about his observations on his recent trips to Europe, and he grew convinced that the explanation lay in the different living conditions in the U.S., which reflected the "dark side" of American prosperity and privilege.

American prosperity after WW II was a source of national pride. Americans enjoyed unprecedented affluence, including widespread availability and affordability of various mechanized time and energy saving devices: cars, televisions, escalators, elevators, and electric household appliances. In contrast, post-WW II Europe was ravaged physically and economically. Conditions remained the same or cruder than they had been before the war. Europeans couldn't afford the latest technological wonders and mechanized devices. Without cars, Europeans had to walk or ride bikes; without escalators and elevators, they had to climb stairs to apartments, offices and shops.

Kraus, who always thought climbing stairs was one of the best exercises, started thinking about this. And the pieces to the puzzle started falling into place for him: American children's lives were too easy, he realized. Modern conveniences meant that children weren't getting enough built-in exercise in the course of their everyday life, unlike previous generations of children.

Of course, in theory, public school gym classes were supposed to compensate. But in practice, as Bonnie Prudden's home exercise classes showed, that hadn't happened. Clearly, the American public school gym programs weren't successfully making children physically fit. Something was wrong with these gym programs. But what?

Kraus thought again about the harder European lifestyle, its impact on children, and the contrast with America. Then he thought also about the contrast he had seen between the European gym and American gym programs.

In Europe, the goal in the gym programs was fitness for all children. Kraus was particularly impressed with the Swiss gym program: a full hour of daily exercise—running, swimming or gymnastics, plus calisthenics and stretching. In addition, Swiss children and their teachers devoted one afternoon a week—often on a Saturday—to an active outing, such as hiking or swimming. And children who lived within two miles of school walked to school every day, while those further away biked to school.

Furthermore, Swiss gym teachers believed that setting a personal example of fitness was an important part of their job. They kept themselves strong and trim, came to class in gym clothes, ready to demonstrate the exercises personally. Kraus recalled an exceptionally fit sixty-five-year-old Swiss gym teacher explaining, "I must be able to chin myself, run and jump better than the children; otherwise I can't do my job. If I'm not fit, what does that say to the children?"

When Kraus contrasted this to the American school gym programs, the differences popped out starkly. In the American gym programs, the emphasis was on team sports, particularly football, baseball and basketball. A proverbial light went off in Kraus' head. "Sports by themselves don't get you fit," Kraus said, "You need to be fit to play sports."

The more Kraus thought about American gym programs, the more problems he saw: In most team sports, the activity level is stop-and-go instead of the crucial, sustained movement that children need. Plus, team sports cater to a small number of children who are the stars—generally the fittest or tallest—who get most of the playing time, while the others sit on the sideline. Kraus elaborated, "The children who benefit from team sports are the ones who already are fit and need them least. The ones who are overweight and out of shape are the ones who need exercise in school the most, but with team sports, they're the ones who sit on the bench."

But as an entrenched American tradition, competitive team sports were beloved by school administrators, coaches, and many parents. As Kraus noted, team sports brought prestige and status to the school, but trying to de-emphasize or eliminate them, Kraus realized, would be unpopular. Kraus commented, "Instead of lavishing attention on the gifted athletes, schools should institute broad, non-competitive exercise programs that benefit all the students. Instead of picking the most physically gifted and welding them into winning teams for the glory of the school (and the coaches), the emphasis should be on all the students."

On top of that, Kraus saw, ironically, many American gym teachers didn't apparently value fitness themselves. Kraus was always amazed, when he started attending conferences of gym teachers, to see that unlike Swiss gym teachers, American gym teachers were often fat, out of shape, and had poor posture. "They didn't look different than any group of under-exercised office workers," Kraus put it. "They didn't look as though they could demonstrate exercises to children; and they were not setting a good personal example of fitness to the children." What message did that send to children about fitness?

But schools could do only so much, as Kraus saw it; parents needed to be held responsible for their children's health and fitness, too. While American children needed to be more active *in* school, they also needed to be more active *out of* school. Kraus was among the first to decry the perils of children watching television, insisting instead that, in the non-politically correct language of the time, "Children shouldn't be watching Cowboys and Indian shows on television. They should be outside, running around, *playing* Cowboys and Indians."

So what was Kraus'solution? He returned to the impressive public school gym programs he had seen in Switzerland. Why couldn't the American public schools adopt something similar?

Kraus proposed an hour daily, starting in kindergarten, of calorie-burning activities, such as running, jumping, and when possible, swimming. He also wanted to see intramural team sports postponed until fifth grade, and then offered only as an option, after school and gymnasium hours. Kraus thought through the details carefully. Cost would be minimal; there would be no need for special uniforms, equipment, or facilities. And as Bonnie Prudden's home exercise classes showed, schools did not even need specially trained, highly degreed, or well-paid gym teachers to run the program. Indeed, in a pinch, schools could use other fit teachers, or fit volunteer parents.

The more Kraus thought about his children's fitness campaign, the more convinced he grew that he had found the answer in his proposed exercise program. After all, setting up and running it would be easy, inexpensive, and safe. Who could argue with that? Who would want to? He would soon find out.

27

The Road to the White House

◆

1952–1954, New York and Washington, D.C.

In 1952, Kraus produced the first of many medical papers discussing how contemporary Americans—adults as well as children—needed to exercise to compensate for their affluent, easy daily lives. Kraus wrote, "Just as we do not receive enough vitamins in reducing diets and have to supplement them either by stressing special kinds of food or with pills, so we will have to bring back in to our lives the minimum amount of exercise necessary for a healthy existence."

Throughout the early 1950's, Kraus continued to churn out a huge array of articles about the importance of exercise for children and adults. Appearing in medical or health publications such as the *New York State Journal of Medicine, Journal of the American Association for Health, Physical Education and Recreation,* and *The Research Quarterly,* the articles helped generate coveted speaking invitations at state-level American Medical Association conventions. Then in June of 1954, he was invited to speak at the national AMA convention in Atlantic City. This was Kraus' big break.

At the national AMA convention, Kraus summed up his life's work: getting and remaining fit through exercise was key to physical and emotional well-being. Lack of exercise causes or aggravates a wide range of diseases, including cancers,[1] heart disease, obesity, diabetes, arthritis, joint problems, depression, mental disorders, and back pain.

For these, Kraus termed the coined the wonderfully descriptive term, *hypokinetic* diseases, from the Greek, meaning diseases caused or exacerbated by lack of motion. Kraus concluded his presentation with a warning: unless people started

116

exercising more regularly and more often, rates of hypokinetic diseases would soar.

Doctors in the audience shook their heads at what they considered a far-fetched, preposterous notion. After all, this was the same year that the chief medical statistician for the American Cancer Society, Dr. Cuyler Hammond, rejected the equally farfetched notion that cigarette smoking causes lung cancer. Quoted by journalist, Alistair Cooke, Hammond had quipped, "carbon in tobacco smoke probably neutralizes some toxic agents, and that if the filter removes those carbon particles 'filter cigarettes would do more harm than good.'"[2]

As a basis for his work, Kraus had conducted various informal studies, even trying out the K-W tests on a group of Shawangunks climbers in their fifties; "the age when most doctors start telling their patients to slow down," Kraus said. In addition to climbing, hiking or skiing on weekends, all the climbers worked out regularly during the week. None had back pain; all passed all the K-W tests easily. "If anything, the climbers were insulted by the suggestion that they might not pass the K-W tests," Kraus said.

"'Slow down!' Hmph!"[37]

Kraus also looked at other medical research, such as the landmark British study conducted in 1953 comparing the fitness of two kinds of London bus workers.[38] The London bus drivers and bus ticket takers shared the same demographics and lifestyles, but showed dramatically different health patterns: The drivers were overweight and unhealthy, with high amounts of Kraus' hypokinetic

---

1.   This was another highly controversial Kraus finding, although today widely accepted. See, *Wall Street Journal*, 8/24/04 D1, "Obesity is Linked to Cancer Risk…" Extra weight sharply increases likelihood of disease in breasts, colon, and organs. Obesity is already known to increase the risk of heart disease, diabetes, arthritis and high blood pressure. Now there is something else to add to the list: cancer. Scientists say it is increasingly clear that weighing too much is linked to about a dozen cancers. An article in this month's *Nature Reviews Cancer*, an oncology journal, points out that obese men are twice as likely to develop colorectal cancer as normal-weight men. Excessively heavy men and women also area as much as three time as likely to develop kidney cancer…The American Cancer Society estimates that excess weight will be a factor in at least 90,000 deaths from cancer this year—or 10% of the expected 564,7000 cancer deaths in the U.S…obesity is being partly blamed for a rise not only in common types of cancer but also some rare forms, including liver cancer.

2.   To his credit, it must be added that by 1957, Hammond publicly reversed his position.

diseases. In contrast, the ticket takers—who walked up and down the aisles and stairs of the double-decker buses constantly—were slim and healthy.

But other than his research at Columbia Presbyterian Hospital, Kraus never conducted official, formal scientific tests, funded by the N.I.H. or some other national science organization. When critics pointed, as many did, to the lack of "scientific grounding" in Kraus' research and conclusions, Kraus shrugged his shoulders. He didn't care. He knew he was right. More importantly, Kraus knew from his patients.

At the national AMA convention, the most controversial part of Kraus' presentation was his section on children's fitness. Kraus presented the results of the K-W testing of American and European children, informed his audience that American children were in poor shape because they didn't get enough exercise, and warned that without drastic changes, American children would be in even worse shape. Then Kraus outlined his plan for fixing the problem by replacing competitive team sports in the public schools with a daily exercise program of running, stretching, and calisthenics.

This was groundbreaking news, and though his presentation won the Honorable Mention Award at the Conference, many of the eminent doctors in attendance didn't want to believe Kraus' report. They stood up in the audience, shouted and shook their fists, "How dare you! How could American children be in worse physical shape than children in countries America beat in the war?…You're insulting America and our children…You, who sound like Hitler!…Go back where you came from, you traitor to America!"

"I never came so close to being lynched in my life," Kraus said.

And in fact, the prestigious medical association would fight Kraus, throughout his career, on his campaign to improve American children's fitness. Kraus never received any endorsement or acknowledgement from the AMA. In 1957, a spokesman for the AMA, writing in the AMA Journal, condescendingly referred to the "so-called Kraus-Weber test" and charged that Kraus confused "the terms health and fitness."[39] In 1961, during one of the many times when Kraus tried to gain support from the AMA for an article he wrote to publicize the problem of unfit American children and the need to exercise, Kraus was flatly rejected.

The AMA's Director of the Department of Health Education, Dr. W.W. Bauer (not to be confused with Zurich's Dr. Bauer), wrote to Kraus coldly, on official American Medical Association letterhead, "We would hope, of course, that you would not introduce into [the article] the controversial aspects of testing, or the international comparisons of fitness in which, as you know, we do not see eye to eye with you."[40]

Yet Kraus still hoped. And his hope seemed justified when a wildly unlikely chain of events a few months later made Kraus the honored guest of none other than the President of the United States.

In the summer of 1954, one of Kraus' many medical articles on K-W testing of American children appeared excerpted in *The Winged Foot*, a magazine sent to the members of the prestigious New York Athletic Club. There it was read by John Kelly, Junior, member of the super-athletic Kelly family of Philadelphia.

Kelly's father, John B. Kelly, Senior, had won the gold medal in rowing in the 1920 Olympics; Kelly Junior, would go on to win the bronze medal in the same event in the 1956 Olympics. Other family members competed on the international level in swimming and other sports. The Kelly family was also wealthy and well connected. A self-made millionaire, Kelly Senior was the father of Princess Grace of Monaco and a friend of Senator James Duff of Pennsylvania.

Kelly Senior and Senator Duff had been discussing an article in the March 1954 edition of *U.S. News and World Report,* "What's Wrong with American Youths?: They're Not as Strong as Europeans." The article reported that one-third of men drafted for military service during 1950–1953 flunked the routine military physical. Citing Kraus' research, the article concluded, "Life may be too easy for U.S. youths. They are growing weak because they get too little exercise in modern, pampered living."[41] It was an article that summarized Kraus' findings nearly perfectly, and won plenty of speculation.

Poor physical fitness among American youth—particularly boys—was a touchy topic during the Cold War. The *U.S. News & World Report* article explained, "It's a vital question whether the U.S. can afford to risk any further increase in physical defects among the group it must depend on for future fighters when man-power resources already are small compared to Russia and China."[42]

When Kelly, Junior had read an excerpt of Kraus' article in the New York Athletic Club, he had called his father. Kelly Senior later told Kraus, "My son called me on the phone. He said to me, 'You know how you're always telling me that children today are in worse shape than when you were young? The other day, I read an article by a doctor who had tests proving that.'"

"I'd like to read that article," Kelly had told his son. He did, and afterwards, he looked up the author. A Dr. Hans Kraus in Manhattan. Kelly figured it couldn't be hard to find him. It wasn't.

Kraus received a call from Jack Kelly, Senior, who introduced himself and suggested a lunch meeting at the New York Athletic Club. Over an excellent meal, Kelly, Senior listened thoughtfully as Kraus described the K-W tests and findings.

Periodically, Kelly Senior shook his head in dismay, "I've been saying the same things for years, but I never had proof. What you're done is very important. Unless we do something about this problem of unfit children, our country will face a major crisis."

They finished their coffee and stood to leave. "The President needs to hear this directly from you," Kelly said. "I'm going to make sure that he does." Kelly said he would talk to Senator Duff about the K-W tests, and through him, gain Eisenhower's ear.

They shook hands and left. Kraus thoroughly enjoyed the lunch and the conversation. He just didn't expect to hear from Kelly again.

28

The Report That Shocked Eisenhower

✦

1955, New York and Washington, D.C.

But Kraus was wrong. Kelly and Duff had indeed spoken to Eisenhower, warning the president, "Here we are, only a few generations removed from the frontier, and one of the most serious problems facing us now is the physical deterioration of our youth."[43]

A few weeks later, Kraus found in his mailbox a thick white envelope with gold embossing. The return address was the White House, Washington, D.C.

> *The White House*
> *Washington*
> *June 29, 1955*
>
> *Dear Dr. Kraus,*
>
> *Would it be possible for you to attend such a luncheon that I am planning for Monday, July eleventh, at half past twelve, at the White House?*
>
> *With best wishes,*
> *Sincerely,*
> *Dwight Eisenhower*

As his guest of honor, Eisenhower wanted Kraus to present his K-W children's test results to a group of American fitness experts and sports celebrities. Kraus accepted, and made sure that Bonnie Prudden was also invited. In this era when ladies wore hats and gloves, Prudden bought a new hat suitable for meeting the President.

Prospects for Kraus' children's fitness campaign had already begun looking brighter. Kraus' articles were the talk of the town; American children's poor fitness had quickly become front-page news. *Sports Illustrated* was so intrigued by the story that it had dispatched one of its rising stars, Bob Boyle, to write a feature on Kraus' talk at the White House.

As part of gathering background material, Boyle spent a weekend with Kraus in his house in Gardiner, where Kraus put the reporter through the K-W tests. During the hamstring flexibility test, when Boyle bent over to try to touch his toes, he could barely get his fingertips to his knees. Kraus warned Boyle that he would develop back pain unless he started stretching and exercising.

"I'm too busy to exercise." Boyle replied. "I'm a busy guy, and naturally tense. That's just me."

Kraus shrugged. He had little doubt what would happen.

At the luncheon, Eisenhower assembled an audience that included Vice President Richard Nixon and forty-odd of the country's leading sports celebrities. Throughout the presentation, as Kraus talked, everyone expressed great concern and shook their heads repeatedly. No one expressed more shock than Eisenhower, who had grown up in a small town, had been a high school sports star, and considered fitness an American virtue.

Newsweek Magazine reported, "The President was appalled by what Dr. Kraus and Miss Prudden told him. Right after lunch, he dashed off a note in green White House stationery to Nixon."[44]

Bob Boyle wrote his story faithfully, with the headline, "The Report that Shocked the President." In the story, which ran on August 15, 1955, Boyle warned, "the U.S. is rapidly becoming the softest nation in the world…At the [White House] luncheon, held in July 1955, it seemed to be the consensus that Americans, deprived by modern comforts of the physical exercise that was a natural part of their ancestors' lives, would have to take conscious and positive action to reestablish and sustain their vigor."[45]

Boyle didn't mention in the article that while he believed exercise was important, he didn't bother exercising himself. Nor did he mention Kraus' warning to him to start exercising or expect back pain. Boyle went on to build an impressive career with *Sports Illustrated*, but his personal story with Kraus was just beginning, to be continued in the next decade.

Other leading magazines followed with cover stories on Kraus' findings, including *Newsweek's* ("Are We Becoming a Nation of Softies"?),[46] *U.S. News and World Report* ("Is American Youth PHYSICALLY FIT? The Findings That

Shocked Eisenhower."),[47] and *Cosmo Magazine* ("Are We Becoming a Nation of Flabby Giants?)[48]

Eisenhower seemed good to his word: He soon set up a series of meetings and appointed Vice President Nixon as the interim head. On September 15, 1955, Nixon wrote to Kraus, "The President has asked me to serve as Chairman of the Conference on Fitness of American Youth which he has called...The Conference will consider the positive measures that can be taken to encourage youth participation in wholesome recreation activities and to improve the health and physical development of our young citizens [so]...we can improve the standards of health, recreation and physical fitness for America's youths."[49]

Then in September of 1955, Eisenhower nearly died from a heart attack. He was hospitalized for seven weeks and spent five months recovering. Attending Eisenhower was the renowned cardiologist, Paul Dudley White, a strong advocate of fitness and exercise.

If anything, one might think that Eisenhower's own brush with death would have strengthened his support for Kraus' children's fitness campaign. Paul Dudley White would become such a strong fan of Kraus that in 1961 he wrote the foreword for Kraus' book, *Hypokinetic Disease: Diseases Produced by Lack of Exercise*. Indeed, months later, Eisenhower seemed, in fact, to be holding true to his promise of supporting Kraus' efforts.

In July of 1956, Eisenhower passed Executive Order 10673, establishing the President's Council on Youth Fitness and appointed his own Cabinet as its first members, a powerhouse roster which included the Attorney General, Secretary of Defense, Secretary of Commerce, Secretary of Labor, Secretary of Health, Education, and Welfare, Secretary of the Interior, Secretary of Agriculture, Secretary of Housing, and the Home Finance Administrator.

The country's leading authorities in children's fitness were quick to laud Kraus' children's campaign. Harvard Professor Dr. Jean Mayer conducted similar studies showing that American children were increasingly growing fat; and agreed with Kraus that the culprits were too much television, and not enough fresh air and exercise.[50]

Yale University Head of Physical Education and U.S. Olympic Swimming Coach Robert Kipputh concurred. "These [American] youngsters just don't use their bodies much anymore. Traveling around the world with swimming teams and seeing what kids in other countries are doing on very meager diets makes me wonder whether we are really doing right by our youngsters in this country," Kipputh said.[51]

Throughout the course of the rest of the decade, American children's poor fitness and Kraus' children's fitness campaign made headlines. *U.S. News & World Report* wrote optimistically, "The significance of any long term trend to softness in American youth is very much in the minds of the nation's leaders, starting with President Eisenhower himself…The odds are heavy that you'll be hearing a lot more about youth fitness in the years ahead…All up and down the country, things are stirring in many schools, colleges and cities and communities where new [fitness] programs are being launched."[52]

Kraus' protégé, Bonnie Prudden emerged as a national fitness spokesperson and media darling. Gracing numerous national magazine covers—even a 1957 *Sports Illustrated* cover—Prudden had her own regular weekly television spot, where she demonstrated exercises in sexy, form-fitting outfits that were precursors to Lycra and Spandex. She also wrote several best selling books on children's fitness, starting in 1956 with *Is Your Child Really Fit*, and produced a series of popular fitness records, *Keep Fit/Be Happy*. Many have called Jane Fonda the pioneer of television fitness gurus. But they forgot about Bonnie Prudden, some thirty years earlier.

To many, success for Kraus' children's fitness campaign looked assured. With support even from the President, how could Kraus not succeed and make American kids exercise?

Hans Kraus and his adored mother, Ella Kraus, Trieste,
spring of 1914, shortly before the outbreak of WWI.

Hans Kraus, his sister Sisi, and their father, "*Schöne* Rudi" Kraus, Trieste, 1914.

Rudi and Ella Kraus, 1920's. Like many wealthy Triestine, they were avid travelers.

At the Wandervogel Camp, the Austrian Alps, summer of 1921. It was the defining moment of Kraus' life. Afterwards, he broke his life into two parts: "Before Marcus," "After Marcus."

Friends from the Wandervogel Camp,
Austrian Alps, summer of 1921.
Marcus, age 18, is in the lower right.
Picture was taken by Hans Kraus
a few days before Marcus fell
and died on the Pluider Kogel.

Marcus, age 18, picture taken by Hans Kraus
on the ridge between the Block Kogel and
Pluidel Kogel, a few hours before Marcus
died. Austrian Alps, summer of 1921.

Vienna, early 1920's.

Medical student, Austrian Alps, mid 1920's.

Medical resident,
wearing his motorcyclist jacket, Vienna, early 1930's. Photograph was
taken in the backyard of the Kraus mansion near the Schoenbrunn Palace.

The great Italian climber of the
pre WW II era, Emilio Comici,
whom Kraus partnered in the
Dolomites during the 1930's.
"The most beautiful climber I
ever saw," Kraus said of
Comici. "He moved like a
dancer on the rock."

The formidable Rudi Kraus, late 1930's, shortly before engineering the escape of many family members and friends from Nazi Germany. As with nearly every aspect of Rudi's life, it was on his own terms that Rudi somehow managed to flee Hitler.

Ella Kraus, Vienna, late 1930's.

Skiing with Fritz Wiessner, Catskill Mountains of New York State, early 1940's. Kraus and Wiessner formed one of the great partnerships of all time in rock climbing.

Second ascent of the climb, Gelsa, Shawangunk Mountains, 1941. Note the sneakers, bought for 39 cents.

High in the Shawangunk Mountains, 1940's. Throughout his life, Kraus
was known for remarkable hand strength in climbing and in medicine.

About to surmount an exposed overhang,
Shawangunks,
1940's.

Top pitch,
High Exposure,
Shawangunks,
first ascent by Kraus
in 1941. Even today,
it is considered **the**
great classic climb
of the Shawangunks.

Dr. Kraus, late 1940's.

About to summit in the Shawangunks, top pitch of unidentified climb, 200 hundred feet off the ground, 1940's.

Aerial traverse
in the Dolomites,
1947.

"King Kraus"…sometimes
called, "Papa Kraus,"
Shawangunk Mountains, 1953.
Rarely has one man so
dominated a climbing area
as Kraus dominated the Shawangunks for nearly
two decades.

Kraus and soul mate, the
great Italian
alpinist, Gino Solda,
in the Dolomites,
1953.

Traversing a wildly exposed section of
cliff in the Dolomites, 1950's.

In his New York office, early 1950's.

Bottom pitch of the climb, "Horseman," Shawangunks, 1953.

Kraus' presentation at the Eisenhower White House about unfit American children made headlines news and prompted schools, gyms and Y's across the U.S. to give fitness tests to children and adults. Here, in 1956, as part of Kraus' highly publicized campaign to get Americans to exercise, he gives K-W fitness testing to an assembly of national Y officials. Kraus stands in the back row, right, in a suit.

1959, North Face of the Grand, the Tetons.

Demonstrating "state of the art" aid climbing techniques
in the Shawangunks, late 1950's.

Hans and Madi Kraus, the Dolomites, 1959.

Kraus on his favorite kind of rock,
exposed and overhanging,
the Dolomites, 1959.

The Patriarchs of the Gunks. Kraus with Fritz Wiessner,
backyard of Kraus' house near the Shawangunks, 1970's.

1970's. Photograph was taken for one of the many medical conferences where Kraus spoke about the importance of exercise and fitness.

Kraus and protégé, Dr. Norman Marcus, Lenox Hill Hospital, New York City, 1993.

Hans Kraus, shortly before his death at age 90. "I'm very much at peace," he said. "I know I've helped a great many people who would otherwise still be in pain."

29

Talk, Talk, Talk

✦

1955–1959, Washington, D.C.

Yet from the beginning, Kraus wasn't sure about the fate of his children's fitness campaign. Sure, there was a lot of talk about the problem, committees formed, meetings convened, heads bobbing sympathetically, in unison. But so far, nothing more.

Bonnie Prudden expressed Kraus' and her own disgust when *Sports Illustrated* interviewed her in 1956 about children's fitness. "'Talk, talk, talk,' she says, her mobile face expressing deep scorn," the *Sports Illustrated* article reported, "'The country is disappearing while we sit around and talk about it. It's like the story somebody told me of the people who argued about which fire hydrant to use while the church burned down.'"[53]

From the start, Eisenhower worried Kraus. In the two-page *Sports Illustrated* photographic spread of the July 1955 White House lunch, everyone posed seemingly jovial and light-hearted. The exception was Kraus, standing behind Eisenhower, looking stern and intent. Kraus liked the way Eisenhower looked people straight in the eye, shook hands firmly, and said good things. But from the start, Kraus didn't see meaningful action from the man, and he didn't see signs of that changing.

Once Eisenhower started setting up the President's Council, he gave more cause for concern. The signs were clear: Eisenhower didn't give the Council a budget or any ability to enforce. The idea, supposedly, was that it would operate through powers of persuasion. But anyone who has worked in business, administration or government knows that this kind of structure is powerless, usually reflects low priority, and invariably fails. It also might have looked impressive that Eisenhower appointed his Cabinet officials to sit on the Council. But the Cabinet

144

members were solely figureheads; Bonnie Prudden couldn't recall a single instance when a Cabinet member ever showed up for a Council meeting.

Moreover, Eisenhower's picks to run the Council were telling. For the interim Council head, he tapped Vice President Nixon—not someone known for personal commitment to fitness, who likely viewed his involvement as dilatory, politically expedient, and a concession to the President. And for the permanent head, Eisenhower skipped over Kraus or a Kraus recommendation, and instead chose Dr. Shane McCarthy.

Like Nixon, McCarthy also knew little about physical fitness. But McCarthy knew lots about public relations. In McCarthy's first year as Council head, he embarked on a "publicity tour" giving eighty-eight speeches spanning 50,000 miles. But as *Sports Illustrated* noted, McCarthy talked a great deal about the importance of children's fitness. And McCarthy thoroughly rejected Kraus' proposal to replace public school team sports with exercise programs, but then failed to put forth ideas or solutions of his own.

Sports Illustrated was blunt in its criticism of McCarthy. "Many people who would like to help say they have been bewildered and frustrated by [McCarthy's] failure to offer specific recommendations which they had expected to hear," it reported. "Over and over his eager and sometimes wary listeners heard him say that the Council has no advice to offer on how to achieve fitness and should have none ('Fitness can not be dictated.'), that the government is not prepared to spend any money on fitness ('Fitness can't be bought by dole.') and that the function of the Council is to persuade the American people to do something about their unfitness. ('We are not doers—but stimulators.')"[54]

Eisenhower proceeded to set up yet more worthless children's fitness initiatives. To augment the Council, Eisenhower established the President's Advisory Committee. Again, the concept sounded good: Bring together informed leaders from all of the fields related to children's fitness, such as child development, psychology, journalism, sports, and youth organizations like the Boy Scouts and the YMCA. Then give them an official platform from which they can work together with the President's Council on Youth Fitness.

But the Advisory Committee was as meaningless as the Council. This time Eisenhower included Kraus and Prudden on it, but kept adding more members, until finally there was a whopping 119 members—too many to accomplish much of anything at all. Eisenhower also used the position as Committee Head as another political honorarium, this time naming the President of TWA Airlines, Carter Burgess, whose resume listed the State Department and a role as Assistant

Secretary of Defense for Manpower but included nothing about health, or children, or fitness.

Kraus watched and shook his head sadly. He was left pondering questions: *Why did Eisenhower do this? Why these meaningless programs and powerless measures virtually guaranteed to fail?* Particularly troubling was that Eisenhower had seemed genuinely shocked by the problem initially and then sincere about improving American children's' fitness, and by 1956, was indoctrinated by Paul Dudley White in the importance of exercise.

The likely answer is that children's fitness was probably important to Eisenhower, but not as important as many other pressing issues the President faced: the recession of 1956, the Cold War, losing the start of the "Space Race" to the Soviets, a bitter de-segregation battle. Eisenhower had likely expected that Kraus' children's fitness campaign would be politically safe and easy; not requiring much time or effort, but in return, generating widespread and popular grassroots support. After all, who wouldn't want to see children in better shape?

The reaction of some of the doctors at the 1954 national AMA meeting was a harbinger. Eisenhower was likely surprised that the issue of children's fitness turned out to be so controversial, stirring up organized and bitter resistance from several powerful special interest groups. These included a highly sensitive group, in fact, one that seemingly would have embraced Kraus' children's fitness campaign the most: Public school gym teachers.

30

Copperheads

✦

1955–1959, Washington, D.C.

In a way, the gym teachers' opposition was understandable. As *Sports Illustrated* noted, criticizing the gym programs meant criticizing the gym teachers.

The union for the gym teachers—the American Association of Health, Physical Education and Recreation[1]—like other unions supporting public schools teachers, was well organized and powerful. And it determined to fight back from the attack, as they saw it, on the way the gym teachers were doing their job.

At stake was much more than bruised egos. To the gym teachers, Kraus and his children's fitness campaign were threats. It was nothing less than a fight for survival. The gym teachers felt they had already been festering as second-class citizens in the teaching hierarchy with less training, lower status, and lower pay. They wanted to re-make themselves into "physical educators"—graduate degree holders who discussed lofty fitness theories, were the peers of other teachers, and garnered equal prestige and pay.

Kraus recalled, "At one of these conferences, one of the officials from the teacher's organization pulled me aside before dinner.

"'You don't understand,' he told me. 'We've spent most of our careers trying to get away from the label of gym teachers. Now we've reached the point we're considered educators, respected members of the teaching profession, and we're not going to go back. If you persist in trying to make us back into gym teachers, we will fight you tooth and nail.'

"Isn't that funny?" Kraus continued, "I hadn't understood what he was saying at first, because my father used to kid me that I wasn't really a doctor, but an

---

1.   Now renamed the AAHPERD, or American Association for Health, Physical Education, Recreation and Dance.

147

exercise teacher, because mostly what I did for my patients was to give them exercises. I didn't mind it. I knew what I was doing was right for my patients. But it wasn't enough for the gym teachers. They didn't want to be seen that way. They didn't care about doing right for the children. They did what was right for them, not the children."

This wasn't just Kraus' opinion. *Sports Illustrated* reporters supported Kraus, writing in one of many articles, "the attitudes and values of the individual [gym] instructor often are the biggest stumbling block to progress. Those who should be most interested in furthering the President's fitness program—the physical educators—are doing the least to better fitness."[55]

And so the gym teachers struck back. First they attacked the K-W tests, charging the tests were worthless because fitness couldn't be measured. "Fitness is a constantly changing quality," they claimed disingenuously, "It is not possible to design a single set of standards for all age groups and persons."[2]

It didn't matter that this contradicted medical evidence. Kraus fired back, "You can measure aspects of physical fitness, such as cardiac fitness, in a single set of standards for all age groups and persons, when you look at blood pressure, cholesterol levels, and pulse rates. Why not also strength and flexibility?"

Then the gym teachers countered that even if you could measure physical fitness, it was worthless to do so. Physical fitness was too narrow a concept, they charged—somewhat amazingly, considering, their job. Yet physical fitness, they insisted, must be looked at within the broader context of "total fitness," integrating its "mental, emotional, social and spiritual components."[56] A shocked Kraus remarked sadly, "Before the gym teachers were brought in, the debates about children's fitness were a lot of talk, but at least they were about fitness. But…they started talking about how physical fitness wasn't enough, how fitness was only part of the problem, how you needed to look at the larger picture, consider other aspects, such as emotional, spiritual, mental and financial fitness. They took the focus off physical fitness, which was the point."

Well, anyway, the gym teachers argued, this was all unimportant, because under their leadership, American children were in superb physical condition: taller than ever, living longer, enjoying unprecedented standards of living; and winning many Olympic medals. To which, Kraus retorted that these were irrele-

---

2.   *Sports Illustrated*, 8/5/57, p 31–32. "The chief professional organization in the field, The American Association for Health, Physical Education and Recreation, has failed to take the lead because its own members disagree on what fitness is."

vant fitness measurements—height didn't mean health, longer life spans had come from better hygiene and medical breakthroughs such as vaccines and penicillin, and the small number of American Olympians didn't reflect overall American fitness levels.

But the gym teachers' most successful strategy was asserting that if there was a problem, it was the *tests*, not the children. They argued that Kraus' tests were too "European," slanted toward European-type skills; if you put American children through different—more appropriately "American" tests, like timing how long it took to run between baseball bases—you would get different test results.[57]

So the gym teachers developed their own fitness tests. Instead of measuring minimal strength and flexibility, the gym teachers' tests specifically measured skills taught in their gym classes, like throwing softballs. Not surprisingly, the performance of the American children on these specially designed gym teacher tests was much better than their performance on the K-W tests. Afterwards, the gym teachers proudly reported: see American children are, after all, in excellent shape.

The gym teachers soon won a lot of important allies. In fact, a great many other teachers and parents rallied to their support. For the teachers, partly it was a matter of defending one of their own. For both teachers and parents, partly it was continued denial and disbelief at Kraus' bad news; and partly the success of the gym teachers' effective strategy of positioning opposition to Kraus in grand concepts like national interest.

Although Kraus' children's fitness campaign took place ten years after WW II, the memory of it was still raw. Organized calisthenics, like the program Kraus advocated, summoned up painful recollections of Nazi propaganda films featuring blond Hitler Youth doing push-ups and jumping jacks. Looking for more excuses to reject Kraus' findings, many parents and teachers pulled out the ultimate argument: that Kraus' children's fitness program was *un-American*. "Calisthenics and gymnastics are totalitarian and the proper physical activity in a democracy is team sports," parents and teachers insisted, "[calisthenics and gymnastics] would 'Hitlerize' youth…physical fitness under government tutelage sounds awfully similar to Hitler's and Mussolini's youth programs."[58]

Kraus was bewildered. He could survive High Exposure. But he was on terrain outside his abilities with the gym teachers. The same traits that made Kraus extraordinary at scaling exposed, dizzying Shawangunks rock also made him ineffective at persuading large, divisive, self interest groups. Instead of strict self-reliance, Kraus needed the ability to shape relationships and form coalitions. Instead of raw determination, he needed to be able to compromise. Instead of assessing situations in absolute terms, he needed to tease, promise, prioritize, cajole, encourage, back off, butter up, water down, debate, re-focus, trade off, and gain buy in.

At one meeting, Kraus and Prudden were so fed up, they simply walked out—certainly not the most politically adept gesture.

"The weekend before, Bonnie and I were climbing in the Gunks," Kraus recalled. "As we hiked up one of the talus trails to the base of the cliffs, I nearly stepped on a copperhead. They were very common then at the cliffs. And I killed it.

"As I walked out of the meeting with the gym teachers, I turned to Bonnie, who was also there, and said to her, 'To think, I killed that copperhead, which wasn't hurting anyone. Why did I do that? And here we were at this meeting and the people were far deadlier than that copperhead, far more poisonous.

"I never killed a copperhead again."[3]

---

3.   Little has changed in fifty years. On the AAHPER website, the organization's mission statement barely mentions fitness, instead, focusing on promoting the AAH-PER. Routinely, the media report on American children's obesity and poor fitness: nearly half of all New York City public elementary schoolchildren are overweight or obese;[22] children's obesity has caused heart problems, Type 2 diabetes, and various debilitating health problems formerly considered elderly diseases to be now common among the young.

31

Indefatigue-able

◆

1955–1959, New York, the Dolomites, the Bugaboos, and Dallas

If the second half of the decade was dispiriting to Kraus as he watched the sad downward spiral of his children's fitness campaign, it was at least happy in other areas of his life.

Even by the mid 1950's, Kraus was still very much in his prime. "Indefatigue-able" was how several people described him at this time. A woman who had an affair with him said, "He had such beautiful, powerful legs and never seemed to tire."

She didn't elaborate.

Climbing partner Howard Friedman, added, "Hans had these enormously powerful shoulders and hands, and it expressed in the way he moved on the rock. He could lean way back and hold on with just a few fingers. He wasn't a beautiful climber, but you could look at him when he climbed up an overhang, hanging out into space, and see extreme confidence."

Even without his Gunks training program, Kraus continued to mentor and train a coterie of up and coming climbers, such as Ken Prestrud, with whom he sang Gilbert and Sullivan songs as they walked to and from the cliffs.

Prestrud recalled, "We used to sing a lot in the car driving up to the Gunks, walking into the climbs, sometimes even on the climbs, or after a day at Schlueters. Hans loved American college folk songs or Gilbert and Sullivan. But about this time there was more of an air of sweet melancholy. Hans joked and sang as much as ever, but his songs increasingly were about the passage of time and passing of youth and life's possibilities."

Most notable among the new crop of climbers was Jim McCarthy—no relation to Shane McCarthy—a Princeton student who in the 1950's became one of the best American climbers of his generation. Nearly twenty-five years separated the two men, yet their rapport was instant. Until Kraus' death, they remained the closest of friends. Like Kraus, McCarthy was propelled up the rock more by impressive muscle and will power than inherent technique or talent. Like Kraus, too, McCarthy was highly educated, articulate, erudite, and staring down his own set of complex father-son dynamics.

McCarthy was a novice climber when Kraus spotted him at the Gunks and offered to lead him up a route. A few weeks later, McCarthy watched from a few yards away as a Princeton friend fell while climbing, and died. McCarthy's first reaction was to quit climbing. Kraus talked him out of it; just as a few years later he talked McCarthy out of becoming a climbing bum. Kraus felt that unless you were born into a mountaineering family, climbing should remain an avocation only; it was important to do something with one's life besides climb. McCarthy instead went to law school, became a successful trial lawyer, and president of the American Alpine Club.

With Kraus as his mentor, McCarthy soon climbed at the top standards, and then pushed difficulty levels into new territory. In 1958, *Sports Illustrated* honored McCarthy with a cover photo and the headline, "Cliffhanger," featuring him dangling inverted as he climbed the huge rock ceiling in the Shawangunks known as Foops. McCarthy had made the first ascent of Foops, seconded by Kraus, who returned to make its second ascent.

Each weekend, about 100 climbers visited the cliffs of the Shawangunks. To older timers, like Kraus and Prudden, they were starting to feel downright crowded. The Shawangunks popularity was partly fueled by word of mouth, but also aided by advances in climbing gear making the activity more safe and comfortable. Ropes were now more often constructed of nylon, rather than hemp, because it was lighter, more flexible, less water absorbent, and far stronger. Pitons were also lighter and stronger, and made from chromium-molybdenum alloy (nicknamed "cro-molly") rather than iron.

The new generation of climbers was also different. The older climbers typically were former skiers and hikers, used to the outdoors and nature. In contrast, the new climbers were typically recruited by the newly organized university-climbing clubs that sprang up in northeast universities like Harvard, Yale, Princeton, Rensselaer Polytech, and Syracuse.

Kraus saw these new climbers as young, inexperienced, ignorant, fired up, feckless and fearless; a dangerous brew, he realized as he recalled his boyhood climb with Marcus. He felt uncomfortable around them, particularly since he no longer ran the climber's training program. Whatever the reason, but perhaps not surprisingly, the first fatality at the Shawangunks occurred at this time. The victim was a university climber.

Two university climbing club students had been attempting an exposed, intimidating route called High Corner. One of the climbers had never climbed before, and the other had climbed just once previously. Piecing the story together afterwards, the second-time climber admitted that he encouraged his friend to take the lead. His friend did, got up about forty feet, fell, and hit the ground.

As always in the era before organized rescue, whenever there was any kind of accident in the Gunks, Kraus was the first one called. As soon as he got there, Kraus could see that the young victim was unconscious and unresponsive. Kraus guessed, correctly, that he had broken his neck. The young man lingered in a coma a few days before dying.

The serious accidents started to pile up. A young man in his twenties, also seconding High Corner, tied incorrectly into the rope. When he slipped on a traverse near the top of the cliff, the rope didn't cinch tightly by the knot at his waist and catch his fall. Instead, the knot opened, the rope slipped through, and the climber fell 200 feet to the ground. This time the victim was dead by the time that Kraus arrived at the scene.

There was also a young woman who survived a bad accident, but with grievous consequences. A ski instructor, she was hiking with her fiancé down the non-technical but steep break in the cliffs known as Roger's Escape Hatch, when she slipped and fell 100 feet to the bottom. When Kraus reached her, he could see she had no feeling below her waist and guessed correctly she would be permanently paralyzed.

Between medicine and the mountains, Kraus had seen more than his share of poignant deaths. In many ways, he was emotionally hardboiled—he thought birthday and holiday celebrations silly, artificially manufactured displays of affection. His attitude extended to death. "There's too much fuss made over death today," he would say, "People don't even want to say it. They don't say, 'You die.' Instead they say, 'You pass away.' But that's absurd. You die."

But Kraus' bluntness wasn't because he was unaffected by death. Quite the opposite was true, particularly those of young people in the mountains. The personal side of tragedy always touched Kraus deeply. Kraus always remembered that the first young man who died on High Corner was the only child of a widow; no matter how many times Kraus told the story, he always included that poignant detail. Or, more happily, he would be sure to include in the story about the woman who was paralyzed on Roger's Escape Hatch that she went on to marry her fiancé and have children.

As much as Kraus loved the Shawangunks, he yearned for true wilderness areas with higher cliffs, longer routes, fewer or no people, and even greater unknowns and adventure. It remained important to Kraus to get away each August to the "real mountains."

Kraus looked for regions where getting there was part of the adventure: often the last point of civilization was an isolated farm, from where he and his partners hitched tractor rides until the road ran out. From there they hiked rough terrain for several days, toting eighty-pound backpacks. Kraus' favorite area continued to be the Tetons, where a few years earlier he had led a sweet natured young man named Art Gilke up the classic Grand route. Gilke would die in 1953 on K2 in one of climbing's most wrenching yet heroic sagas.[1]

Kraus also climbed outside Seattle (summitting the classic Liberty Bell route), the Wind Rivers (staying with transplanted Shawangunks climber, Betty Woolsey, now full time ranching), in Aspen (then a sleepy, completely non-chic country town), and the Bugaboos (a perennial favorite). On Kraus' first trip to the Bugaboos, Kraus had another premonition. Partnered by John McCarthy, they had warmed up on pleasant but easy routes like Bugaboo Spire, the Second Pigeon, and Mount Marmolata. Now they were fired up to tackle a greater challenge, like an early ascent of Snowpatch.

Kraus led up about twenty feet, when he knew the rock didn't want him. He recalled, "Suddenly, I didn't want to lead. I don't know why, but the rock was telling me, 'Don't go up.' Whenever I got that feeling, I always obeyed it."

Their route was remote, but they were not alone. On a neighboring route was aspiring Himalayan climber, Nick Clinch, who in 1958 would lead the first—and only—American expedition to make a first ascent of one of the fourteen eight-thousand meter Himalayan peaks, Hidden Peak. Clinch had never met Kraus, but knew him by reputation. Clinch watched in amazement as Kraus calmly down climbed, handed the leader's rack to McCarthy, and said, "I don't feel right about leading today, Jim. I'm going to turn it over to you."

---

1.   It's still debated today whether a grievously sick Gilke might have committed suicide on K2 in order to spare his teammates the likely suicidal task of attempting to lower him down the mountain in a storm.

Clinch recalled, "I was blown away by that. I had never seen anyone of Kraus' stature do that before. It took so much self-confidence and maturity. It was a lesson in judgment that I never forgot."

Somehow Clinch and Kraus inadvertently mixed up their ice axes, and didn't realize it until they were back in the States. They arranged to swap axes at the annual AAC dinner in Philadelphia. Kraus, elegantly decked out in formal tuxedo, attracted curious glances as he boarded the train at Pennsylvania Station, carrying Nick Clinch's ice axe.

32

Madi

✦

1959, New York, the Dolomites, and Dallas

Even more significant during this period were the milestones in Kraus' personal life. He and a longtime girlfriend broke up. His divorce to Susie finally came through. And after three decades of tumultuous love affairs—which he wasn't always fastidious about keeping consecutive—he fell head over heels in love.

In the last year of the decade, Kraus, the consummate ladies' man, morphed into Kraus, the confirmed family man. The inspiration behind the transformation was Madi Springer-Miller, twenty-six years younger, from a prominent Stowe, Vermont, skiing family.

Madi first met Kraus she was a little girl, when he and Wiessner came to know her father through overlapping northeast skiing circles. An outstanding athlete in her own right, Madi excelled in skiing. When she started to race in college at Middlebury, she quickly established herself as one of the best in the world, particularly in the downhill.

Twice the national ski champion, Madi made the 1956 U.S. Olympic ski team as an alternate and became the first woman to ski the infamous "Lip" of Tuckerman's Ravine, on Mt. Washington, in New Hampshire, still an impressive feat today.[1] She won one World Cup race, at Stowe, beating the reigning downhill world champion.

---

1. *Not Without Peril*, Nicholas Howe, p. 277. "By spring, snow has banked up against the headwall 150 feet deep, and skiers come from all over America to hike up from the highway and test nerve and technique on some of the steepest skiing anywhere on the planet. 'Going over the lip' making the vertiginous plunge from the higher snowfields down into the bowl, is a major rite of passage. In fact, going up over The Lip can be as scary as most people would want."

Yet Madi was gentle, modest and reserved. Her skiing style reflected her personality: smooth, serene, graceful, understated, effortless looking. She didn't like to talk about herself or her achievements. Few people, in fact, were aware of them.

For nearly twenty years, Madi had been there under his nose. When did it hit Kraus that Madi was the one? When did it occur to him that a stream of gorgeous woman paled beside her quiet presence? Madi was outdoors oriented, tall, attractive, but different from his usual type: glamorous, gregarious, and immaculately groomed. As Kraus passed his fifty-year milestone, substance sparkled more brightly than pure style.

They married in 1959 and honeymooned that August. Madi had been to Europe during her ski-racing career, but Kraus was eager to show her the Dolomites. Photos show them beaming, gazing dreamily, very much in love. They stayed with Kraus' close friend, Gino Solda. A rapport continued to develop as it had since the two men first met in 1947, and Kraus began visiting and climbing with Solda on subsequent August trips. Their friendship lasted until Solda's death in the early 1990's.

During World War II, Solda had been a leader in the Resistance. Since the war, he had worked as a mountain guide, and established himself as one of the top climbers in the world, known for first ascents of hideously exposed and difficult aid climbing routes in the Italian Alps. Local Italian newspapers followed his exploits with as much fanfare as American newspapers today report NFL games. When Solda made a first ascent in 1959 in the Italian Alps, headlines trumpeted, "Daring Enterprise by Solda in the Moiazza Group." The article described in detail how he ascended the daunting 350-meter high southeast face characterized by "extreme exposure."[59]

In Italy, Gino Solda was a living legend, hounded by autograph seekers wherever he went. However, he maintained a down-to-earth demeanor, a fine sense of humor, and a humble perspective on his fame. On one climbing trip, as Kraus and Solda approached a mountain hut where they planned to camp for the night, they could see climbers and hikers clamoring toward them, no doubt to ask for Solda's autograph. Kraus started to kid his friend, but Solda replied, "Not this time, you'll see."

As the crowd approached, Solda told them, "The autograph you really want is not mine, but of this man here."

Gesturing to Kraus at his side, Gino explained, "This man is a very famous American climber, very famous. If I were you, I'd want *his* autograph."

Kraus laughed, remembering, "The crowd murmured in awe. After all, Gino had said I was very famous, and everyone believed the great Solda. I tried explaining, but it did no good. For the rest of the time we were there, people were asking left and right for my autograph. Gino of course thought this enormously funny."

Like so many of Kraus' close friends, there was a striking physical similarity between the two men. One year younger than Kraus, Solda was equally short and muscular, and could have passed as a brother. There were strong emotional ties, too: Both had both seen death and suffering; had few illusions about life, and yet maintained an optimism rejuvenated by their closeness with nature and time spent in the mountains. They were compatible in little ways, too: Both loved to sing when climbing or at night in the mountain huts; and of course, both loved a good laugh.

On this trip, Kraus, Solda and Madi often climbed as a threesome, including making the first ascent of a peak Kraus named, Cima Madi. But another climb left a long-term physical impact. Solda and Kraus were looking forward eagerly to climbing the south face of the Sisilla together. It was everything they loved: breathtaking exposure, intimidating traverses, complex route finding, strenuous vertical faces, bulges and roofs.

It was also difficult and dangerous for either leader or second.

Solda led the first pitch without hammering in a piton, even though on the Sisilla, where the route weaves and slants, pitons can be critical to the safety of the second as well as the leader. It's not clear whether Solda couldn't place pitons, or whether Kraus concluded, as Emilio had done, that Solda overemphasized Kraus' climbing abilities.

On the Sisilla, without pitons securing the rope in place along the traverses and diagonals, the length of rope was longer than the length of the pitch. If Kraus fell, he would hit the ground. Even though Kraus was seconding, any fall could be fatal.

The problem was that Kraus thought he might fall.

It was at a bulge on the first pitch. To reach the hold above it—a thin edge with room for one hand—Kraus decided he needed to crank a one-arm pull up to get his body to swing out and his feet to kick loose in the air. The one-arm pull up was no problem; he could still do several. But the overall move was at the upper range of his ability. Still, he had no choice.

As soon as Kraus started the move, he felt a twinge in his shoulder. Immediately he knew he had torn or pulled something. But he managed to get through the climb. "I had no choice." Kraus explained. But he wondered if he had done permanent damage to his shoulder.

Kraus decided this was a great opportunity to experiment on himself. Could he cure himself without resorting to trigger point injections? For the rest of his honeymoon, he tried a range of treatments, including massage, heat, exercise and ethyl chloride. (Kraus never traveled anywhere without a cache of ethyl chloride.) When he and Madi returned to New York, he added electro-therapy. But nothing worked.

A month went by, and while Kraus was still holding out on the trigger point injections a weekend came that was unusually cold; it actually snowed at the Gunks. Kraus decided, uncharacteristically, that he wouldn't climb the next day. The pain in his shoulder was annoying and sometimes woke him up at night. So he thought, I'll take a sleeping pill, a strong one with codeine, and get a good night's sleep.

But the next morning, he and Madi awoke to brilliant sunshine, warm temperatures, and near perfect climbing conditions. Friends from New York had driven up to climb with them. He still felt groggy, but didn't want to let his friends down by not climbing. Kraus figured, "Heck, I'll pick an extremely easy route, something like Southern Pillar."

The first route Kraus put up at the Gunks, Southern Pillar is steep, but like a ladder. Even the first time, Kraus had climbed it without a rope. By then, he had climbed up and down it nearly hundreds of times, and always without a rope. Kraus saw no reason now, for the first time to tie into a rope and hammer in pitons.

The first pitch of Southern Pillar ends about sixty feet up, at a wide ledge usually covered with small, loose pebbles. On the day that Kraus attempted it with his sore shoulder, it was also dusted with snow. At the ledge, Kraus reached up with his right hand; and for some reason, it slipped. For some reason too, he lacked his usual balance and care; and he couldn't catch himself.

He fell.

Madi and Kraus' friends watched in horror and disbelief as he hit the ground. They assumed they were watching him die. Instead, Kraus cautiously started moving fingers and toes, then arms and legs, sat up slowly and started checking himself out for damages. He had several minor cuts on his head, a sprained ankle, and some swelling on his back with an impressive sized hematoma.

Kraus walked with his friends to the car and instructed them in a litany of symptoms that could signal a brain, spinal or other internal injury. They drove him to the nearest hospital, where doctors looked at him, took x-rays, and amazingly found no serious injuries at all. Kraus credited luck with getting off so lightly—along with his thick, strong back muscles, which protected his spine from serious damage.

The next week, Kraus was back on the rock, at least for a psychological climb. He said, "Fritz led me up a very easy climb, I don't remember which one. I do remember it was the most painful one I ever made. Afterwards I spent the rest of the day in bed. But I was convinced I had to do that, so that I wouldn't have any fears or hesitation afterwards."

The next weekend, Kraus returned to Southern Pillar. He climbed unroped up to the ledge where he fell, pulled himself up carefully, and stood for a long time looking out. Then he carefully climbed down the route. And he did that again, ascending and descending the climb several times before he was satisfied.

A few weeks later, Kraus was scheduled to give a medical talk in Dallas. Nick Clinch had since moved to Texas, and picked him up at the airport. Clinch recalled, "Kraus looked terrible. His face was banged up, he was limping, and his body looked pretty busted up too. He said he wouldn't have come, except that he was giving a paper.

"So I asked him, 'What's the subject of your talk?'

"'Prevention of sports injuries,' he told me."

Clinch recalled, laughing, "I never forgot that."

PART IV
CAMELOT 1961–1963

33

The White House Calls

✦

June 1961

The next two years passed fairly contentedly for Kraus, with more of the same. More climbing. More skiing. More medical articles about the importance of muscles. More medical conferences about the importance of fitness. More frustration with other doctors. Howard Friedman recalled attending a lecture Kraus gave to a group of prominent cardiologists. When Kraus explained, "The heart is a muscle, you must use it to keep it strong," some of the doctors laughed. More fighting with the AMA. More miracle cures for Kraus' own patients.

Kraus and Madi moved into a modest two-bedroom apartment on Manhattan's Upper East Side—a block that is now chic and expensive, but not so in 1959—where Madi still lives. They also custom-built a country house near the Shawangunks, nestled among trees, near the base of the cliffs, where they spent every weekend. The small, simple ranch-style house reflected their personalities: straightforward, modest, practical, and private. They never bothered to expand or update it, or make it more comfortable or more chic.

With a settled home life, the first of the two Kraus daughters, Ann, was born, followed soon by Mary. Kraus, who before his marriage to Madi, was indifferent to children and assumed he wouldn't have any, found himself bombarded by a new set of powerful emotions. He was glad to have daughters, rather than sons, freeing him to dote and adore without as much emotional baggage that had saddled his relationship with Rudi.

Still, when Ann hiked as a young girl with her father in the Shawangunks, the shadow of her grandfather, Rudi, hovered nearby. "I said I needed to rest because I was tired. And my father told me, 'No, I wasn't tired,'" Ann recalled, laughing. "Sometime later I said to him that I needed a drink because I was thirsty. And he told me, 'No, I wasn't.' Then I said I needed to stop to pee. And he told me, 'No, I didn't need to pee.'"

Life could have passed happily for Kraus indefinitely. Then, in June of 1961, Kraus got a phone call from the White House. On the line was one of Kennedy's White House doctors, Dr. Gene Cohen, a renowned endocrinologist from New York Hospital, who had secretly treated Kennedy for his Addison's Disease since 1956.

Kennedy's Addison's Disease remained a closely guarded secret from the American public until sealed documents were opened in the 1980's. For good reason: the knowledge that Kennedy had Addison's Disease could have been an overwhelming political liability. Many historians believe that Kennedy would not have been elected president in 1960 if his Addison's disease had been public knowledge.[60] They had a good point: The disease used to be known as a death sentence.

A rare malfunctioning of the adrenal glands,[1] Addison's Disease destroys the adrenal cortex, which produces several hormones controlling crucial responses to stress and inflammation. There are several degrees of disease severity, but Kennedy had the worst type—"Classical Addison's"—which wipes out the adrenal glands. During Kennedy's lifetime, his adrenal glands completely withered, so that one of the doctors performing his autopsy—Dr. John Humes of the Bethesda Naval Center—reported no trace of adrenal glands left in Kennedy's body.[61]

Before the 1940's, there was no treatment or drug for Addison's Disease, and patients were doomed to die within five years of diagnosis. But Kennedy was lucky in his timing. When he was diagnosed in 1945, doctors had recently discovered that cortisone was an effective antidote for the disease. Early cortisone treatments for Addison's Disease were crude—either daily injections or surgically implanted in pellets under the skin—and didn't completely eliminate flare-ups. Patients survived, but didn't flourish.

Photographs of Kennedy from the late 1940's to the mid 1950's show a man who was thin, sallow, and sickly. Dr. Larry Sonkin, a noted endocrinologist who trained under Gene Cohen, recalled that he and other endocrinologists assumed Kennedy had the disease. "You could tell, just by looking at his photo in the

---

1.   According to the official Addison's Disease website, there are no accurate statistics on the incidence of Addison's disease in the United States. A study in London showed thirty-nine cases per million population as of 1960. www.medhelp.org/nadf/

newspapers," Sonkin said. Ironically, Addison's Disease produces two side effects that suggest good health: hyperpigmentation that makes the skin look tanned, and unusually plush hair.

By the late 1950's, the situation of an Addison's patient under the care of a skilled endocrinologist like Gene Cohen took a quantum leap for the better. The new generation of cortisone analog drugs not only worked extremely well, but taken once a day as pills, also dramatically improved the patient's quality of life. Daily life for an Addisonian became like that of a thyroid patient in 2005: dependent on daily medication, but leading a completely normal life.[2]

By the time Kennedy was running for president in 1959, he looked like he could have been a climber partnering Kraus at the Gunks: tanned, trim, seemingly toned, turning out that dazzling smile and glowing with apparent health and "vi-gah." Kennedy and his supporters saw a supreme opportunity to market his athletic, outdoors image. Staged photos showed him sailing, swimming, playing football; often bare-chested, muscles rippling in the sun.

Kennedy's appearance became a huge asset in his presidential campaign. An aide to Kennedy's main rival, Lyndon Johnson, declared grumpily, that Kennedy "appears so healthy that it's almost illegal."[62] Even sophisticated media, such as *The New York Times,* were bowled over, "Crowds responded warmly to a masculine presence, a lithe figure, a suntanned face and a natural smile." *The Times* gushed, "He gave an impression of vigor and directness…Many observers of the Kennedy campaigns agreed that nothing quite equaled the effectiveness of the candidate himself."[63]

But one side effect of Kennedy's disease still remained. Addisonian patients—like others with endocrine and metabolic conditions—often also had muscle problems. In fact, it was Kennedy's muscle pain that first brought Kraus and Gene Cohen together. Through the interconnected elite New York medical circles, Kraus and Cohen found they often shared the same patients: many of Cohen's patients had muscle pain, while many of Kraus' turned out to have underlying endocrine conditions. The two doctors began formally referring patients to each other on a regular basis, and developed a mutual high regard.

When Kraus received the call from Gene Cohen, asking him to treat one of his patients for back problems, Kraus wasn't surprised. The difference was that

---

2.   It was the same situation, as Larry Sonkin pointed out, of the first President Bush, who, while in the White House, developed Grave's Disease, a thyroid condition requiring daily medication.

Cohen was asking Kraus to come to the White House to treat the President of the United States.

This was the chance of a lifetime for most doctors. They would be overjoyed! They would be elated! They would be overwhelmed!

They wouldn't be Kraus.

He listened to Cohen, neither flattered nor excited, as Cohen explained that he was seriously worried about Kennedy's worsening back problems and that Kennedy's current White House back doctor wasn't helping him. To Cohen's surprise and dismay, Kraus politely refused, "No, I really can't, Gene." Kraus explained to Cohen that he was sympathetic to Cohen's worries, but added, "You know I can't see Kennedy unless his current back doctor personally asks me. It wouldn't be ethical."

Kraus didn't bother adding that he also realized that treating the President of the United States would be a total commitment, consuming what little free time he had on weekends for his family or to climb, already interrupted by his regular practice and his unofficial practice of treating—for free—all injured climbers at the Shawangunks. Without having met Kennedy, Kraus wasn't sure he was willing to take on that commitment. Kraus explained further, "Too many people judge other people on their rank or money. But to me, it wasn't that. What mattered was whether I felt they were a good person. I couldn't treat anyone I didn't like."

Furthermore, Kraus knew from Cohen that Kennedy had been through several failed back operations. That gave Kraus pause: Even a single back operation could permanently incur so much damage, that it could be too late, even for Kraus. "Once someone has had a back operation, even once, you never know," Kraus explained. "Backs don't like to be operated on."

After the conversation, Kraus hung up and forgot about it. "So it was the White House and the President. I could be very arrogant at times. It was no big thing to me." Kraus said.

But it was a big thing for Cohen. It would take Cohen six more months, banding together with another Kennedy White House doctor, and threatening a "palace coup" against Kennedy's White House back doctor. And in the meantime, Kennedy continued to grow alarmingly worse.

But Cohen had determined that Kennedy needed Kraus, and that if anyone could still help Kennedy, it was Kraus. Cohen was determined he would make sure, somehow, that Kennedy got that chance.

34

Kennedy's Back

✦

1917–1955, Washington, D.C.

Kennedy's bad back, unlike his Addison's Disease, wasn't a secret to the American public. Acute back pain, such as his was, would have been impossible to conceal completely anyway; and a "sanitized version"—attributed by aides to an epic PT 109 wartime rescue and Harvard football injuries[1]—cast Kennedy in a heroic, sympathetic light.

A bad back doesn't sound all that serious. Unfortunately, for Kennedy, it was. Throughout his adult life, it crippled him; twice, it almost killed him.

Then Kennedy met Kraus.

Kennedy's back problems had started in childhood,[64] but didn't become serious until college, when he was involved in a car accident as a Harvard sophomore.[65] After that, they grew steadily worse. In June of 1944, doctors at the prestigious Lahey Clinic decided that the twenty-seven-year-old's problem was a ruptured disc and operated on him.[66] This was the first of three disastrous back surgeries. Almost immediately, the doctors realized the operation had been a major mistake[2] and even questioned their own diagnosis. But they were completely confounded and never did arrive at an alternate diagnosis, other than noting that

---

1. *My Twelve Years with John F. Kennedy*, Evelyn Lincoln, p. 50: "I had learned that when he was at Harvard he had injured a spinal disc in football scrimmage and had never completely recovered. And that when his PT boat was struck by a Japanese destroyer during the war his back was injured seriously once again."

2. Kennedy's naval records, 8/44, recorded: "An 'interesting' [sic] complication of the surgery when the surgeon at the Lahey Clinic may well have failed to get to the bottom of the situation…The post op muscle pains he had were apparently very severe…The pathology seen at operation was not evidently a clear cut disc."

young Kennedy was "a "high strung individual" and that his back pain might be due partly to stress and emotional factors.[3]

By 1947, when Kennedy entered politics as a Congressman, his back was in terrible shape. He climbed stairs with difficulty, was in great pain, and used crutches.[67] His brother Robert was prompted to say that "over half of his days were spent in pain."[68] With superb political instinct, though, Kennedy made sure to hide the crutches when in public.[69] Few photos exist of him on crutches; just as Kennedy also made sure not to be photographed wearing his prescription eye-glasses.[70] (Fashionable and athletic sunglasses were a different matter.)

Although Kennedy's first back operation was worthless, two years later, doctors decided to do it again. However, the proposed second operation was much more complex and dangerous: a double disc fusion wherein bone was grafted and a metal plate would be inserted in his tissues. Kennedy described the operation to close friends as "the one that kills you or cures you."[71]

Additionally, this second back operation was also riskier because Kennedy's Addison's Disease had by now compromised his immune system. Any type of major surgery on Addison's patients was rare; even minor post-op infections could induce shock and prove fatal. When the operation was performed in October of 1954 it made medical news, garnering a write-up in the American Medical Association Archives of Surgery. The author was careful not to mention Kennedy by name; simply, "A man 37 years of age."[72]

Unfortunately, Kennedy's second back operation was also a tragic failure; not only did it hurt Kennedy's back even more, it also nearly killed him. Three days after the surgery, infection set in, induced shock and sent Kennedy into a coma. Kennedy hovered near death and the Catholic Church gave him last rites.[4] However, as before, Kennedy proved extraordinarily tough and rallied, although he faced several more months of hospitalization and the fear he might not walk again. Then his medical news grew worse.

The area where the doctors had inserted the metal plate grew infected, creating an "open, gaping, very sickly looking hole."[73] Four months after the doctors had operated to put the plate in, they decided they needed to take it out. A third

---

3.   Kennedy naval records, August 1944, John F. Kennedy Library: "a high strung indi-
       vidual who has been through much combat strain. He may well have recurrent discs
       and incomplete removal [sic], but better bet is that there is some other cause for his
       neuritis."
4.   The first time Kennedy received the Last Rites of the Catholic Church was in 1947,
       when returning on the boat to New York from London newly diagnosed with Add-
       ison's Disease.

painful, dangerous back operation was needed, which took place one year later, in February 1955. Again, this operation was a complete fiasco. Infection again set in. Again, Kennedy was expected to die and received last rites of the Catholic Church. And yet again, Kennedy proved amazingly tough.

Sadly, again, this third operation also left his back in even worse shape than before. By this point, Kennedy was on crutches continually, couldn't walk down even a few stairs without help, and could barely put any weight on his left leg.[74]

In desperation, Kennedy decided to try yet another new doctor. He hadn't yet heard about Kraus, but through another of his doctors, Kennedy learned about Dr. Janet Travell, of New York Hospital. For the next six years—until he discovered Kraus—Kennedy put his back in Travell's care. This decision would create difficult ramifications for Kennedy, the country, and not incidentally, Kraus.

35

Rumors

✦

1955 to May 1961, Washington, D.C.

Maybe it was Janet Travell's athletic, wealthy, WASP persona. Maybe it was her enormous personal charisma and extraordinary bedside manner. Regardless, more so than with his previous back doctors, Kennedy quickly developed a high comfort level with Travell and was soon seeing his new doctor on a regular basis.

Travell's diagnosis was novel: She found some contributing mechanical factors, such as one leg was shorter than the other.[75] Mostly, using "skillful medical detective work," as she described her process in her textbook, *Myofascial Pain and Dysfunction*,[76] she focused on an obscure and little understood muscular condition: *trigger points*.

Travell, who proudly called herself, *The Trigger Point Queen*, was not the first to identify the condition.[1] By the 1960's, there was already a small group of doctors—including Travell and Kraus, of course—who could identify these small hard lumps of dead muscle fiber located deep in muscle. Caused by continual, ongoing muscular tension, whether originating from a physical injury or emotional stress, trigger points cut off the blood flow to tiny, microscopic bits of muscle fiber. Over a period of time, the oxygen-deprived muscle fibers die, harden, and leave scar tissue. Kraus, who had formally trained in massage techniques while in Vienna, found he could easily identify trigger points by touch, feeling lumpy clots instead of the smooth, silky, resiliency of healthy muscle, reminiscent of fine bread dough.

To the patient, trigger points are extremely painful, raw, and sore, somewhat like deep, fresh, black and blue bruises. But trigger points also set up a vicious

---

1.   As noted in Chapter 11, the credit for first identifying trigger points goes to the German orthopedist, Max Lange, who wrote about the condition in 1913.

cycle of muscle problems: By keeping the muscle perpetually tensed, shortened, and unable to relax when needed, they weaken surrounding muscles and disrupt normal muscle functioning. Eventually, even ordinary, daily emotional and physical stress can produce painful, disabling spasm, causing more pain. The body tightens in response, the spasm grows worse, the body produces more pain, with more tightening, more spasms, and more pain…and so the cycle continues.

Treatment to eliminate trigger points was extraordinarily painful—trigger point injections, where the doctor jabs an oversized, thickened needle repeatedly into the sore and painful muscles to break up the scar tissue. In fact, many doctors, including Kraus, found that the injections were so painful, that they scared off many patients. And many trigger point physicians—although not Kraus[2]—began experimenting with ways to cut the pain and make the injections more palatable, such as trying smaller needles or incorporating pain-killing medications.

Travell, who prided herself on increasing the "comfort level" of her patients, started to fill her trigger point needles with the non-narcotic pain killer, procaine,[3] replacing the simple saline solution that Kraus used in his trigger point injections. Not only did Travell's trigger point injections now hurt less, but to Kennedy and Travell's other patients, they also gave hours of pain relief afterwards.

The problem was that the pain relief was temporary and came incidentally from the procaine, not from the treatment. Kennedy would not have realized this; likely, after so many years of suffering, he wouldn't have cared. Grateful and overjoyed to find some measure of relief, Kennedy didn't sweat the details. Commenting about a different treatment from a different—and in this case, questionable doctor—he purportedly told his brother Robert, "I don't care if it's horse piss [if] it works."[77] [4]

To Kennedy, Travell's injections were a godsend. The pain killing effects of the procaine meant that for the first time in years, he could work for hours at a stretch without incapacitating back pain. When Kennedy ran for president in 1960, he called Travell a "genius[78] and credited her injections for keeping his

---

2.   Partly this was because Kraus felt that ability to deal with pain was part of a strong moral character. But more importantly, he didn't want to introduce modifications that might undermine the efficacy of the injection.

3.   Of note, procaine is rarely used today, except to treat irregular heart beats and illegally as an anti-aging nostrum. Adherents claim procaine reduces wrinkles, restores muscle mass, and enhances sex drive.[33] Interestingly, no one has conjectured whether Travell's procaine injections played a role in the infamous Kennedy libido.

political career alive.[79] The last part was almost certainly true, but the reason was also as much Travell's literary aptitude as her medical prowess.

During the Democratic convention, someone—probably Richard Nixon or Lyndon Johnson—leaked "rumors" that Kennedy had Addison's Disease.[80] Kennedy knew he needed to squash these "rumors" to receive the Democratic nomination[81] so he declared himself "the healthiest candidate for President in the country;" a direct jibe to his main rival, Lyndon Johnson, who had suffered a severe heart attack in 1955. In a news conference on November 10, 1960, Kennedy outright lied to the press, declaring that he "never" had Addison's Disease.[82]

But the press wasn't satisfied. To drop the "rumors," they demanded that Kennedy show them two things: a signed statement from Kennedy's doctor specifically stating that Kennedy didn't have Addison's Disease, and a signed statement from his doctor stating that he didn't take cortisone for Addison's Disease. The problem for Kennedy, of course, was that both were facts, not "rumors."

But when the Kennedys turned to Janet Travell for help, she exceeded their wildest expectations. Travell's medical statement, which she and Robert Kennedy pressured Gene Cohen to co-sign, was issued to the press at the 1960 Democratic Convention and was a masterpiece of misinformation, obfuscation, confusing jargon, and misleading references. Without actually lying in it, Travell brilliantly and completely bamboozled the press.[5]

When Travell denied outright facts, she added subtle medical qualifiers beyond the understanding of non-doctors. When she conceded medical truths,

---

4.   Even so, Travell couldn't eliminate all the pain from her trigger point injections: Travell's medical records showed that Kennedy sometimes screamed in pain from them. [http://www.ibsgroup.org/other/NYTimesNov172002.htm]. When a close friend of Kennedy's, Red Fay, developed muscle pain, Kennedy sent him to Travell; he then called Travell's office after Fay's treatments to find out whether Fay *also* screamed in pain.

5.   *Office Hours*, Janet Travell, p. 333. *New York Herald Tribune*, 6/6/1960, p.1 and 6. Medical statement at the 1960 Democratic Convention included, "Your [Kennedy's] health is excellent. Your vitality, endurance and resistance to infection are above average. Your ability to handle an exhausting work load is unquestionably superior…With respect to the old problem of adrenal insufficiency, as late as December 1958, when you had a general check up with a specific test of adrenal function, the result showed that your adrenal glands do function." Of note, nothing in this was an outright lie. Dr. Larry Sonkin noted, "If Kennedy's adrenal glands had not been functioning at all, he would have been dead in twelve hours."

she buried them under confusing medical jargon and convoluted grammar. For instance, in order to describe Kennedy's back as "entirely well," Travell stated that his back pain had "disappeared under further treatment," which was true when considering her pain killing injections. Travell denied that Kennedy had Addison's Disease, describing his condition in medical mumbo-jumbo instead as a "depletion of adrenal function from which he is now rehabilitated." Travell also denied that Kennedy took cortisone for Addison's Disease, but didn't add that in fact her patient took a stronger adrenal medication, based on cortisone, but with a different name.

Travell's statement put "rumors" about Kennedy's Addison's Disease to rest throughout his presidency. The reality wouldn't surface until sealed documents were opened two decades after Kennedy's death.

After his election, Kennedy didn't forget Travell and her invaluable services. Travell became his first presidential appointment, made at 8:00 a.m. on January 21, Kennedy's first day in office.[83] Kennedy took the unusual step of rewarding Travell with two positions on his White House medical team: naming her both his White House back doctor—the first woman on any White House medical team—and also his Chief White House physician.

Political observers were shocked. Travell was an unusual choice for the top medical role both because she was practicing as a specialist (instead of a generalist in internal medicine) and a civilian (instead of a military doctor). As the *Washington Post* noted, "The appointment ruffled a few feathers among members of the Washington establishment, especially in the military, which had regularly staffed the White House position since the early 1920's."[84] It would not be the first time that political pragmatism played a role when a president chose his White House physician.[85]

And plenty of insiders, Gene Cohen and later Kraus among them, conjectured that genteel blackmail on Travell's part highly motivated Kennedy to keep Travell content and loyal, so she was not tempted to go to the press to reveal any of his medical secrets.

Certainly, the Kennedys treated Travell differently than the other doctors.

Alone among Kennedy's medical team, the Kennedys doted on Travell as a friend and social equal. And Travell responded,[86] thrilling to the proximity to money and power—what Kraus later disparagingly called "Potomac Fever"—frequent jaunts to the Kennedy mansions in Palm Beach and Hyannisport, chatting with servants, hobnobbing with Joseph Kennedy and other Kennedy family members, scribbling casual, off-the-cuff mentions of the White House in her personal correspondence and name dropping throughout her autobiography.

Travell's social flair, in fact, outperformed her medical skill with Kennedy's treatment. Despite hundreds of Travell's procaine injections, Kennedy was so stiff and in so much pain that he often worked from his bedroom, stretched out flat on his back, lying on his bed.[87] Kennedy had so much trouble climbing stairs that he boarded Air Force One hoisted from the type of airport cherry picker used by airplane engine mechanics.[88] To get through a news conference or major event, Kennedy had Travell buoy him up with seven to eight procaine injections, at one time, in the same spot.[89]

Inevitably, more "rumors" about Kennedy's back problems started leaking. The Kennedys needed to squelch this new set of "rumors" before the press picked up on them. Travell tried to come through again.

She quickly issued another reassuring press statement denying there was no reason for worry over Kennedy's back. Kennedy "was in wonderful condition," she declared, and his back only became a minor nuisance *after* he became President, due to the unusually cold winter of 1961 and less time to play sports.[90] Travell insisted that during the fall 1960 campaign, under her care, Kennedy had been entirely well, and had actively golfed, swam, and played tennis.[91]

If Travell wasn't worried, others close to Kennedy were. They included Kennedy's devoted, adoring, long-time personal secretary, Evelyn Lincoln—who had begun working for Kennedy in 1953 when he was a junior Senator[92]—and both other White House doctors: endocrinologist Gene Cohen,[93] and Travell's assistant White House general physician, the unassuming, gentlemanly Navy internist, George Burkley.[94]

By the spring of 1961, Kennedy's inner circle was split into two camps over Janet Travell and her back treatments of Kennedy: Aligned on one side were Burkley, Cohen, and Evelyn Lincoln, who distrusted Travell. On the side, though, was the powerful bloc of Travell and her supporters, who included the Kennedy clan, and Kennedy aides Theodore Sorenson and Pierre Salinger, both of whom recognized Travell's immense political value.

Throughout the spring of 1961, relations between the two camps were highly tense and stuck at stalemate. That changed in May of 1961.

36

Desperate

✦

May 1961–October 1961, Ottawa and Washington, D.C.

Kennedy was in Ottawa for a ceremonial tree planting. When he bent over to shovel a small amount of dirt, he threw out his back. Television cameras caught his face screwed up in pain, and his fierce efforts to hide it.[95]

Ottawa was a turning point for Kennedy. Afterwards, he walked even more stiffly, rose from chairs with even more difficulty, resorted more to crutches, and spent more time in the heated White House pool.[96] Some in his Secret Service speculated that Kennedy would be in a wheelchair in his second term.[97]

Amazingly, even after Ottawa, Travell still insisted that Kennedy was just fine, and continued to give Kennedy her procaine injections, now up to an astounding six times a day. Travell issued a widely publicized statement from the White House: "There is no serious concern about the President's health," she declared.[98]

But Cohen and Burkley watched and worried. Both doctors grew convinced that Travell valued her prestigious position over her patient's welfare; that she would do nearly anything to hang onto her prestigious White House position. Their distress wasn't just that Travell's treatments weren't helping; as George Burkley stated in a sealed interview in 1967, he and Cohen worried that Travell's treatments[99] "were actually harmful."[100]

By now, Cohen and Burkley were desperate to find a new doctor for Kennedy. Cohen had been telling Burkley about a terrific back and muscle doctor he knew in New York. Burkley was eager to hear more about this Hans Kraus.

Cohen told Burkley how he had met Kraus because their specialties overlapped. His patients with thyroid or endocrine problems often also had ancillary muscle problems, while Kraus's patients with widespread, generalized muscle

175

pain—the kind where patients told him, "Doctor, I ache from head to toe"—often turned out to have previously undiagnosed gland problems. Kraus himself had become one of Cohen's patients after Cohen pointed out that people who were short in stature and had the tendency to develop trigger points often also had thyroid problems. Over many years, Cohen came to know Kraus well personally as well as professionally. When interviewed in 1995, Cohen called Kraus nothing less than "one of the great unsung medical pioneers of the century."

While normally unethical for any doctor to approach another doctor's patient, Cohen and Burkley felt that circumstances were exceptional, and they had no choice. By June of 1961, when Cohen first called Kraus to see Kennedy, the doctors were desperate. As they watched Kennedy grow worse over the summer, they grew even more desperate. They kept beseeching Travell to call Kraus for a second opinion. And Travell kept refusing.

As Burkley recalled in 1967, in the stiff and elliptical style he used in his sealed Oral History for the John F. Kennedy Library, "At that time, I had attempted to secure the aid of a physical medicine specialist, Doctor Hans Kraus of New York, and had requested contact with him from Dr. Travell. She had resisted doing this, and I said if she did not call him personally, I would call him."[101] The loyal Evelyn Lincoln, who had remained allied with Cohen and Burkley, also supported the idea of approaching Kraus. Lincoln would later write to Kraus, "I was keenly aware of Kennedy's physical problems and I was in a position to know which doctors helped him and those who did not. When (Gene Cohen) recommended you I had full confidence in you."[102]

Finally, in October of 1961, Burkley and Cohen issued their ultimatum to Travell: Either she personally called Kraus to invite him to see Kennedy, or else they would go to Kennedy themselves, explain that Travell was inept, should be fired, and Kraus brought on as her replacement.[103]

Given those options, Travell had no choice. "At that point he was called," Burkley said about Kraus.[104]

37

The Arrangement

✦

October 1961, Washington, D.C.

On October 14, 1961, Travell phoned Kraus to invite him to the White House to examine Kennedy. The next day, Kraus flew to Washington.

Always known for her great charm, Travell met Kraus at the airport and during the drive back to the White House, chatted like an old friend, even insisting that Kraus join her and her husband for dinner that evening as their guest at an elegant restaurant before Kraus flew back to New York. Kraus remembered that Travell and her husband Jack Powell made engaging dining companions. For the time being Kraus did not detect any of Travell's political jockeying. That would soon change.

At the White House, Kraus set up temporary shop in Travell's office. He started his exam, as usual; by labeling a manila file with the patient's name, although in this case he did take the precaution to mark the folder merely "K" and kept it separate from his other patient files in his Manhattan office. He then jotted down basic patient statistics: "K" was forty-four years old, six feet tall, and weighed 179 pounds. Next, Kraus felt Kennedy's muscles for trigger points and other muscle anomalies, put his patient through the Kraus-Weber tests, and observed how stiffly and awkwardly Kennedy moved.

What Kraus did *not* do would surprise many: He didn't read Travell's medical notes; it was clear to him that Travell had failed. Nor did he look at Travell's x-rays or take x-rays of his own.

Kraus' deeply rooted conviction that x-rays were overused started when the prominent Herr Professor Doktor at the Vienna University hospital soundly chewed out the young medical resident for relying on x-rays to make, rather than support, a diagnosis. The appearance of even more sophisticated MRI and CAT scan imaging techniques reinforced Kraus' belief that high tech, sexy, expensive diagnostic testing had pushed aside invaluable, old-fashioned physical exams based on touch and observation. Kraus would say, with a sigh, "Doctors don't touch their patients anymore."[1]

Kraus also knew that when it came to backs, what you see isn't necessarily what you *really* see. His studies had shown that most people's spines look "imperfect" on x-rays, but that there's no correlation between these imperfect looking spines and back pain. And he had treated many people suffering back pain whose x-rays looked fine.

But Kraus' old fashioned physical exam and K-W tests told him a lot about Kennedy: Kennedy was so weak that he couldn't do a single sit-up and he was so tight that his leg muscles felt "as taut as piano wires." When Kraus asked his patient to touch his toes, Kennedy's fingertips dangled a good twenty inches off the floor, not even reaching his knees.[105] It was clear to Kraus that whatever else was going on with Kennedy's back, Kennedy was in abysmal shape.

Kraus wasn't sure how much he could help Kennedy, considering Kennedy's back operations and subsequent treatments. But from the little Kraus had seen of the man, he had a good feeling about him, and wanted to try to help him. And Kraus had no doubt about one thing: Kennedy needed to exercise. Otherwise, his muscles would grow weaker and tighter, causing only more pain and immobility. Kraus delivered his assessment to Kennedy bluntly, "You will be a cripple soon if you don't start exercising. Five days a week. And you need to start now."[106]

Kraus described his conditions for treating Kennedy. On his part, he laid out what Kennedy could expect from him: Kraus would make the huge concession of flying to Washington to treat Kennedy, rather than insisting, as Kraus did with all his other patients, that Kennedy come to his office in Manhattan.[2] Kraus would also commit to treating Kennedy personally at least three times during the week, and would train the three White House therapists so that they could supervise the two additional weekly exercise sessions in Kraus' absence. Kraus would also commit, on a moment's notice, to fly to Kennedy for emergencies, whenever he needed him, wherever he was, no matter how often; a considerable personal sacrifice for Kraus, since it meant giving up his weekends of climbing.

---

1.   Kraus would often draw a parallel between the evolution of medicine and climbing. "Doctors don't touch their patients," he would say, "It's all second hand now, like in climbing, where climbers [on indoor plastic climbing walls] don't touch the rock.

2.   Kraus did not make that exception for Robert Kennedy, the Attorney General. Like Kraus' other patients, when Robert wanted a treatment, he had to come to Kraus in his New York office.

Then Kraus got to the crucial part: what he expected from Kennedy and the other White House doctors. Kraus explained to everyone in the room that to him, this was his most important condition, on which he was absolutely unyielding and completely unwilling to compromise. It was the only way he would work with any patient, whether president of the United States or a Gunks climber: "I must have absolute control," Kraus announced.

As Kraus looked around the room, he explained: He would brook no interference from any doctor, whether Travell or even Cohen or Burkley. He would entertain no second opinion, unless he sought it. If the other doctors, or Kennedy, didn't like his conditions, that was fine with him. In that case, he simply wouldn't take Kennedy on as a patient.

But Burkley and Cohen were thrilled, and quickly agreed to Kraus' conditions. Dissenting votes did come from Kennedy and Travell, although for different reasons.

Travell didn't want to be fired or give up any power, but she would not have much choice if the President agreed to the change. Kennedy didn't want to draw attention to his health problems by having reporters notice Kraus' regular presence in the White House. "I don't know; what if the reporters start writing again about my health problems?" he asked Kraus.

"It's your decision," Kraus shot back smartly, to Kennedy, "but when you get worse, what will they write then?"

Just as Kraus had an uncompromising condition for Kennedy, so too, Kennedy had one for Kraus. His was equally simple to express: absolute secrecy.

Kennedy insisted that Kraus get no publicity for being his back doctor, and instead remain hidden and operate completely behind the scenes. If the press tried contacting Kraus, he wasn't to speak to them, even off the record, and instead refer them to Kennedy's press secretary, Pierre Salinger. It was the way all the Kennedy doctors worked—except Travell, who was trusted to say the right thing, and who loved the limelight.[3]

Neither Kraus nor Kennedy mentioned payment. In fact, Kraus didn't even raise the issue for over a year—and then in a letter to Evelyn Lincoln, simply requesting reimbursement for plane fares. He never even charged for his time or the

---

3.   After George Burkley became Kennedy's Chief White House physician, Burkley had no outside contact, recalling, "I had never had any direct relations with the press, because I felt that any information that was of significance to the press would be given through the channels of the press secretary."

actual treatments. But this wasn't because he was trying to curry favor with the Kennedys or treat Kennedy with special favor.

As Kraus sat in the White House the first time, he decided that treating Kennedy would be a privilege and his form of public service. Kraus hadn't been able to fight for America in World War II, but if he could heal its President, it would be his way of giving back to his country. He wasn't going to let financial arrangements, or anything else, get in the way.

But he had another reason as well. Kraus didn't want to charge Kennedy before he was confident that he was really helping him. It wasn't a matter of special favors for a special patient—although Kraus would go on to have many, as rival doctors keenly and enviously noted. The first thing that Bruce Grynebaum, former Vice Chairman of the N.Y.U. Rusk Institute Department of Rehabilitation Medicine, volunteered about him was that "Kraus captured all of the 'carriage trade.' He treated all the famous people who had back pain. Kraus must have made millions. *Millions.*"

But Grynebaum, like most people, didn't realize that Kraus had a sliding scale of fees. He charged his wealthy and celebrity patients his usual amount, charged middle class patients much less, and there was a considerable group of patients Kraus charged nothing. It was a point of honor for him when his long time accountant, Tony Uzzo, sat him down when he did Kraus' taxes, and informed him, "Hans, you really can't afford to take on more 'free patients.'"

The arrangement between Kraus and Kennedy added another layer to Kennedy's presidential health cover-up. Kennedy fired Travell from her dual roles as his back doctor—replaced by Kraus—and his Chief White House physician—replaced by her former assistant, George Burkley.[107] (Gene Cohen remained Kennedy's endocrinologist.) But Kennedy was careful about how he made the changes; he didn't want to call attention to his health issues. No public announcement was made about the new appointments; rather, great pains were taken to hide them. But the President would need a cover story for the press to account for Kraus' sudden and constant presence around him.

It's not clear who masterminded the cover story, but a likely candidate would be the brilliant and utterly devoted aide, Theodore Sorenson, who ghostwrote Kennedy's *Profiles in Courage,* and then stood back while Kennedy took all the credit and won the Nobel Prize for Literature.[108] Regardless, when the press picked up rumblings among Kennedy's medical team (The *Washington Post* reported on the front page, "Dr. Travell quitting as Kennedy's doctor,"[109] while The *New York Times* wrote that Travell was fired[4]) the White House was ready. Pierre Salinger told the press that Travell remained Kennedy's back doctor, but that a New York specialist, named Hans Kraus, had been brought in to consult with Travell as a "physiotherapist." Kraus' role wasn't as Kennedy's *doctor*, Salinger emphasized; he was merely giving Kennedy fitness exercises.

To help maintain the fiction, when Kraus stayed overnight to treat Kennedy for the weekend, holidays, and emergency flare ups that occurred regularly when Kennedy visited his family, Kraus stayed tucked away discreetly at small *pensiones*. In contrast, when Travell visited, she had been feted at parties and dinners as a houseguest at one of the Kennedy compounds, or else stayed publicly, amid great fanfare, at local grand hotels, such as the Breakers in Palm Beach.

The arrangement started smoothly, but soon Kraus saw a problem emerge. Kennedy was on the phone constantly throughout the day, and he saw no reason to stop taking calls during his back treatments. Kraus laid down the law: "No calls, none, no matter who they're from. I don't care."

After some argument, Kraus relented, slightly, and was willing to compromise. "Okay, the only exception I'll allow is in case of national emergency," he said.

Enlisting the support of Evelyn Lincoln, who was already adept at handling unwelcome visitors and callers, Kraus warned her, "If you want the President to get well, you have to curtail all of those telephone calls and leave him *incommunicado* during the hour of his treatments."

A few weeks passed; Evelyn Lincoln held all of Kennedy's calls as she promised. Then one day, Evelyn Lincoln buzzed Kraus during a treatment session. "I'm very sorry, Dr. Kraus. There's a phone call for the President, and this one he needs to take." She added, apologetically. "It's his mother."

Kraus replied gently, thinking of his own adored "mutter," Ella Kraus, "Of course. I understand. Mothers are important."

Afterwards, Kraus softened his no-calls stance during treatments: Exceptions for national emergency or Rose Kennedy.

---

4. *New York Times*, August 2, 1997, in Travell's obituary: "Early in her White House days, Dr. Travell was the focus of some political infighting, enough that one newspaper speculated that she might be forced to resign. As she recalled later in an interview, she became aware of the dissension and approached the President. 'I will do anything I can for you as long as you wish.' Dr. Travell told him [Kennedy]. 'But I am ready to leave at a moment's notice, if that is your pleasure.' Kennedy replied, 'I don't want you to leave. If I do, I will let you know.'"

38

Kraus in Action

✦

October 1961–Winter 1962, Washington, D.C.

So Kraus sprang into action. Burkley set up a small area next to the swimming pool with gym equipment where Kraus put Kennedy through his exercises. For the next two years, Kraus spent more time with Kennedy than he did with his own family.

Despite Kraus' reservations, after only six weeks from when he first started treating Kennedy, the inner circle saw remarkable improvement. After two months, even outsiders couldn't help but notice. In a rare press reference to Kraus that slipped into the press, on December 14, 1961, The *New York Times* reported, "President's Back Reported Better. 'Back Apparently is Tremendously Better.' About six weeks ago, New York expert, Dr. Hans Kraus, began coming to the White House to supervise a series of muscle strengthening exercises. Dr. Kraus still makes the visit once or twice a week. Presidential aides said he has done wonders for the President." (Undoubtedly to Kennedy's relief, the article downplayed his treatments, as Kraus was treating him at least three times a week.)

Over the course of 1962, under Kraus' care, Kennedy continued to make steady progress. Cohen sent Kraus a note, "Well done! Equivalent to Mt. Everest—as you rightly said, this is round one of the New Year but a good one…"[110] When early in 1962, Kraus re-tested Kennedy for strength and flexibility of the back, hip, stomach, and leg muscles, he was already much stronger. By then, he could do ten sit-ups, knees flexed and straight. He was also a lot more flexible; when he bent over to touch his toes, he was only twelve inches off the floor.[111]

In March of 1962, Kraus' back records on Kennedy revealed a significant milestone. The additional padding in Kennedy's famous rocking chair, which had been installed to cushion his aching muscles, was removed.

The rocking chair was an example of Travell's brilliant marketing acumen. Travell proudly claimed that she was "responsible for bring[ing] back the rocking chair" to American culture when she recommended it to Kennedy for his bad back. Kraus was dubious about a rocking chair's medical utility, but Travell recommended it broadly to patients with back pain and made it into a personal trademark. As for Kennedy, if nothing else, the rocking chair garnered a great deal of sympathetic publicity, generated terrific photo opportunities, and evolved into an icon of his presidency.[1]

Encouraged by Kennedy's progress, Kraus continued to put his patient through his K-W exercises five times a week. While not painful or uncomfortable, Kraus' exercises can be monotonous and tedious. Whenever Kennedy started merely going through the motions—undermining their benefits—Kraus delivered a stern lecture.

Kraus' treatments of Kennedy consisted almost entirely of exercise. Only a few times in the two years that he treated Kennedy did Kraus deviate, finding that Kennedy had developed a trigger point from stress, requiring a trigger point injection. Apart from the name, Kraus' trigger point injections had little in common with Travell's or those of other practitioners. Kraus targeted different spots in the muscle, "needled" only once with longer and thicker needles, used brute force to break up dense scar tissue like breaking up a thick block of ice; and crucially, started the K-W exercises within three days after the injection. Kraus also never used procaine, just plain saline solution or else the mild, non-narcotic, lidocaine; which unlike procaine, does not provide pain relief afterwards. From experience Kraus knew he could even "needle dry," without any fluid in the needle, but that was unbearably painful for most patients, to the point where many balked at finishing their treatments.

Over the course of the fall of 1961, Kraus increasingly grew aware of the politics of being a Kennedy White House doctor. Travell had resented being fired, even though she publicly retained her former titles and prestige. Underneath her charm and vivacity, she found ways to practice political gamesmanship. Travell

---

1.   When Sotheby's auctioned Kennedy's rocking chair in February of 2005, it fetched $96,000 by an anonymous bidder.

kept Burkley from seeing her White House medical notes for four months and took several more months before clearing out her White House office so that he could properly establish himself there.[112] She also maintained the charade that she was Kraus' boss, supervising his treatments of Kennedy because she had wanted a second opinion.

Wearing large dark sunglasses and a large scarf pulled low over her face—parking her car at the far end of the airport parking lot, "for extra security," she explained—Travell kept insisting on meeting Kraus at the airport and driving him back to the White House."

Then came December of 1961. Travell saw a chance to get rid of Kraus for good. Kraus' indoctrination into White House politics would now be complete.

While visiting his parents for Christmas in Palm Beach, Kennedy suffered a relapse of back pain, which Kraus attributed to stress. As arranged, Kennedy sent a plane for Kraus. Settling back comfortably into his seat, Kraus snapped open *The New York Times*, and prepared for a relaxing flight. What he read there filled him with shock and anger.

Travell had called a press conference to announce that she was Kennedy's back doctor; she was worried about Kennedy's back, and she was convening Kennedy's medical team for a consultation over his back treatments.[113] Travell itemized to the press the doctors who were supposedly reporting to her and were huddling together in Palm Beach. The list included the surgeon responsible for Kennedy's disastrous 1954 back operation. Travell's list did not include Kraus.

Kraus didn't care about the publicity—he would have been equally furious if his name had been on Travell's list—but he cared intensely about his patient and the arrangement that he had made with him. The newspaper story meant that Travell was seeing Kennedy, and that Kennedy and Travell were breaking their side of the arrangement with Kraus: Kraus had agreed to complete secrecy, in return, Kennedy had agreed that Kraus would have complete control.

Kraus practiced medicine the way he led rock at the Gunks: exuding complete confidence, demanding complete control, and thereby assuming complete responsibility for his decisions and their consequences. Kraus still sputtered in anger thirty years later when he recalled the episode. "I saw red," he said. "When she met me at the airport, I chewed her out and gave her a piece of my mind."

Kraus' blood continued to boil when he reached the Kennedy compound. In front of everyone there, Kraus lambasted Travell again, and then he turned his criticism on the President. He reminded Kennedy of their agreement, and concluded, "I won't treat *you* again if *she* touches you."

Kennedy nodded.

Burkley, like Cohen, was by now a staunch fan of Kraus. Burkley turned icily to Travell, "Do you understand? Keep your hands off the President."[114]

After the episode in Palm Beach, Travell wasn't yet ready to concede defeat, but she did stop meeting Kraus at the airport. When they ran into each other in the White House, they treated each other with chilly correctness.

For the next few months, Travell continued to talk to Kennedy about taking a pain killing procaine injection when the pain flared up. One time she succeeded. When Burkley found out, he reprimanded Travell. When Kraus found out, he flew immediately to Washington and demanded to see Kennedy.

Kennedy was surprised to see Kraus, even more when Kraus announced that he was resigning. "Why are you saying that?" the President asked him.

Kraus bluntly informed him, "Mr. President, you obviously aren't happy with my services."

Unused to such directness, Kennedy demurred, "No, no, I'm very pleased..."

"Well, Mr. President, I can't treat you if any other doctor touches your back and interferes with my treatments." Kraus again reminded Kennedy of their agreement; Kraus was holding up his end to ensure complete secrecy, and Kennedy needed to hold up his end to ensure Kraus maintained complete control.

As Kennedy listened meekly, Kraus continued, "The poorest of my patients has the benefit of my services as I see fit. No other doctor is to interfere with my treatments. The President of the United States should have no less."

Kennedy was not accustomed to people talking to him in this way; all his life, he had been treated deferentially: as a boy, as the son of one the richest men in America, and as a man, as the most powerful person in America. It must have been quite a sight: the 5'6" Kraus sternly lecturing the leader of the Free World like an errant schoolboy.

Kennedy agreed, "No, no, it won't happen again."

After that, it never did.

39

Kraus in Camelot

✦

1962, Washington, D.C.

Like others in Kennedy's inner circle, the more contact Kraus had with Kennedy, the more Kraus admired him. Even though Kraus had voted for Nixon in the 1960 election, Kraus soon was caught up in the Kennedy spell. As he would say, "Kennedy was very easy to like. He treated a person like a person. He was a really likable fellow."

For Kraus, the turning point in his relationship with Kennedy was Monday, October 22, 1962. It was a day that Kraus was scheduled to treat Kennedy. It also was the day the Cuban Missile Crisis came to a head. Afterwards, Kraus' devotion to Kennedy was absolute, although his reasons were personal rather than political.

When Kraus boarded the plane in New York in the afternoon to fly to Washington, events were not yet public, but from the moment Kraus arrived in D.C., he sensed something was wrong. At the airport, Kraus' White House limo driver was tense and nervous. Approaching the White House, Kraus saw a large number of barricades and security guards. When the Security Police stopped Kraus' car, they sternly followed procedures with expressionless faces; always before, when they saw Kraus, they smiled and waved him in casually, often pointing to their backs and kidding, "Ouch!"

Inside the White House, Kraus saw lots of grim faces and people running around. Someone finally told him that Kennedy would be late, and asked him to wait downstairs in the West Wing Dispensary. At that moment, Kennedy was in fact upstairs in the Oval Office, delivering his historic televised speech. At 7:00 p.m. that evening, Kennedy had begun speaking to the world.

Good evening, my fellow citizens: This government, as promised, has maintained the closest surveillance of the Soviet military build up on the island of Cuba. Within the past week, unmistakable evidence has established the fact that a series of offensive missile sites is now in preparation on that imprisoned island. The purpose of these bases can be none other than to provide a nuclear strike capability against the Western hemisphere...

Kennedy announced he was issuing an ultimatum to Khrushchev to remove the missile bases, that the U.S. would quarantine Cuba until he did, and that the U.S. would retaliate if Khrushchev launched a nuclear attack. While people around the world sat glued to their televisions wondering if Kennedy's speech signaled the start of WWIII, Kennedy walked stiffly downstairs to the Dispensary still wearing his thick television make up and he took his doctor's hand gently.

"I know, Doctor, you've come a long way to take care of me," Kraus recalled Kennedy said, "but please forgive me. Tonight, I simply have no time." Then aides whisked Kennedy away to deal with averting nuclear holocaust.

Kraus recalled, "I was struck that after such a momentous occasion, Kennedy took the time to personally come down to excuse himself. It only took a minute, but almost anyone else"—Kraus rattled off Eisenhower, Nixon, Robert Kennedy, and Lyndon Johnson—"would have sent an assistant or secretary down to say, 'Get rid of this guy, this doctor. I'm busy.'

"You know, I really liked Kennedy before that incident. But after that, I liked him even more."

Kraus observed that the President treated the people around him in a similarly thoughtful way, and in return Kennedy's domestic staff at the White House and Kennedy compounds doted on him. They began to dote on Kraus, too, when they saw how much he helped Kennedy. Evelyn Lincoln became an adoring fan of Kraus, as did Kennedy's personal maid, Providencia, always called, "Provie." Feisty and direct, Provie became particularly protective of Kraus.

When Kennedy suffered a sudden flare up of back pain while visiting his family in Palm Beach, Kraus flew down, as usual, to treat him. At the Kennedy compound, Kraus was asked to wait in a room adjoining Kennedy's bedroom. Some time went by; Kennedy still hadn't emerged. Provie popped in and out doing her chores. After a while, when she saw Kraus still waiting, she asked him, "What, you're still here and he isn't here yet?

"Don't worry, it's okay," Kraus told her.

Unsatisfied with this, Provie marched into Kennedy's bedroom. Kraus could hear her voice easily through the wall.

"Get in there. The Doctor has flown down to treat you and is waiting for you."

Kennedy soon emerged from the bedroom, looking somewhat sheepish, as Kraus recalled, and apologized profusely.

While it was clear to Kraus that Kennedy earned the loyalty from those around him, he was aware that there was a flipside to Camelot; there was one person to whom the President could not stay loyal. Kraus knew that the President was a womanizer, but after his own bitter first marriage and divorce, Kraus was sympathetic to what he considered Kennedy's plight of being trapped in a loveless, emotionally barren marriage. It was telling to Kraus that in the fierce debate over Kennedy's back treatments, Jackie was conspicuously absent, even though Kennedy's aides, brother, and secretary were all passionately involved.

Kraus had only occasional contact with Jackie. One time, for instance, at the President's request, he gave a talk to Jackie and the other Kennedy wives about the importance of exercise. Despite little interaction with her, Kraus was convinced that Jackie was glamorous and beautiful, but shallow and dull; much like Kraus' first wife, and the myriad women Kraus had known before his second wife, Madi. Regarding the stream of charming young women he saw enter and leave the White House, Kraus shrugged his shoulders. "How could you not see it," he said, "We all saw it."

Kraus also came into firsthand contact with the dirty side of politics. Assuming that the phones in Kraus' New York office, Manhattan apartment, and Gardiner country home were tapped, Kennedy installed "red lines" so that he and Kraus always had secure direct access. As a precaution, when Burkley, Cohen and Kraus needed to talk on the phone, they always used pay phones. Kraus, then, wasn't surprised when he arrived at his office one Monday morning to find the door open, drawers pulled out, and patient records dumped across the floor.

Everyone in the White House assumed the break-in was the work of J. Edgar Hoover, since Hoover was well known for his efforts to gather political dirt on Kennedy and other senior politicians.[115] Nonetheless, it was a bungled affair; Kraus had outsmarted the culprit through the simple precaution of labeling the file, "K," and keeping it in an unlocked drawer in another part of his office.

Anyway, Kraus pointed out, "Even if Hoover had gotten his hands on Kennedy's files, all that would have happened is that he would have discovered that Kennedy did exercises."

The Kennedy White House also had unusually heartwarming moments. When Kraus gave Kennedy a weekend treatment in the family's Palm Beach compound, Kraus was present when a beaming five-year-old Caroline rushed in. She wanted proudly to share the news with her father that she won a race on her pony, Macaroni, and rewarded Macaroni with a bowl of Coca Cola. Watching the young girl, Kraus thought of his own daughter, Ann, who was close in age. "How lucky this little girl is to have such a young father. One day, he'll be alive to walk her down the aisle at her wedding." Kraus assumed that he himself would not have such a chance with Ann.

But the charming scene also held a special poignancy for Kraus, underscoring the trade-offs he had made in starting a family when he was well into his fifties and then agreeing to treat Kennedy. Now that Kraus finally did have a family, he had less time than ever for his wife and daughters.

Even Kraus' climbing was colored against the backdrop of his family. He had little time to climb during the Kennedy years, but on the rare occasions when he did, there was a marked difference. Now he seconded more as often as not, or led routes several notches within his ability. Kraus' days of leading first ascents, soloing, or pushing limits while leading hard, dangerous terrain were over. Kraus explained, "I didn't want to die when my daughters were young."

Kraus' next to last first ascent took place during this time, from the far safer position of being the middleman on a three-person rope team. Still, Rib Cracker, in the remote Millbrook section of the Shawangunks, was strenuous and exposed.

Jim McCarthy, who led the party, which included fellow climber Werner Bischoff, recalled, "Hans was tied into the middle of the rope, with Werner last. Hans was in Washington a lot treating Kennedy and he wasn't climbing much. There was a tough section on a traverse, and I figured what the hell; I'd help him out a bit with the rope, and gave it a tug to 'help' him over the hard part.

"The problem was that Werner, who was tied to the belay at the other end, thought the rope had gotten stuck. So he began tugging on his end, to free it, as he thought. The harder I tugged from my end, the harder Warner pulled from his.

"There was Hans stuck in the middle—this before modern harnesses, mind you, so Hans was just tied into the rope—being pulled by the two of us from each direction. I was trying my damnedest to pull Hans across the traverse, while there was Warner trying to pull him back.

"You can imagine; Hans was pretty sore around the middle from the rope pulling him in each direction. He found out a few days later that we had cracked several of his ribs. He thought it pretty funny, and that was how the route got its name."

Even though the fifty-seven year old Kraus wasn't climbing much, in 1962, he was invited to join the American expedition attempting to summit Everest for the first time. This was incredibly prestigious: Everest had been summitted first in 1953 by Edmund Hillary and Tenzing Norgay, and in 1956 by a Swiss team. It was a point of national pride that Americans finally made it to the top. An all-star team was assembled, supported by *National Geographic* and the astronomical budget of $400,000. But Kraus didn't think twice; he turned down the berth because he felt he couldn't leave Kennedy.

After the expedition successfully placed Mt. Rainier guide, Jim Whittaker, on the summit, *National Geographic* bestowed its highest honor, the Hubbard Medal, on the expedition's organizer, Norman Dyhrenfurth—the first time the award was bestowed on a mountaineer.[1] Kraus suggested to Kennedy: Why not recognize the expedition's efforts? Why not a ceremony in the White House Rose Garden to celebrate American achievements in mountaineering?

This was the kind of thing Kennedy loved, and he took up the suggestion enthusiastically. He included in the honors other leading American mountaineers, such as Kraus' friend, Nick Clinch, who led the only American first ascent of a Himalayan 8,000 meter peak. Kennedy's remarks bore the distinctive and unmistakable influence of Kraus. "In presenting this award I carry on a great tradition," Kennedy announced to the thrilled assembly, "demonstrating that the vigorous life still attracts Americans, and also particularly mountain climbing, which is a special form of the vigorous life."[116]

Nick Clinch recalled the occasion. "It was very nicely done, of course. Kennedy had a way with words, and there must have been 200 press members there. Of course, everyone on the expedition wanted to have their picture taken shaking hands with Kennedy."

Kraus watched the ceremony in the Rose Garden without any pangs of regret, his devotion to Kennedy far outweighing desire for Everest. Kraus said, "I couldn't leave Kennedy for three months. He needed me."

As an afterthought, Kraus added, "Still, it's not easy treating a President. You're at the beck and call of the White House. I got calls in the middle of the night. On

---

1.   Previous Hubbard Medal winners include Charles Lindbergh and Admiral Peary.

weekends, I got called away from the ski slopes, when I was out on a climb, or out running."

Madi Kraus recalled a time when Kraus was on one of his usual five-mile runs through the woods in the Shawangunks. The White House had called on the "red line" at their Shawangunks house. "I picked up the phone and explained that Hans was out running," Madi said, in her characteristically gentle but firm manner, "and I'd give him the message to call as soon as he got back from his run. But that wasn't good enough for the White House. They kept insisting I should go running after Hans to bring him back. Finally I said to them, 'Look, I can't run that fast. You'll just have to wait until Hans gets back'"

Despite the constant contact with trappings of power, Kraus never developed "Potomac Fever." Sometimes, Kennedy arranged to fly Kraus on Air Force Two, or another government plane or helicopter used only by the senior-most officials. When Kraus walked up the ramp, smartly attired Air Force officers snapped to attention and saluted; inside, he usually found himself the sole passenger, waited on hand and foot by the plane's crew. "At first, it all made me feel very important," Kraus recalled, "But pretty soon you get used to it, and realize it's no big deal." Kraus was perfectly content to fly the commercial shuttle to Washington for his scheduled treatments.

Usually it was a Kennedy aide who called to say Kennedy needed Kraus, but not always. Sometimes it was Kennedy himself. Kraus remembered, "There was one time I was particularly displeased at being interrupted. It was my day in New York. After the office, I had gone to the New York Athletic Club where I lifted, ran, and got into shape. When I got home that night it was late, and when the phone rang, I picked it up, very disgruntled at being disturbed again.

"'Who's this?' I must have barked into the phone.

"Then I heard this voice on the other end, very quiet, apologetic, sheepish even. 'It's *me*,' JFK said," Kraus laughed.

40

A Converted Kennedy

✦

Late 1962–Spring 1963, Washington, D.C.

Kennedy's recovery was not straight uphill. As with any muscle injury, there were occasional bumps. But after just one month, Kraus could discern a pattern: Kennedy's relapses always took place on weekends and holidays.[117]

When Kennedy spent Thanksgiving of 1961 with his family at the Hyannisport compound, Kennedy was hit with severe back spasms. As had already become their routine, Kennedy called Kraus and sent Air Force Two for him. Six weeks later, when Kennedy spent Christmas with his family in Palm Beach, Kennedy suffered another relapse, this time far worse.

Actually, neither relapse should have been surprising. On top of Kennedy's nearly unimaginable professional pressures—like keeping nuclear war at bay—was great personal stress, including his marriage. Then devastatingly, Joseph Kennedy had suffered a debilitating stroke in December of 1961. Confronting a parent's mortality is always wrenching for a child, but particularly so for Kennedy, who owed his political ambitions and achievements to his father's open and behind the scenes efforts.[118] It had to tear at Kennedy to watch his once all-powerful father dribbling, disabled, half paralyzed, and confined to a wheelchair.

Nonetheless, diligently doing his Kraus exercises, Kennedy learned to deal with his personal stress. As Kennedy continued improving, Kraus' visits to the White House tapered off. By late 1962, Kraus was down to seeing Kennedy twice a week, with markedly fewer weekend emergencies. Then it was once a week. By the spring of 1963, Kraus sometimes saw Kennedy only once every few weeks.[119]

This didn't mean that Kennedy did his exercises less often. Kraus had trained head White House therapist "Chief" Hendrix in the K-W exercises. Hendrix, who always traveled with Kennedy—including the last trip to Dallas—made sure that Kennedy, whom he adored, faithfully followed Kraus' directives and exercised five times a week. Kraus and Hendrix grew so close, that after Kennedy's death, Hendrix called Kraus from the Johnson White House and asked if he could join Kraus in his office in Manhattan. "He was the best therapist I ever saw," Kraus said of Hendrix, who would work for him until Hendrix retired in the 1980's.

Under Kraus' influence, Kennedy came to appreciate the amazing power of exercise. "I have called for a higher degree of physical fitness in our nation," Kennedy declared in December of 1962.[120] This was different than the characteristic Kennedy clan attitude toward sports. The Kennedys as a whole were physically active, but brought up to view sports as another testing ground for identifying winners from losers. Even their highly publicized family activities—touch football, ski outings, sailing matches, or rounds of monopoly—which for others might be in the spirit of simple fun and games, in the hands of the Kennedys morphed into deadly serious competitions.[1]

The intensity with which the Kennedys played these supposedly fun family games surprised visiting school friends. One recalled that Joseph Kennedy "really did preach that winning was everything." Kennedy and his siblings grew up listening to their father intone, over and over again, like a mantra, "We don't want any losers around here. In this family we want winners."[121]

In contrast, Kraus' view that exercise was an end in itself—to enhance daily life by increasing physical and mental well-being—was a novel concept to Kennedy. But under Kraus' influence, Kennedy became an ardent convert. Pierre Salinger recalled that during 1962, Kennedy believed "that his administration had to make a very public showing of the importance of being physically fit."[122]

To put his words into action, Kennedy began climbing stairs instead of taking elevators.[123] The President even tried to persuade Pierre Salinger—who described his fitness regimen as "the occasional run to the corner for cigars"—to take up distance hiking. Kennedy half-kidded his pudgy aide that he could be an inspiration to millions of other out of shape Americans.[124] Bearing obvious shades of Kraus' influence, Kennedy also came up with the idea of a fifty-mile hike for the Marine Corps, inspired by workouts, Kennedy read, the Marines had done during Teddy Roosevelt's era. The point, as Salinger put it, was that Kennedy

---

1.   In the 1990's, Kennedy cousin, Michael Kennedy, died from a reckless game of touch football while skiing with other Kennedy cousins.

wanted to show that "today's Marine Corps officers are just as fit as those of 1908."[125]

By the end of 1962, Kennedy was close to living up to his political image of "vi-gah." When *Time* Magazine picked Kennedy for its 1962 'Man of the Year,' another reference to Kraus slipped out. Admiring Kennedy's physical fitness regime, the reporter wrote: "Kennedy is a buff for physical fitness for himself and others, at one point suggested that his aides all lose at least five pounds—and that portly Press Secretary Pierre Salinger lose a good deal more. He swims twice a day in the heated White House pool, has taken up a rigorous series of calisthenics under the direction of New York University's Dr. Hans Kraus to help his ailing back. He does his nip-ups in the White House gym, in his bedroom, even on board the big presidential jet while flying off to important meetings."

Watching Kennedy's excitement over exercise gave Kraus renewed hope for the campaign Kraus had launched in 1955 under Eisenhower to improve American children's fitness. By 1962, though, the President's Council on Physical Fitness had degenerated into a parody of Kraus' intentions. Instead of following Kraus' original vision to offer meaningful exercises to get children into shape, the President's Council mutated into a meaningless feel-good program that offered pins and badges to children for meeting extremely low standards of sports skills.

Through Kennedy, Kraus saw another chance. He waited until Kennedy had become a diehard convert to exercise, and after one treatment at the end of 1962, he presented Kennedy with a two-page document on the poor fitness levels of American children and how the problem could be solved by introducing calisthenics and jogging in the public schools.

Kennedy was very interested. "How would it be best to do this?" he asked Kraus. They discussed possibilities. "Should we establish a foundation devoted to health and fitness or make this an act of Congress?" Kennedy mused aloud.

Kennedy wanted Kraus to discuss the idea with Robert, the Attorney General. Kraus knew Robert slightly already, from treating him occasionally for a chronic but minor sprained leg muscle from tennis. Kraus found Robert very different from his brother. "I didn't like him very much," Kraus admitted. "I mostly treated Robert in my office in New York. He wasn't an easy patient. Unlike JFK, he was haughty, aware of his importance, and lacked his brother's human touch. He was almost always late, but unlike his brother, didn't bother to apologize. He would come in, surrounded by his aides and his large retinue, and immediately take over the phones. I said to him, "You can't do that; this is a doctor's office. You have to leave at least one line open.""

When Kraus and Robert met in July of 1963 to discuss Kraus children's fitness campaign, Kraus saw quickly that Robert had a different agenda. Robert listened perfunctorily, then steered the conversation toward the infighting among the Kennedy doctors. It seemed to Kraus that Robert was looking for political grist, unlike the subject of children's fitness, which had become, in Robert Kennedy's view, dated and politically useless.

Summer turned into fall; Kraus didn't hear anything further from Robert. He must have felt mild disappointment, but Kraus was neither surprised nor distressed. JFK was a young man, in good health. A second term looked like a sure thing. There was plenty of time.

41

A Cured Kennedy

✦

May 1963–October 1963, Washington, D.C.

By May of 1963, the previously unthinkable happened. Kennedy was so well that Kraus gave him permission to resume playing golf—grudgingly, though, because Kraus was no golf fan. By Kraus' exacting standards, golf was not a sport: it did not provide real exercise and, worse, it caused stress for most players and tightened their muscles. Kraus strictly warned Kennedy, "A couple of holes would be okay, but avoid driving practice."[126]

Kennedy's back records showed no muscle complaints until July, when Kennedy had a minor muscle pull from racing someone in the White House pool.[127] Kraus' notes don't mention the other swimmer's identity, but they do refute the claim of a Pulitzer Prize winning journalist that Kennedy first began wearing his back corset after he strained a muscle chasing a woman in the White House pool.[128] Actually, during the summer of 1963, the only back pain that Kennedy suffered came from minor golf injuries. Golf aficionados take note: when Kennedy asked how to strengthen his handgrip for golf, Kraus told him the best way was simply wringing a wet towel.[129]

Kennedy's return to playing golf after two years was noted with surprise in the press. Elucidating another rare mention of Kraus, *Time* wrote on July 6, 1963:

> *Ever since May 1961...John F. Kennedy has stayed off the golf course. So it came as a surprise when, early this month, newsmen spotted the President swinging vigorously away on the course at Hyannisport...To help his ailing back, Kennedy has for two years been doing special calisthenics under the guidance of Dr. Hans Kraus, a Vienna-trained New York physician who thinks that much back trouble is related to muscular weakness. On his recent trip to Europe, Kennedy noted how*

greatly his back had improved in the course of those two years. He endured the jos-tling and the strenuous pace without noticing any pains, and upon his return he exultantly told friends that his back was no longer troubling him. With Dr. Kraus's O.K., he decided to take up golf again. Last week at Hyannisport, he got out on the course again and swung away.

By the summer of 1963, Kraus' work with Kennedy was done. Kraus said, "I con-tinued to see Kennedy at Burkley's insistence, but my work with Kennedy was really over. If he had been a regular patient, I wouldn't have continued to see him at all." In August of 1963, Kennedy was finally so well that Kraus decided he could take his annual climbing trip. The only vacation Kraus allowed himself, in traditional European fashion, each year he would shut down his practice in August and climb for the month in Europe or a wilderness area like the Bugaboos in Canada.

But first, Kraus needed to arrange for a replacement, "just in case." But this wasn't so straightforward or easy. A suitable candidate didn't immediately present itself to Kraus.

"The politically smart thing to do," he realized, "would have been to pick someone I worked with from N.Y.U. But no one else there was interested in exer-cise." Instead, Kraus finally chose Dr. "G," who had a personal interest in fitness. Kraus first met the charming young doctor in Europe when Kraus gave the K-W tests to European children. Afterwards Kraus mentored Dr. "G" in New York and trained him in his immediate mobilization techniques. Now with Dr. "G" set as his back up, even Burkley conceded that Kraus was ready to go.

Leaving Madi in New York with their two young daughters, Kraus traveled to the Dolomites, to visit Gino Solda, who lived in the small Italian mountain town of Recoaro. The highlight of the trip was to be an ascent of the Spigolo Gialo. As part of the training, Kraus and Solda made first ascents of several neighboring peaks, including a particularly beautiful one they summitted by two different routes on the south face and east ridge.

An ardent JFK admirer, Solda named the peak Cima Kennedy—an even greater honor than ordinarily, since it was rare in Europe to baptize a mountain after a living person. (A brass plate marked simply 'John F. Kennedy' was inserted into the base of the cliff, which Kraus learned to his sorrow, was stolen the fol-lowing year after Kennedy's death.)

A few days after the ascent of Cima Kennedy, Solda rushed into Kraus' bed-room in the middle of the night. "La Casa Bianca! La Casa Bianca!" he called out excitedly.

It was the White House on the phone. Burkley explained to Kraus that Kennedy had twisted his leg playing golf. It was a minor injury, which Burkley initially had Dr. "G" treat; but Kennedy still wanted to send an Air Force jet to Italy to bring Kraus back to look at it. "So there was no Spigolo Gialo," Kraus said, sighing.

The next day, the White House plane arrived, and flew Kraus directly to Washington. Kraus found the injury as minor as Burkley had described it, and soon took care of it. Afterwards, Kennedy sent a telegram thanking Kraus for cutting short his vacation. The telegram became one of Kraus' most prized possessions, always kept in his bank safety deposit box, along with his Kennedy medical records.

> *I have just learned that you cut your vacation to come up here.*
> *I am extremely sorry that this was permitted although I am gratefull [sic] to you*
> *for your kindness in coming.*
> *John F. Kennedy*

By September of 1963, it was clear even to Burkley that Kennedy was cured. Kennedy's muscles were so strong and flexible, Burkley declared, that Kennedy could execute "a series of exercises which would do credit to a gymnast."[130] Evelyn Lincoln concurred, noting in her bestselling 1965 autobiography, "It was due to Dr. Kraus' persistence that the trouble in the President's back almost vanished."[131] Nearly thirty years later, in a letter she wrote to Kraus from her house in Chevy Chase on July 29, 1993, Lincoln added that it was due to Kraus that Kennedy, for the first time in his life, could fully play with his children. "And a thing he was able to do, [sic] was to pick little John up and toss him around—something that had been lacking in his life. And all of this was made possible because of your treatment."

It has long been noted that the office of the American president exacts a personal toll, graphically etched across the outsides of the men who sat in the Oval Office. Over the course of a single term, most Presidents age far more than the four-year genealogical period: FDR, Johnson, Nixon, Carter all come to mind as victims of this accelerated process.[132] Renowned Presidential historian, Michael Beschloss noted an unusual thing about Kennedy. Without knowing anything about Kraus or his treatments of Kennedy, Beschloss wrote that Kennedy was a rare American president who looked better at the end of his term than at the beginning.[133]

42

Male Bonding

✦

Autumn 1963, Washington, D.C.

Despite Kraus' assertion that things between himself and the President were "strictly business…mostly we talked about the exercises," a bond of friendship developed. Evelyn Lincoln recalled Kennedy saying to Kraus, "I wish I could have known you years ago."[134] And then there was the time that Kraus gave Kennedy a climbing demonstration.

It took place in the early autumn of 1963 after a treatment. Kraus and Kennedy were in the dressing room next to the White House pool, and Kraus was recounting the first ascent of Cima Kennedy. Kennedy furrowed his brow.

"I don't see how you people manage to climb. How do you do it?" he asked.

Kraus tried explaining, but Kennedy still looked puzzled. Noticing the walls near the pool were decorated with horizontal rows of tile, with spaces between each sharply edged tile row, Kraus had a better idea.

Grasping a tile edge, Kraus hung off his hands, and first walked his feet up by pressing them against the wall in a technique climbers call "smearing," and then with his hands in the same position, walked them up by balancing them carefully on the narrow tile edges in a technique called "edging." Next he inserted his fingers into a space between the two tile rows, twisted his fingers so that they jammed and formed a secure lock, hung his weight off his jammed fingers, and again walked his feet up the wall, called "jamming," or "crack climbing."

Kennedy watched the demonstration wordlessly until Kraus was finished. "Now I understand how you climb," he told Kraus.

On the plane ride back to New York, Kraus started laughing. "It occurred to me that I made the first ascent of the West Wall of the White House," he said.

The rapport between Kraus and Kennedy shouldn't have been surprising. There were key similarities between the two men, in make up, values and motivation. It started with their fathers. Rudi Kraus and Joseph Kennedy were both self-made, wildly successful businessmen and larger-than-life characters to their families. Both consciously had created closely-knit clans and carefully crafted rigid expectations for their eldest sons. (John F. Kennedy had inherited the mantel when the plane of his older brother, Joe, was shot down over Europe during WWII.)

Both Rudi Kraus and Joseph Kennedy were also establishment outsiders and renegades, comfortable bending or making up rules in business, and controlling and judgmental in their personal lives—dominating "family psychic space,"[135] in the words of a Kennedy historian. What another historian wrote about Joseph Kennedy also applied to Rudi Kraus: "Joe Kennedy ran his family like a tribal chieftain. When he gave an order he expected it to be unhesitatingly obeyed."[136] Both men also blessed and burdened their sons with a huge, overwhelming, irreparable debt: For Kennedy, it was fiscal and behind the scenes help that paved his way to the White House. For Kraus, it was fiscal and behind the scenes help that paved his way out of Nazi Germany.

All in all, the result was a complex legacy of love, gratitude, respect, adoration, stress, and resentment. Kraus and Kennedy responded in similar fashion to their childhood forces: Despite wealth and privilege, both developed simple tastes—oblivious to fashion,[1] furnishings, food, wines, and most high culture—and a common touch—they were comfortable with state heads or domestic workers alike. Both filled the same role to their siblings as advisor and protector, chose professions of service, and remained almost childishly indifferent to money.[137]

Both Kraus and Kennedy developed wit and irony; confidence yet selfishness. Both were direct yet domineering; admired yet emotionally self-contained. Both

---

1.   One of the few exceptions in Kraus' life was during the 1950's when he adopted the fashionable, European-inspired climbing attire. Otherwise, he retained complete indifference to attire. Jane Taylor, who spent many years in the Shawangunks, recalls, "We were having a picnic [in the Gunks] with a New York friend of ours who was terribly into haute cuisine, so we had pulled out all the stops on this picnic—lugging up "tablecloth," napkins, wine glasses, wine, paté—you name it. It was a beautiful day and we were spread out close to the edge of the cliff, eating and sipping away, when suddenly two hands plopped down on the rim of the cliff. Then, two more hands. Then, two very scruffy, sinewy, man-mountain guys hauled themselves onto the ledge, looked at us, nodded, and walked off. It was Hans and his brother, and we were all too flabbergasted to say a word—not even offer them a glass of wine!"

Kraus and Kennedy were also keenly aware of their mortality from a young age.[2] Even as teenagers, both were obsessed with death, talked about it often, lived their lives intensely and didn't expect to reach old age: Kennedy, in his twenties, told several friends he didn't expect to live past forty-five;[138] Kraus was so bold on his first ascents because he accepted the prospect of dying on them. Both prized toughness above all other traits. Even unconsciously, they would have recognized a kindred soul in the other.

Despite the Kennedy public relations mill's portrayal, to the contrary, Kennedy himself was mediocre at sports, but since college, had virtually worshipped star athletes.[139] Kraus' climbing, fitness, and boldness would certainly have impressed the young President. One Friday night, returning from treating Kennedy, Kraus' plane developed landing gear problems and made an emergency crash landing. After helping the crew deploy the emergency chute, Kraus calmly arrived home still covered with the thick, white runway safety foam. Despite the close call, Kraus was his usual unflappable self on Monday back on the shuttle to Washington. "He had real physical guts," many people said about Kraus, whether on or off the cliffs.

But neither was Kennedy short of heroism himself. Kraus, on his part, was aware of Kennedy's heroic WWII PT 109 rescue, his resiliency coming back from three botched back operations, his cool response to the Cuban Missile Crisis, his acceptance of the possibility of assassination, and his stoic attitude toward painful medical treatments. Kennedy's close friend, Red Fay, recalled watching Kennedy give himself a cortisone injection for Addison's Disease.

"'Jack,' I said, 'the way you take that jab, it looks like it doesn't even hurt.'

"Before I had time to dodge, he reached over and jabbed the same needle into my leg. I screamed with the pain.

"'It feels the same way to me,' he commented flatly."[140]

Both Kraus and Kennedy shared another basic drive: Wildly attractive to women, for most of their lives, both were extraordinary womanizers—although Kraus reformed after being smitten with Madi. Of Kennedy's womanizing, Kraus said, "Everyone knew. You couldn't help but know. Anyway, so Kennedy liked to sleep with a lot of women." He paused, smiling, "So had I."

---

2. For Kraus, the pivotal experience was the death of Marcus. For Kennedy, it was the deaths of his older brother, Joe, and older sister, Kathleen, "Kick," in airplane crashes in the 1940's.

A former lover of Kraus' said, "Hans once told me that every time he entered a crowded room he looked everyone over and asked himself which of the women he would enjoy sleeping with and which of the men he could beat in a fight.

"Had he chosen to follow either path, his chances of success were excellent. He was a very sexually attractive man, which was immediately apparent to most of the women present."

43

The Back Corset

◆

October 1963, Washington, D.C.

Even though Kennedy was cured, he couldn't stop exercising. If he did, his muscles would again weaken and tighten, again causing pain. Kraus told Kennedy that now he needed to shift from physical therapy exercises to exercises designed for staying in shape. But as is common among people who suffer chronic bad pain—the psychological adjustment lags behind physical progress—Kennedy did not quite dare give up the trappings of his infirmity just yet.

In the fall of 1963, Kraus knew that he still had one last piece of unfinished medical business left with Kennedy: the President had to throw out his back corset.

Kennedy had worn the back corset continuously since his car accident while a sophomore at Harvard. It was a formidable contraption. Dr. M.T. Jenkins, one of the Parkland Memorial Hospital doctors who worked on Kennedy after he was shot, described it as a tightly laced brace, held in place by wide ace bandages making figure-eight loops around Kennedy's torso and thighs.[141]

Kraus understood Kennedy's stubbornness about his back corset. Kraus explained, "Kennedy still saw himself as a 'bad back,' rather than as a healthy person who might occasionally suffer a strained muscle." Sometimes it took years for his patients' mental image to catch up to their physical reality: He wasn't surprised, therefore, when in March of 1963, Kennedy had developed two trigger points from tension, and before Kraus eliminated them with his trigger point injections, Kennedy asked Kraus whether he should try crutches again.[142] "Don't even think of it. Throw those things *out*," Kraus retorted.

Kraus vehemently opposed artificial supports—whether canes, crutches, girdles, braces or back corsets—and wanted Kennedy to stop wearing his back corset as soon as possible. He explained, "Because muscles atrophy without physical activity, a person should be strengthening his muscles rather than relying on these things."

When in the spring of 1962 Kennedy's improvement had hit a temporary plateau, Kraus theorized the culprit was the back corset, by interfering with normal muscle function and recovery. Both Cohen and Burkley agreed with him: "Kennedy had worn his corset too long." Back then, Kraus had launched his campaign against Kennedy's back corset. But in this, Kennedy, ordinarily an easy, ideal patient, had proven himself stubborn. Throwing away a brace he had depended on throughout his adult life was a big, scary step. But Kraus kept pushing, explaining to Kennedy, "Your corset isn't needed [anymore] since there are enough muscles in your hips and low back to support it without outside help."

Kennedy was also reluctant to stop his therapeutic Kraus exercises, even though Kraus kept telling him he was ready for the next step: a well-rounded, moderate exercise program—one that Kraus designed for normal, healthy individuals with office jobs and essentially sedentary lives. A scaled down version of the demanding regime Kraus himself pursued throughout his life, Kennedy's prescribed program included three-times-a-week weight lifting, stretching, relaxation exercises, calisthenics such as sit-ups and pull-ups, and jogging three miles.

Finally, in October—the last time Kraus saw Kennedy—Kennedy agreed. Kraus confidently jotted down in his medical notes that Kennedy had assured him that after the New Year he would throw out his corset and begin Kraus' regular exercise program.[143]

Many historians have speculated that Kennedy might have survived the assassination three weeks later if he had not been wearing his corset.[144] The second bullet, which hit him in the back of the neck, rendered him unconscious, but was likely not enough to kill him. The normal physical response would have been to slump over. But even though presumably unconscious, Kennedy's rigid corset held him upright, presenting an easy, stable target for the third, fatal bullet. [1]

That bullet shattered Kennedy's skull and brain.

---

1.   Robert Dallek, in his 2002 biography of Kennedy, An Unfinished Life, went as far as to conclude, "Were it not for a back brace, which held him [Kennedy] erect, a third and fatal shot to the back of the head would not have found its mark." An Unfinished Life, p. 694.

44

The Assassination

✦

November 1963, Washington, D.C.

Even after Kraus stopped treating Kennedy in October of 1963, their relationship continued. The next month, for the first time ever, Kennedy invited Kraus to a State Dinner.

> *The President and Mrs. Kennedy*
> *request the pleasure of the company of*
> *Dr. and Mrs. Kraus*
> *at dinner*
> *on Monday, November 25, 1963*
> *at eight o'clock*
> *on the occasion of the visit*
> *of*
> *Dr. Ludwig Erhard*
> *Chancellor of the Federal Republic of Germany*

At the least, the occasion suggests gratitude. And the timing suggests that Kennedy intended to bestow on Kraus a public role, at last.

Kraus was thrilled. Even he wasn't immune to the Camelot charisma. But more importantly, Kennedy's invitation gave Kraus renewed hope for his children's fitness campaign. If Kennedy decided to acknowledge Kraus publicly, it would give Kraus a powerful platform for another attempt to reform American public school gym programs.

Kraus and Madi arranged to leave their two young daughters with his mother and enjoy a rare weekend to themselves. Kennedy happened to be out of town, in

Dallas, Kraus knew, but they planned to fly down to the capitol on Friday, stop by the White House anyway, and see the sights. They had plenty of time. The dinner to honor the West German Chancellor wasn't until Monday, November 25.

Late on Friday morning, November 22, Kraus had a dentist appointment in Manhattan, a few hours before they were scheduled to leave for Washington. As Kraus' dentist drilled, he listened to the radio. Kraus was sitting in his dentist's chair when he heard the news of Kennedy's assassination.

That night on the Washington shuttle, instead of accompanying Madi, a grief-stricken Kraus sat next to a grief-stricken Gene Cohen. The two doctors found Kennedy lying in state in the East Room as family, friends, aides and dignitaries filed by to pay their respects. Kraus took his place in the second row, sitting immediately behind Jackie, Caroline and John John. As Kraus knelt, he remembered the poignant scene of Caroline proudly telling her daddy about her pony, Macaroni, and how he had been envious of the President, assuming that the young JFK would walk his children down the aisle at their weddings.

On Monday, instead of attending a State Dinner, Kraus joined Gene Cohen and George Burkley on the lawn of the White House to watch Kennedy's funeral procession.

Before Kraus returned to New York, Jackie summoned him to a meeting. The young widow said, "I want to thank you for all you did for my husband."

All Kraus could say was, "I appreciate that very much." He nodded. There wasn't much else to say.

Over the course of Kraus' long career, he became known among his patients for his "miracle cures." That included Kennedy. A week after Kennedy's death, Burkley expressed his gratitude to Kraus. Burkley wrote from his office in the White House:

> *The White House*
> *Washington*
>
> *Dear Hans,*
>
> *Just a note which in no way can express or convey the deep appreciation of your personal and professional value in the care of President Kennedy. Without your management the President would have been unable to carry on his active program which astounded the entire world. More important you returned to the President a full life allowing him to enjoy the activities and sports he so dearly loved. You will*

always remain on the top of the list by those who dearly loved and worked with the President.

Sincerely,
George G. Burkley[145]
Physician to the President

Kennedy aide Kenneth O'Donnell recalled how Kennedy, on the last day of his life, turned to him and declared "I feel great."

"He said to me, 'My back feels better than it's felt in years.'"

O'Donnell went on to explain. "A new treatment of calisthenics had strengthened [Kennedy's] back muscles...Along with his good health, David Powers, [another Kennedy aide] and I never saw him in a happier mood."[146]

Evelyn Lincoln mirrored these sentiments in a letter she wrote twenty years later to Kraus, adding, "I have often stated that in the last six months of President Kennedy's life he was in the best health he had ever been."[147] And in a rare, relatively candid television interview with the news program 20/20, in 1993, Lincoln publicly described how on the day Kennedy died he had finally achieved "vig-ah" and robust health for the first time in his life. Lincoln said emphatically, "He was in the best [health] he had ever been. He was really in good health."[148]

Like Burkley, Cohen and the other doctors on Kennedy's medical team, Kraus remained devoted to Kennedy after his death. He treasured his Kennedy White House memorabilia, including the presidential PT 109 tiepins that had been the rage of Washington, and the presidential matchbooks, some of which he had sent as coveted gifts to Gino Solda and other friends in Europe. Kraus explained, "Kennedy had this vision and he could make you feel that you were part of something bigger."

When Kennedy died, Kraus' sorrow was enormous for the loss of a charismatic leader, a man whom he had grown to love, and his favorite patient. Thirty years later, when he described hearing the assassination over the radio he still paused to find words for his grief. And he found that he could not.

Finally, he said, "That was a very sad time. When I heard the news, I cried."

Kraus looked away. Thirty years later, he cried again.

PART V
NEW YORK 1964–1996

45

Fame

◆

1964–1965, New York City

Like so many others in the JFK inner circle, after Kennedy's death, Kraus was left with a feeling of emptiness. Kraus wasn't interested in treating Presidents again; for two years he had been at Kennedy's beck and call, every weekend and holiday, without time for himself, his family, and his climbing. No one else would be worth that sacrifice again.

Circumstances made Kraus' decision an easy one. When Lyndon Johnson asked him to stay on as a member of his Presidential medical team, Kraus turned him down, as much because Kraus came to dislike Johnson as for those other reasons.[1] Kraus also turned down requests afterwards to treat other Kennedy family members, because JFK was the only one he liked.

Kraus didn't want to "market" his Kennedy experiences, unlike Travell and many Kennedy aides, who by 1965 had already come out with Kennedy memoirs. Kraus, like Kennedy's other White House doctors, Gene Cohen and George Burkley, felt that was "unseemly." Anyway, Kraus had given his word to Kennedy, promising secrecy, and Kraus was not a man to break his word. He would continue to honor the secrecy just as he protected his "K" file.

Yet even without capitalizing on his Kennedy connections, Kraus' practice finally took off. Kraus' newfound fame was reflected in a 1963 *Time* article. The magazine ran multiple-choice current events quizzes on timely topics for its readers. One of these quizzes was about medicine: Who discovered the oral polio vaccine? Readers had to pick from among four towering, presumably famous,

---

1. Mostly it was Johnson's personality, but Kraus could also never forgive Johnson for holding a party in the East Room one month after Kennedy's body had lain there in state.

medical giants: Edward Jenner, who discovered the smallpox vaccine; Albert Sabin, who discovered the oral polio vaccine; Jonas Salk, who discovered the injectable polio vaccine (and who, coincidentally, had also been a patient of Kraus); and Hans Kraus.

Kraus didn't care about fame for himself. But he realized it would be useful to attract more patients he could heal, offer another platform to exhort Americans to exercise, and maybe even, open another chance to re-launch his children's fitness campaign. In 1965, Kraus' fame spread even wider. The occasion was his third book, which became a bestseller without even mentioning Kennedy.

Before *Backache, Stress and Tension*, Kraus had written two other books, both dense literary efforts, closer to medical tomes for doctors than as mass market reading: In 1956, Kraus had published *Principles and Practice of Therapeutic Exercises*, which had been written in long hand, much of it in a tent on rest days during a climbing vacation in the Tetons. In 1961, Kraus had followed it up with *Hypokinetic Disease,* one of the first books to link heart disease to sedentary living, which featured a forward by renowned Eisenhower cardiologist, Paul Dudley White. Kraus gave a copy to Kennedy, and was delighted to see it on Kennedy's White House nightstand.

Then, in 1962, Kraus cured the head of the large publishing company, Simon & Schuster, who had suffered from back pain for many years. Delighted, Schuster began urging Kraus to write a book for the popular mass market. But when Kennedy was alive, Kraus had neither the time nor inclination. That changed when Kennedy died.

Kraus enjoyed recounting what happened next. "I submitted to Mr. Schuster two pages and a table of contents," Kraus recalled. "After a short while, I received it back, with red and blue corrections over it. When I picked up the manuscript, an interoffice memo from one of his editors fell out of an envelope. I still remember what it said. 'This is terrible. For god's sake, tell this guy to get a good ghost-writer.'"

As it happened, Kraus knew the perfect "ghost" for his book: Bob Boyle, who had written the 1955 *Sports Illustrated* article, "The Report that Shocked the President." In the intervening years, Boyle had made his way in desperation back to Kraus. This time, though, not as a journalist, but as a patient. Although Boyle had been a high school athlete and wrote about sports for a living, when he first met Kraus in 1955, like many sportswriters, he had little interest in his own fitness. Only twenty-nine, Boyle hadn't exercised in years, was overweight, and was out of shape.

As part of the research Boyle conducted for the *Sports Illustrated* article, Kraus put Boyle through the K-W tests. And Boyle had flunked. Like many men, Boyle passed the strength tests fine, but his problem was flexibility. Like many men's, his hamstrings were tight. So tight, in fact, that when Kraus asked Boyle to touch the floor, after much grunting and straining, Boyle could barely reach his knees.

Kraus had warned Boyle, "Unless you start exercising to loosen these muscles, you're going to develop back pain."

Boyle had dismissed the warning from Kraus at that time. If someone asked him about exercise, Boyle would agree it was important, it would be really nice for him personally to exercise, maybe eventually he would, but for right now, he was too busy. Then one day in 1960, without warning, Boyle's back went out.

The day before, while driving his car in icy conditions, Boyle yanked the steering wheel to avert skidding into traffic. He didn't think anything of it at the time, but the next day he felt a little pain in his lower back. A few minutes later, when he went to pick a piece of paper off the floor, it hit.

Boyle recalled, "Wham, I fell down. It was as though someone had swung an axe into the base of my spine. I was flat on my face and I couldn't move my legs. I stayed there for a half hour until my wife found me. She called the volunteer fire department. They came, put me in a stretcher—boy, did that hurt—and took me upstairs to bed. My wife called our doctor, and he called an ambulance. I spent a week in the hospital in traction."

Over the next two years, Boyle's condition grew steadily worse. He lived in constant pain, and his life was miserable. He had days when he couldn't get out of bed. And, just as he would begin to feel better, every few months his back would go out again. Periods between attacks grew shorter. His doctors put him in a brace, gave him a cane, tried traction, prescribed bed rest, and then admitted him for month-long hospital stays. Nothing helped; Boyle was so immobilized, he thought of himself as a paraplegic. As a last resort, Boyle's orthopedic surgeon recommended surgery, although he offered little hope that it would help.

Desperate, Boyle remembered the back doctor's warning from seven years before, and went to see Kraus. He recalled, "Hans told me to relax, there was nothing wrong with me. He told me that in six months, coming to his office three times a week, he could cure me.

"Hans told me, 'You have enough strength, but you need to stretch to loosen the muscles and get rid of the tension which doesn't give the muscles a chance to relax and heal.'

"The first thing Hans told me to do was to get rid of the brace and cane because they made things worse. Then he gave me exercises, which I had to do *exactly* as he told me to, twice a day."

Boyle continued, "Let me tell you, after six weeks, I felt great. After three months, Kraus cured me. I consider what he did for me a miracle. I wouldn't be walking today if it weren't for him.

"After that I did my exercises religiously. To this day, whenever I start to feel tight, I make sure to do the exercises twice a day, exactly as he told me."

Boyle became a devoted friend and convert to Kraus' way, and so he was thrilled to become Kraus' "ghost." In *Backache, Stress and Tension,* Boyle combined thinly veiled autobiographical and biographical vignettes to discuss back pain causes, preventative measures, and exercise treatments in a breezy, easily readable style. He even unsparingly described his own tough lesson about back pain, using the pseudonym Pete Hamilton. The book also included the K-W tests, so readers could test their own strength and flexibility, and predict their likelihood of developing back pain. And it provided drawings and descriptions of the K-W exercises, so readers could do them on their own.

Backache Stress and Tension sold over one million copies. Kraus made the book tour circuit and appeared on many television and radio interview shows to discuss it. "It's no big deal to be on television," Kraus commented. "Sure, the first time, you might think it is, and they put the thick television makeup on you. But you quickly get used to it." To Kraus' amusement, he became widely acclaimed as the 'Back Doctor.' He recalled, "Twenty years before, when I cured Cookie of his bad knee, I was 'the Knee Doctor.' Some called me the 'Ski Doctor.'" He shrugged, "Now suddenly, I was the 'Back Doctor.'"

But it was another aspect of the book that was more gratifying to Kraus. For the rest of his life, Kraus received heartfelt letters from devoted readers. This one, postscript three months before his death, was typical. In it, a woman named Janice Mayer poignantly wrote:

> Twenty-eight years ago, I read your book, *Backache, Stress and Tension* and to this day, I am grateful to you for writing it. My back used to 'go out' at least twice a year for about two weeks at a time. Three or four doctors did nothing but prescribe, what I later found out, the wrong exercises. Since I found the right ones, I've been fine. I've tried to convert other people, but usually without success. I think of you often when doing my exercises, and wish you continued good health.

46

Golden Years

♦

1965–1986, New York City and the Shawangunks

Then came the golden years for Kraus in medicine. His practice continued soaring, his large office on Central Park South was always bustling, and his six therapists—supervised by "Chief" Hendrix, Kennedy's former White House therapist—were kept busy non-stop.

Kraus took his professional success in stride, remaining remarkably modest and hard working. Often on evenings and weekends, after he finished treating patients, Kraus continued to read medical articles and wrote his own for medical journals and mainstream magazines, turning out a steady stream in which he exhorted Americans to exercise. When asked how he had managed to get so much done, Kraus insisted, "It's really very simple. I worked during the day, and wrote at night."

He did wish that Rudi had been alive to see his success. Rudi might have been stubborn and overbearing, but he would have gladly admitted he was wrong, when over half a century ago, he warned his oldest son he would starve as a doctor. For many years, Rudi had a point. A couple of tough times, it was touch and go. By now, Kraus didn't have to worry about starving, or any question of whether he was making his father proud.

Kraus remained hopeful of reviving his children's fitness campaign, even as Americans continued to resist his warnings about the need to exercise and greater affluence produced an even more sedentary lifestyle. On the one hand, that might have been discouraging. On the other hand, Kraus always had his patients. And starting in 1972, Kraus had even *more* patients. Enough to fill a whole city. That's not a literary allusion. It's literal.

That year, Kraus become responsible for the largest and most successful back treatment program ever in the United States. In all, over the twelve years the program ran, it treated an estimated 300,000 people. That is nearly as many people who live in the city of Pittsburgh (estimated population in 2005 of 321,000) or Cincinnati (estimate population in 2005 of 312,000).

And the program had a cure rate of over eighty per cent. The number of back pain sufferers helped by the program could virtually fill the city of Orlando, Florida (estimated population in 2005 of 204,000) or Baton Rouge, Louisiana (estimated population in 2005 of 225,000). [1]

It was a program run by the YMCA, surprising to Kraus because he held a low opinion of most organizations. That was particularly true for the Y. In the 1960's, Kraus had served on the Y's national medical committee. When a new national head was appointed, Kraus—and all the other volunteer members on the medical committee—had received a mimeographed letter, without even a signature, informing him that his "services" were no longer required. Kraus was furious, and swore up and down he would never again have anything to do with the Y. His resolve lasted less than a year.

The man who changed Kraus' mind was Alexander Melleby, a Y official in New York. When Melleby was promoted as head of the Y for New York, one of his first projects was to persuade Kraus to design a back pain program for the Y. When Kraus kept turning down his suggestions to meet, Melleby—who didn't know Kraus' history with the Y—was confused. But Melleby was also persistent and finally Kraus begrudgingly granted a short meeting. Ten minutes was all it took.

After meeting Melleby, Kraus' ire turned to excitement. He found himself thinking, *This Melleby seems really special. Like 'Uncle Bill' Darrach, Sonja Weber and Barbara Stimson at Columbia Presbyterian Hospital. Maybe Melleby is someone who can get things done at the Y.* Throughout his life, Kraus maintained a youthful, American optimism in the ability of one person to make a big difference. By the end of his meeting with Melleby, Kraus was convinced that Al Melleby was such a person, who possessed that rare and precious combination of low ego, high integrity, and greater concern over doing something than being known for having done it.

---

[1] Source for estimated number of participants and cure rate was Alexander Melleby, former head of the YMCA in New York City, who developed and ran the program along with Kraus.

The question still remained: What to do? Melleby learned that after Kraus had cured a fellow Y official after years of back pain, Melleby's colleague had said dryly, "Look at what that guy Kraus does! Heck, all he did was give me these exercises of his—these K-W exercises—and my pain went away! Why can't we offer these exercises at the Y?" The comment made its way back to Kraus. Instead of being upset, as the Y official feared, Kraus was amused. And he began wondering, "Well, why not?

But could the K-W exercises still work even if Kraus didn't customize or supervise them for each patient? Kraus grew convinced the answer was yes. After all, the exercises corrected the problems causing over eighty percent of back pain, and readers of *Backache Stress and Tension* kept writing to tell him that the exercises were so simple and straightforward that they worked when people did them on their own.[2]

A pilot program was set up in several Manhattan YMCAs: one-hour classes of the K-W exercises, twice a week, for six weeks, run by Y staff who Kraus trained. But an unforeseen problem soon emerged. It turned out that the K-W exercises were *too* simple and easy.

Some people couldn't believe they really worked, even some of the trained Y staff. After Kraus first demonstrated them in one training session, a Y staff member had asked, "Okay, now when do we start the exercises?"

"You see," Kraus explained, "He didn't realize he had already done the exercises. He didn't think they counted if you didn't sweat or work hard."

Kraus soon realized this was confusing to the people who signed up for the classes, who on average, had suffered back pain for over eight years. Some in the pilot program dropped out after the second class, shaking their heads in disbelief at the laughably old-fashioned exercises. (They had a point: The most high tech and expensive pieces of equipment in the program were the gym mats on the floor.)

From then on, the Y staff was trained to announce in the first class: "The exercises which you are going to learn and perform during this course are very easy to do. In fact, you will question my sanity that these ridiculously easy exercises will

---

2.   Example was letter of Janice Mayer, 12/7/95, also quoted earlier in the book: "Twenty eight years ago, I read your book, 'Backache, Stress and Tension' and to this day, I am grateful to you for writing it. My back used to 'go out' at least twice a year for about two weeks at a time. Three or four doctors did nothing prescribe, what I later found out, were the wrong exercises. Since I found the right ones, I've been fine. I've tried to convert other people, but usually without success. I think of you often when doing my exercises, and wish you continued good health."

help your back. Many have questioned these exercises in the past. All I can say to you is, do as I ask you to do, and most of you will begin to feel a difference in about the fourth week."[149]

The dropout problem went away. When the classes ended, six weeks later, eighty percent of the people in the pilot program were cured. The results were so exciting that the Y expanded the program throughout the YMCAs in the rest of the city, then the state, and then the northeast, and then across the country.

The Y's Way to a Healthy Back became an enormous success. It ran for the next twelve years, treating 30,000 people per year. When follow-up studies were done, the results were stunning—as was true for the pilot program, eighty percent of the people declared themselves cured.[150]

The media sensed a good story. Profiles on the program and interviews with Melleby frequently ran on popular shows like the *CBS Morning News*, ABC's *Good Morning America*, NBC's *The Today Show*, and the *Phil Donahue Show*. Stories ran in newspapers and magazines, including *The Wall Street Journal, New York Magazine, Prevention Magazine, GQ, Parade, Women's Day, Redbook, Glamour, Family Circle, American Family, Ladies Home Journal, Consumer's Digest, Parents, Modern Maturity,* and *House and Gardens Magazine.*

Over 100 large corporations paid their employees to take the Y's back program. Melleby traveled throughout the United States, Canada, and Asia giving speeches, and wrote a successful book, *The Y's Way to a Healthy Back,* which was turned into a video. Whenever Melleby had the chance, he quickly pointed out that Kraus helped write the book, although Kraus' name does not appear as an author. Melleby shook his head in amazement, remembering, "Hans insisted on that. He refused to put his name on it as well. He said that once his name was on it, with the MD, no one would pay attention to my name."

As Melleby explained, his eyes moistened. "I tell you, Hans was just the most unselfish man I ever met."

The success of the Y's back program was particularly remarkable when contrasted with "state of the art" surgical back treatments, which were high tech, expensive, inherently risky and painful, and which often required intrusive and inconvenient hospital stays. On top of that, they rarely worked. Of the 250,000 spinal fusions performed annually in the United States, success rates vary from an estimated high of fifty percent down to only fifteen percent.[151] (That's also taking into account that different doctors have different ways of measuring back operation success, and that some, unlike Kraus, considered the operation successful if the patient achieved only moderate pain relief, only several months out.)

Often surgery even makes the back problem worse. As the *Wall Street Journal* reported, "The trauma of the surgery itself can trigger chronic back problems dubbed, 'failed-back syndrome,' which afflicts as many as one-third of back surgery patients."[152] Failed back surgery is so common that it gave rise to a new medical condition, "failed back surgery syndrome."[153]

The Y's back program was enormously satisfying to Kraus. Wherever he traveled to various Ys to train the staff, he was told amazing and inspiring stories again and again: Stories of people who had given up hope, who felt that back pain had diminished, even ruined their lives, who had tried all sorts of expensive, sophisticated and painful treatments, who were desperate—and who then tried Kraus' Y back program of the K-W exercises. And who were then cured. Kraus loved those stories.

If the 1960's were the start of the golden years of Kraus' medical practice, they were silver years for his climbing. The older Kraus was less physically suited to the new cutting edge climbs. By the first half of the 1960's, the hardest Gunks climbs—put up by Kraus protégé and close friend, Jim McCarthy—pushed into the grade of 5.10. (In contrast, Wiessner's hardest at the Gunks was 5.8; Kraus' hardest climbs were 5.7 using just free ascent techniques.) And by late 1967, the hardest Gunks climbs were firmly 5.11, achieved through new climbing techniques mixing strength, gymnastic training, and elegant footwork.

But climbing the hardest routes didn't matter to Kraus, as it never had. He just as easily relished the exposure of the easy traverse on Three Pines as on the intimidating top pitch of High Exposure. Afterwards, Kraus never failed to come down spiritually refreshed and physically invigorated. With his flourishing practice, happy family life, large contingent of cured and adoring patients—as CBS's Mike Wallace said about his wife, who was one such fan and patient, "She thought the sun and moon rose and set with Kraus"—Kraus no longer felt compelled to push himself on the rock.

Even Kraus' annual August climbing trips underwent an evolution. Now they often were European family excursions, with Madi and his girls, to visit family in Trieste or old friends, like Ko and Gino Solda. And even on these climbing vacations, being a doctor was so ingrained in Kraus' mentality, he never left that part of him behind. Literally, too; he always carried a cache of ethyl chloride with him, wherever he went, ready to use.

Kraus recalled visiting Solda in the Dolomites during an August climbing trip, only to find his friend stuck in bed, leg in a cast. Solda explained that he had hurt his leg in a climbing accident, and that his doctor told him it needed months to heal. No climbing, of course, until then. Solda was extremely upset. He hated being away from the rock, but there were practical considerations, too. Guiding was Solda's livelihood; if he didn't climb, he didn't earn money. But his doctor brusquely waved his concerns aside.

After Kraus examined his friend, he removed the cast, treated Solda's leg with ethyl chloride and movement, and healed him in several days. He and Solda set off happily up the cliffs, and Solda resumed guiding, without any problems. When he saw his doctor later, his doctor was angry. Solda had disobeyed his orders; that was more important to him than his patient healing so quickly.

Kraus was familiar with doctors like Solda's. After Kraus returned to the States, Kraus threw himself back into his efforts to win support from other doctors and the AMA for the Y's back program. He was as unsuccessful as before. Despite the program's success and Kraus' many medical articles, speeches, and convention talks, he never won support of it from the medical community. The AMA never showed interest in it, and few doctors recommended it to patients who complained of back pain.[154] Most participants found out about the program through word of mouth, television stories, magazine articles, or newspaper ads—which the Y ran without testimonial letters, for fear of antagonizing the AMA.

In some ways, this isn't surprising. The Y's back program's most dramatic success stories came from people who doctors hadn't helped, many of whom had been through failed, expensive and painful back surgery. It was common for Y participants to say, as this one did, "I have had back pain for over twenty years and have spent huge sums of money on various doctors and clinics but received no help. I took the YWTAHB program and haven't had back pain since I started the course." When a local Y chapter ran that testimonial from a delighted participant in a newspaper, Melleby was forced to rebuke it.

When Melleby retired in 1986, it signaled the end of the "The Y's Way to a Healthy Back." Melleby's successor had little interest in maintaining the program. He replaced the K-W exercises—calling them "old fashioned"—and fired Kraus' medical advisory board, a handpicked group of six former Presidential physicians, who had volunteered because of Kraus. The Y didn't officially stop "The Y's Way to a Healthy Back." But by the early 1990's, the program had changed so much, that other than the name, it bore little resemblance to the one set up and run by Kraus and Melleby.

Like Kraus' earlier involvement with the AMC and running the Gunks climbers training program, when the Y's back program ended twelve years later, it had to be a relief in many ways for Kraus. The program had extracted a large financial and personal cost from him. Just like with Kennedy, Kraus didn't want terms of payment to get in the way of treating the patient. For twelve years, Kraus spent alternate weekends flying around the country on behalf of the Y, visiting chapters and training Y staff, all of which constituted an enormous, never-ending task. In the end, Kraus had personally trained 5,000 Y staff members, and required them to get "re-certification" with him every six months.

Kraus did this all as a volunteer, never receiving any payment, fees for his time, or even reimbursement for plane tickets. On top of that, he also supplied most of the program's funding, either by paying for it directly or raising donations from friends and patients. And it meant less time for Kraus with his family or on the cliffs.

But Kraus didn't begrudge the time or cost. As a result of the program, Kraus knew there was a virtual city-full of people who had suffered back pain and who were now without pain. That was even more thrilling to him than the top of High Exposure.

47

'A' List...

◆

1965–1990, New York City

The Y's back program took time and effort that Kraus could have devoted to his private practice. But even so, in contemporary lingo, Kraus' private practice became "A list." It included a roster of successful businesspeople—Mr. Schuster of Simon & Schuster might have inspired Kraus' bestseller, but Kraus also treated Schuster's main rival, "Mr. McGraw," of McGraw Hill—famous musicians and conductors, radio and television personalities, doctors and scientists; writers, singers, and even royalty.

Kraus' "miracle cures" using the K-W exercises became so widely known, that anyone famous with back pain made his way to Kraus' office on Central Park South. Kraus now had another new nickname, to his amusement: "Back doctor to the Stars." Mike Wallace explained, "Everyone knew who Kraus was. He was back doctor to all kinds of stars. Athletes, politicians, show business, even journalists. *Anyone* who was *anyone* went to Kraus."

Most of the famous names Kraus treated: Angela Lansbury, Lauren Bacall, Eleanor Roosevelt, Yul Brynner, Danny Kaye, Rita Hayworth, Lunt and Fontaine, Greta Garbo, Fred Waring, Paulette Goddard, Erich Maria Remarque, Jack LaLanne, Jack Benny, Lena Horne, to name a few—passed gratefully on with their lives. Usually they sent tickets to whatever show they were in, and that was pretty much it. A few, though, became good friends: Lowell Thomas, the well known radio commentator; Arthur Godfrey; and Katharine Hepburn, who called Kraus a "real friend" and became so close to Sisi, Kraus' sister and office manager, that Hepburn looked after Sisi's dogs when Sisi had to enter the hospital.

Kraus didn't recognize many of his famous patients. He rarely went to movies, didn't pay attention to "popular culture," and didn't own a television. One day, Kraus' staff was agog when a gorgeous redhead walked into his office, but Kraus had no idea it was Rita Hayworth until someone clued him in. "She was really a nice lady," was all he would say about the heartthrob. There was another extremely famous actress who joked to him, "*I* shouldn't have to *pay* you. *You* should have to pay *me*, for the privilege of seeing *my* legs!"

Kraus' sister, Sisi, was as devoted and protective an office manager for Kraus as Evelyn Lincoln had been loyal and dedicated to Kennedy. Sisi made sure that no one interrupted Kraus at noon when he took lunch—often sharing a brown bag sandwich and Pepperidge Farm cookies with Franz, the only break Kraus allowed himself during the day. Sisi also helped Kraus with the all-important billing questions.

Kraus maintained a complex, multi-tiered and elastic billing system. He charged nothing for climbers, anyone he knew personally, or anyone who he thought would have trouble with his fees. Kraus charged partial payment for middle class patients, and charged regular rates for wealthy patients. If he had any question, he guessed "low," leading Sisi to cry out once, "You're only charging *her* half? Hans, you should have seen that sable fur coat she walked into the office wearing!"

Lynne Rhodes Mayer, a working girl in her late twenties when Kraus treated her knee for a skiing injury, described Kraus' distinctive billing philosophy. "If the $12.00 fee was too much for me," she recalled, "he would lower it to $8.00. If that proved too much after awhile, he would lower it to $6.00. That was, he told me, what it cost to run his office. However, if ultimately, I couldn't pay that, he would treat me free."

Although Kraus billed patients differently, he treated everyone the same. With one exception: Kennedy—partly because Kennedy was president, partly because of Kraus' deep admiration for the man and his uplifting vision for America, and partly because in treating Kennedy he saw he could serve his country. Kennedy would always remain the only patient Kraus ever traveled to see. Anyone else—no matter how powerful, famous or rich—had to come to him. When an Arab sheik offered Kraus huge fees and transport in his private jet for Kraus to treat him in his native country, Kraus was unimpressed and politely refused. The sheik kept upping his offer. Eventually, the sheik gave in and flew to New York, where Kraus treated him in his office and charged customary fees.

Despite constantly rubbing shoulders with celebrities, Kraus never developed a Manhattan version of "Potomac fever." If anything, it was the nonpaying patients he went out of his way to cultivate. He kept finding new streams of free patients: friends of course, even acquaintances; all climbers, even if he didn't personally know them; and anyone he had any contact with, like the workers in his apartment building and office building. Kraus credited his accountant, Frank Uzzo with making sure his finances were sufficiently practical to support his practice and growing family. "Otherwise, I would have run out of money long ago," Kraus said.

One area of patients though, that Kraus didn't treat—though it seemed as though he naturally would because of the sheer regularity of their injuries—was athletes who competed on team sports. Kraus loved treating athletes in general, but explained, "The team athletes had their own team doctor, who wouldn't want them to see me." An exception was skiing star, Billy Kidd, America's bright hope to medal in the 1970 Olympics. As was often the case, Kidd saw Kraus as a last resort.

Back pain in the months before the Games had prevented Kidd from training. The ski team doctors told Kidd he had a herniated disc requiring surgery and couldn't compete in the Olympics. On his own, Kidd made his way to Kraus, who treated him with a combination of exercise, relaxation, visualization, and self-hypnosis. Kidd not only managed to compete in the Olympics, but he also managed to win a Gold medal.

Afterwards, Kidd became a national sports hero, and he didn't forget Kraus. When *Life Magazine* honored Kidd on its cover of the March 6, 1970 issue with the headline, "American First Gold Medal Winner," Kidd sent Kraus a copy. On it, Kidd wrote, "I sincerely thank you for putting me here on this cover and all, Bill." Kidd was typical among Kraus' patients, rich or poor, business tycoon, building janitor, suburban housewife, Hollywood star. They never forgot Kraus or what he did for them.

That included *Sports Illustrated* writer, Bob Boyle. Boyle never needed Kraus to treat him personally again. But Kraus ended up treating Boyle's entire family, and accomplishing more miracle cures. When Boyle's daughter fell down a set of stairs on Christmas Day, Boyle whisked her to see Kraus, even though she had already been to several other doctors. Boyle recalled, "Those doctors told her she needed to be put into traction for three months. I took her to Kraus when the kid could barely walk. He had her back to work in three days and a week later she was running." Boyle did the same with his son, a Yellowstone National Park guide for the rescue squad, who separated his shoulder while guiding. Boyle said, "The doctors out there told him he needed an operation and would be out close to a year. I flew him back to New York to see Kraus, who had him back guiding in two weeks."

Kraus was generally stern and all-business in the office, but there were exceptions. Ken MacWilliams recalled a memorable 5:00 p.m. appointment on November 9, 1965—the day of the big blackout across the Northeast, when the electricity went out at 5:27 p.m. and stayed out for at least six hours. MacWilliams said, "By the time it became clear what had happened and that no one was going anywhere, it was dark. So, always resourceful, Hans turned to a bookcase near his desk and moved it, revealing a disguised and fully stocked liquor cabinet."

Honors poured in next. In 1974, Kraus was voted into the Skiing Hall of Fame; in 1979, he was awarded the American Association of Fitness Directors in Business and Industry "Exceptional Merit Award." In 1981, Kraus was honored in a black tie reception commemorating the 25th anniversary of the President's Council on Physical Fitness and Sports, and profiled in *Sports Illustrated*. "There is an aura of energy about the man," journalist, William Oscar Johnson, wrote, "sizzle and spunk, exuberance, confidence, great physical strength, high-voltage enthusiasm, bursting vitality."[155]

Three years later, the President's Council on Physical Fitness and Sports conferred on Kraus an honorary membership—a completely worthless gesture, in Kraus' mind. Much more meaningful to Kraus was this sentiment from Bob Boyle, mirroring that of so many of Kraus' patients: "I tell you, time after time, Kraus performs miracles. The man has performed more miracles than Lourdes," Boyle said.

48

Twilight

✦

1980–1991, New York and the Shawangunks

For Kraus, by the 1980's, the sun was starting to dip in the sky. Even he couldn't indefinitely stave off the march of time, and was starting to feel the wear and tear of the years, particularly the cumulative impact of injuries.

Kraus had fractured his right wrist and finger from the tragedy with Marcus, broken a tooth and torn his left bicep in a 1924 motorcycle accident, and cracked a bone in his left foot later in the decade. In the early 1940's, Kraus fractured an ankle skiing at Big Bromley, Vermont, and a few years later injured his left arm while glissading a Tetons snowfield. In 1959 he had his sixty-foot fall in the Gunks, when he suffered numerous cuts, gashes and blood clots. In addition, his body bore scars and nagging injuries from jogging, skiing, hiking with heavy backpacks, and running downhill to train for skiing, which Kraus grew convinced was harmful to knees. Big or small, the injuries eventually added up.

Throughout the 1970's, Kraus remained an impressive physical specimen. Billy Kidd recalled how the sixty-five year old always walked the thirteen flights of stairs up to his office, instead of taking the elevator. But by 1980, Kraus had severe arthritis in his back and hands, and both his knees needed surgery. Kraus stopped downhill skiing, although, as he saw it, the sport had become a "yo-yo lazy person's" activity, removed from the mountain spirit that he loved. He was grateful that he could still cross country ski.

Most importantly, Kraus could still climb, although arthritis made it hurt to pull on rock holds and hard to balance on narrow ledges. He had long stopped leading and the climbs he seconded grew progressively easier. But Kraus was happy to be on the cliffs, on any route. His partners were old friends, including

Wiessner. As *Yankee Rock and Ice* wrote, "Lending a distinctive touch was the occasional glimpse, treasured by Gunks regulars, of Hans Kraus and Fritz Wiessner walking slowly together along the carriage road, heads bowed, hands behind their backs, seeming incredibly short of stature and large of spirit, two gnomes from the mythology of the Shawangunks past."[156]

Kraus also partnered long-time friend and fellow Gunks pioneer and physician, Burt Angrist. By that point, Kraus was following Angrist up extremely moderate routes, often followed by good-natured imbibing of copious amounts of Scotch at Angrist's house near the cliffs. Angrist was also one of Kraus' patients. Angrist recalled, "I had to twist Hans' arm to let me pay. I tried explaining to him, 'I'm paying all this money to my insurance company anyway. You might as well bill me. Those sons of bitches owe you money for my treatments.' I had to argue with him to let me pay him."

In 1984, Kraus stopped climbing completely. His last climb was seconding a route in the Gunks named Easy. As its name suggests, at the grade of 5.2, Easy is about as easy as it gets in technical rock climbing. Formerly, Kraus had scampered up and down Easy without a rope, considering it a ladder for moving quickly between the cliff top and bottom. Now, even when anchored with the safety of a rope above him, climbing Easy was simply too hard on his seventy-nine year old frame. Most importantly, it was no longer a joy.

After Kraus had reached the top, he coiled the rope, slung it over his back, and knew it would be his last time. Kraus was with his longtime friend, Jon Ross, who had become the first professional guide at the Shawangunks. Kraus said, "I got to the top and told Jon. 'If it had happened ten years before, I would have been sad. But I was lucky. I pretty much did in climbing what I wanted.'" He quipped, "My greatest regret in climbing was that I didn't get to use 'nuts' [instead of hammering in pitons] or sticky rubber climbing shoes."

Once he stopped climbing, Kraus wanted to find an activity that would put him in close contact with nature. He considered sailing, but unlike his brother, Franz, who owned a boat and was a fine water skier, Kraus had spent little time on the water and had never developed a feel for the waves. After a couple of sailing lessons, Kraus concluded that a person starting such a complex physical activity from scratch needed to be younger. It might have been different if he was "only" seventy-three, rather than eighty-three, and if he was content to remain a passenger, rather than wanting to captain. But that wasn't Kraus.

He had the heart and soul of a sailor, though. Franz remembered sailing with his brother in waters off Trieste, during an August trip while they were visiting family. A storm kicked in, with lightning and thunder; the wind grew strong, the waves grew big, and the boat swayed crazily from side to side. Experienced sailors on the boat grew queasy, but Kraus thrilled to feel close to nature.

In his pragmatic fashion, Kraus looked to other interests that he had never made time for—he had season tickets to the opera and concerts at the Philharmonic—as well walks in the Gunks. Kraus insisted, though, that it wasn't hard for him to watch Wiessner, five years older, still scampering on the talus, hiking and climbing.

When Wiessner visited the Shawangunks, he sometimes stayed with Kraus at his house, sometimes at the luxurious Mohonk Mountain House, overlooking the cliffs. At night, Wiessner would walk to the base of the cliffs, alone, and solo one of his old routes.[157] Many were awed by his boldness. Kraus understood his friend, though, as they faced old age together. Often Kraus wondered whether Wiessner would have minded if he slipped and came to his end on the rocks at the Shawagunks.

It would have been impossible for Kraus not to think somewhat about death. Old friends started dying. In 1983, it was Kowalski. Then Gino Solda. Then it was Wiessner.

Until his mid-eighties, Wiessner was in superb shape, but his decline was swift and marked. One day, Kraus received a phone call from him. "I've had a little stroke," Wiessner explained from his home in Stowe. Immediately, Kraus was on his way to see him. Kraus said. "As soon as I got there, I could see it wasn't a little stroke. His son had to carry him down the stairs. It broke my heart to see him like that."

The next time Kraus visited Wiessner, Kraus took drugs with him in case Wiessner asked for help to commit suicide. Wiessner never did, and Kraus never raised the topic. But Kraus wanted to be prepared to help his old friend. Each time Kraus visited Wiessner, just in case, Kraus brought his doctor's bag, with the necessary drugs. After a series of strokes, Wiessner died in 1988.

Kraus had always thought deeply about death, even before Marcus. Watching his old friends dying reinforced his feeling. "My greatest fear was living too long and burdening my family," he said. Then, when he had to enter the hospital in 1988 for a serious intestinal operation, he realized there was a chance his heart might stop during the operation. Sternly, Kraus instructed his family and hospital staff that he didn't want resuscitation. "No resuscitation, I told them in case my heart stopped during the operation. No resuscitation." If that was how he was intended to die, then so be it. Kraus had accepted the possibility since he was a teenager.

Kraus sailed through the operation, although afterwards he had spasms and stomach pains. At the hospital he tried to get ethyl chloride to treat himself, but was met with blank looks. No one had it, or was prepared to give it to him, even though he was a doctor. Finally, Madi smuggled a bottle of ethyl chloride into his hospital room. Kraus sprayed the painful abdominal area, stretched, and his pain went away. When he tried explaining to the doctors what he had done, he found blank, disinterested stares.

Kraus, though, was one doctor who took his own advice. After his operation, he was back walking in the Shawangunks as soon as possible. With his distinctive appearance, there was little doubt as to who he was. Besides, his photograph was in the guidebooks and hung in the popular hangout and local climbing shop, Rock and Snow.[1] Climbers whispered in excitement when they saw him, pointing shyly, introducing themselves and chatting him up. He still didn't understand the fuss.

Kraus was deeply pleased when the Mohonk Preserve, the non-profit organization who took on stewardship of the Shawangunks after the Smiley family, erected a plaque in his and Wiessner's honor. There was lively debate about where it should go—one suggestion was the base of High Exposure—before it was settled that it should be embedded within a large boulder in the central gathering area of the Shawangunks. Kraus remarked, "It's a very nice plaque, but it says Kraus and Wiessner. It should say Wiessner and Kraus."

At that time, too, the Access Fund, a climbing organization devoted to climbers' causes, held a party in the Shawangunks. To help fundraise, it organized an auction. Local merchants donated outdoors clothes and climbing gear; others gave memorabilia or items of value. Kraus decided to donate one of the old pitons he had placed on the first ascent of High Exposure.

After years of cyclical frost and heat, snowfall and rainfall, ice coating and water drips, the piton had corroded and loosened from the rock. Someone climbing High Exposure had pulled it out with his fingers, brought it down off the cliff, and presented it to Kraus. Kraus thought humorously of his old piton when the Access Foundation was soliciting donations. He wondered whether anyone

---

1.   Rock and Snow was started by Kraus' close friend, Dick Williams, and continues to this day under the stewardship of Gunks climbing icon, Rich Gottlieb.

would bid for it and put it up hoping it might bring in at least a small sum for a good cause.

To his amazement, bidding for the piton started at $500—an exorbitant sum in a sport where there is little money to be made, and where champion climbers live out of their vans to save money, even though comparable achievements in sports like golf or basketball would have made them multi-millionaires. The closing bid for the piton was $900.

The buyer was a female climber from California, visiting the Shawangunks on vacation. Barbara Rogers had been so impressed when she climbed High Exposure a few days before, even though she had led much harder routes, that she decided she had to have the piton. When she returned home, she hung it in a place of honor, and wrote to Kraus in delight. "I never suffered any buyer's remorse over having spent nearly $1,000 on it."

Kraus wrote back to her, "Dear Miss Rogers, I never dreamed that my High Exposure piton would be valued so highly. However, when I placed it, I never would have given it away for anything."

49

Finally Getting It

✦

1980–1991, New York

Throughout this period, despite growing physical frailty, Kraus continued to practice fulltime and write regularly about the importance of exercise in medical journals and books: *Clinical Treatment of Back and Neck Pain* (1970) was followed up by *Care, Prevention and Treatment of Sports Injury* (1981), and *Diagnosis and Treatment of Muscle Pain* (1988). He also kept pushing his understanding of muscles and back pain. In fact, he would say that it wasn't until the 1980's that he finally "got" it when it came to muscles.

Kraus' approach continued to fly in the face of popularly held beliefs: Since the established mantra for muscle treatments had become known as RICE—rest, ice, compression and elevation—Kraus dubbed his contrarian approach MECE—movement, ethyl chloride, and elevation.

Kraus grew convinced that just as there were several causes of muscle pain, so too, there were also several *types* of muscle pain—four, in fact, each needing different treatments. The result was a systematic way to identify the types of muscle pain, treat and cure them.[158]

For instance, muscle spasm occurs when a muscle contracts more than it should, which sets off spasm, setting off pain, leading to more contraction, producing a vicious cycle of pain and spasm that is hard to break. The cause is complex, often hard to identify, tracing back to a chain of events often dating from many years before. As with Bob Boyle, who had bent over to pick up a piece of paper, or Kennedy in 1961, who stooped to shovel a small amount of dirt at the ceremonial ground breaking in Ottawa, the triggering event is often routine, minute, seemingly negligible. Treatment is to break it up by spraying the area with ethyl chloride—alternately, using ice, often along with electrical current treat-

231

ments—and introduce gentle movement as quickly as possible. Once the patient could start to move the muscles again, Kraus put him through the K-W tests to discover the nature of the muscle problem, and treat him with the appropriate K-W exercises.

Secondly, there is muscle pain from tension that occurs when the muscle contracts past the point of need or design. Excessive contraction causes headaches as well as neck, shoulder, or back pain. Kraus believed that the cause is usually emotional: stress from jobs, family, marriage, sex or money. Treatment depends on its origin, but the goal is relaxation, achieved through mental training, as well as, of course, exercises. Additionally, Kraus believed that in some cases, tension pain benefited from tranquilizers, although he was convinced that stress-related tension was the *only* type of muscle pain on which tranquilizers work.

Third, there is muscle pain from muscle deficiency that occurs when a muscle is unable to handle a movement, either because the muscle is too weak or tight. Over time, a deficient muscle causes surrounding muscles around it to work harder. The result is that the surrounding muscles overwork, in turn producing pain. Treatment consists of exercise, including relaxation. Often people don't even realize their muscles are weak or tight, because they're used to them. Contrary to popular perception, Kraus believed in low repetitions for exercise, to prevent otherwise already overloaded muscles from straining, causing fatigue, more pain and stiffness.

Last, the most controversial and arguably least understood type of muscle pain comes from trigger points, which result from tender, dead spots in the muscle tissues—the trigger points—causing considerable pain and impeding normal muscle functioning, thus producing more pain. Trigger points can occur in muscles throughout the body. But they most characteristically crop up in certain muscles: the posture muscles; around the back, hips, and backside. In contrast to healthy muscles, which feel smooth like bread dough, trigger points feel knotty, lumpy, and hard. When the area is pressed, the pain is particularly acute, but it will often hurt even when not pressed.

Causes for trigger points vary. They could be from an injury, prolonged tension, spasm, strain, endocrine imbalance (such as thyroid, adrenal or estrogen deficiency), or lack of exercise or conditioning (very common among people who had surgery or prolonged bed rest). Yet trigger points can also be caused by mundane, chronic, longstanding behavior, like talking on the phone by squeezing the receiver between the shoulder and ear. Regardless, the result is too much muscle contraction, which over time cuts off blood flow, and causes tissues to die from lack of oxygen.

Treatment consists of trigger point injections. An oversized hypodermic needle stabbed into the right parts of the muscle breaks down the dead tissue, in a motion similar to breaking up a block of ice. Needle size varies: the larger and deeper the muscle, the longer and thicker the needle must be to penetrate the muscle. Kraus used big needles for muscles on the thigh or over the backside, smaller ones for muscles over the neck, chest or groin area.

Kraus also came to recognize that there were certain personality types who were prone to developing trigger points. In particular, these were often people, like Kennedy, who internalize stress, do not acknowledge conflict, and are often considered workaholics. Trigger point sufferers may be conscientious, compulsive, responsible, hard working, self-motivated, self critical, with histories of excessive work performance and extreme self-reliance. Often, too, Kraus noted that trigger point patients were pathologically self-reliant from an early age, growing up in a dysfunctional family.

Kraus realized that back pain could be a stunningly complex condition. Many patients had more than one type of back pain; in fact, Kraus came to see that regardless of cause, stress played a large role in most back pain. Kraus occasionally came across a back pain patient whom he didn't have to treat for stress, but it was rare. It was also common for a patient to develop different types of back pain if the initial back pain wasn't caught and treated when it first began. A patient suffering back pain from weakness and stress might very well, over the years, also develop trigger points; and a patient suffering back pain from spasms, exacerbated by stress, might develop trigger points, particularly if he resorted to bed rest, in turn developing back pain from weakness.

The different types of back pain were linked. And the longer a person suffered back pain, the more likely different types of back pain would be involved. Yet in other ways, back pain is strangely simple. The way to prevent it is to keep the back strong and flexible, meeting minimal standards for both, as Kraus pointed out, through the right exercises. While a very strong but tight man could get back pain, a very flexible but weak woman could also get back pain; but the important point in both cases is that a person doesn't have to be Olympics-level in strength or flexibility, just enough to meet *minimal* demands for his or her body, in his or her daily life. Former President of the American Academy of Pain Medicine Norman Marcus commented, "That was Kraus' great contribution to medicine, this idea of minimal standards for strength and flexibility."

As it turned out, Kennedy played a pivotal role in Kraus' understanding back pain. Before Kennedy, Kraus was confident about his approach. After Kennedy, Kraus was sure. Here was someone who had suffered back pain for all his life, who underwent three disastrous surgeries—two of which nearly killed him—and who had been crippled by back pain for most his adult life. Each of the many doctors Kennedy had seen shook their head in complete bewilderment; except Travell, and her opinion doesn't carry much weight, since when Kennedy was under her care his back deteriorated gravely.

When Kraus stepped in, Kennedy was hobbling on crutches, unable to walk normally. In two months, under Kraus' care, Kennedy was much better. In two years, Kennedy was cured. If Kennedy had survived another year, the enduring public image of Kennedy would have been different. When the most recent Kennedy biographer, Robert Dallek, needed an iconic image of Kennedy for his biography cover, Dallek chose one of Kennedy in his rocking chair. If Dallas had occurred one year later, Dallek more likely would have chosen among photographs of Kennedy jogging, hiking, or lifting weights.

But what exactly was wrong with Kennedy's back remains the last unsolved Kennedy medical mystery. Not for want of trying.

Over the years, a wide ranging list of theories have been advanced: Kennedy aides loved suggesting heroic wartime and Harvard football injuries, Travell theorized strain from different length legs, and Kennedy's other doctors, including his surgeons, never did reach a diagnosis. Some journalists conjectured a birth defect;[159] most recently, Robert Dallek concluded weakened bones from Addison's steroid medication;[160] although Larry Sonkin dismissed that possibility, and Dallek didn't realize his source, Theodore Sorenson, had provided incomplete and misleading information.

What about Kraus? He thought about it a lot in his twilight years. To him, the explanation for Kennedy's acute back pain was, in some ways, straightforward.

Just as he had done with other patients, Kraus used the K-W tests to eliminate the possibility of physiological causes. He was left assuming that Kennedy, along with over eighty percent of people with bad backs, had postural muscles that were too weak and too tight to be able to meet the minimal demands of his daily life. Like most patients, Kennedy had exacerbating factors—in his case, the unique double whammy of Addison's Disease along with three disastrous back operations—plus, as was true for most patients, stress.

But that raises the question: How did Kennedy's back get so dramatically weak and tight in the first place?

To answer that took a little detective work on Kraus' part. Kennedy never told the full story of his medical history to Kraus (or for that matter, to his other White House doctors, or close aides, like Theodore Sorenson).[161] But that was common with patients. Kraus had realized that patients often didn't even acknowledge the details to themselves. Remembering his advice from James Joyce, Kraus had learned over the years that he needed to observe patients closely on his own.

With Kennedy, Kraus noticed a pattern to his emergency flare-ups; invariably they occurred on weekends or holidays. Did these flare-ups coincide with the many grave domestic or international crises Kennedy faced? The building of the Berlin Wall, perhaps? The decision to escalate U.S. forces in Vietnam? The growing and bitter Civil Rights unrest? The many confrontations with Khrushchev?

Actually, as Kraus' White House records showed, Kennedy's flare-ups were timed with visits to his parents or his wife. Having treated the domineering Joseph Kennedy and seen the interactions between Kennedy and Jackie, Kraus concluded that Kennedy, like many people, felt considerable stress from his family.

This was a significant finding, not because of prurient curiosity, and not just because it is astounding to note that the man who bravely averted WWIII was more stressed out by his family than foreign affairs! It was mainly important because it affected the way that Kraus had decided to treat Kennedy. It meant that even after Kraus corrected Kennedy's muscular weakness and tightness with the K-W exercises, Kennedy still needed to exercise to deal with his stress. Otherwise, his muscles would again tighten, and his pain would again return.

That much Kraus knew from his partial information and personal observations. Because it was enough for Kraus to treat Kennedy successfully, Kraus didn't dwell on what else might be part of Kennedy's story.

But now the full story can be reconstructed from information from Kraus, Gene Cohen, Kraus' White House medical records on Kennedy, as well as formerly sealed documents in the Kennedy Library. The result, for the first time, is the full story of what was wrong with Kennedy's back.

Kennedy's bad back started when he was a young boy, the same time as his other mysterious, never diagnosed and chronic stomach, intestinal and back illnesses emerged.[162] At least in part, Kennedy's incessant boyhood sicknesses were likely a way to gain attention from his parents. While that part is conjecture, it is reasonable to assume that in a household of nine children—which included a severely

retarded daughter living at home who required disproportionate time and attention—the children were bound to vie for limited parental attention and love.

And that would have been even truer in Kennedy's childhood household.
Kennedy's father was frequently absent on business trips, and when home,
flaunted his affairs to his wife and children. Kennedy's mother responded by
being often physically absent on trips to Europe, and when home, was resentful
and emotionally distant to her husband and children.

Leaving aside conjecture, the fact remains that Kennedy's boyhood doctors
never did reach a diagnosis for his dramatic symptoms, but invariably prescribed
bed rest. Reading over Kennedy's childhood medical records in the John F.
Kennedy Library, one is struck by the extraordinary amount of time Kennedy
spent throughout his childhood and teenager years lying in bed at home or in
hospital rooms for testing—anywhere from several weeks to entire summers. At
prep school at Choate, Kennedy was in the infirmary so often that stories went
around that he was dying.[163] [164]

This, by itself, is not brand new information. Dallek's biography, among others, for instance, took note of Kennedy's many and unending illnesses as a boy.
The difference is that Dallek and others didn't make the connection between
Kennedy's childhood illnesses—whether physiological or psychosomatic—the
amount of bed rest that resulted from them, and the effect of all that bed rest on
the young Kennedy.

In effect, Kennedy grew up as an invalid. Without chances to run around and
play games, the boyhood Kennedy would not have developed normal muscles. By
late teenager years, Kennedy's muscles would have been growing too weak to support his maturing, heavier frame. As an adult, Kennedy was going to be a prime
candidate for developing back pain anyway, but he sealed his fate in college.

Just after the car accident at Harvard, Kennedy started wearing his back corset. Permanently donning an artificial support that keeps muscles from working—whether back corset, brace or crutches—is about the worst thing a back
pain sufferer like Kennedy could do. Even in the 1930's, some people knew this.
The paraplegic Franklin Delano Roosevelt then advised a doctor, "Remember
that braces are only for the convenience of the patient in getting around—a leg in
a brace does not have a chance for muscle development."[165] And some years later,
when Howard Friedman broke his leg while in Europe, Kraus instructed him:
"No matter what the other doctors tell you, Howard," Kraus said, "You need to
start moving around after the operation ASAP."

Kennedy's situation epitomized why Kraus' approach to medicine was so successful. Kennedy became as much an icon for Kraus' medical philosophy as a

much beloved individual patient. That extra layer of meaning further explains Kraus' unblinking loyalty and attachment to Kennedy, "It was so satisfying to build someone up, to start from scratch and make someone so well," he said. Trying to explain his devotion to Kennedy in a different way, Kraus added, his voice mixing happiness and sadness, "Kennedy was my baby."

50

The Other Marcus

✦

1990–1991, New York City

As Kraus grew closer to his ninth decade, he realized that when he died, so too would his hard-earned medical knowledge. Kraus was happy when younger doctors occasionally stopped by his office to observe. However, most had the same reaction as Dr. Norman Marcus, then head of the Pain Clinic at Manhattan's Lenox Hill Hospital. Marcus recalled, "Kraus was gracious, but I couldn't believe what I saw. His methods looked so barbaric. I couldn't imagine stabbing a needle that big into anyone and banging it around. It seemed so insane. I certainly couldn't imagine doing it myself."

Kraus nearly created a medical legacy in his oldest daughter, Ann. The two had always been close, and Ann, so much like her father, knew she wanted a career in medicine. Over the years, father and daughter discussed the possibility she would follow in his footsteps, join his practice and carry on his work. The idea held great emotional pull for both.

But in the end, Kraus discouraged Ann. Partly it was timing; realistically he didn't think he would still be practicing when Ann graduated medical school. Partly it was medicine. The nature of what it meant to be a doctor had changed dramatically from when Kraus first entered the practice. Sadly for Kraus, what changed the most was what to him mattered the most: the human element, which is what had first drawn him to medicine after the tragedy with Marcus.

One is reminded of this when reading the memoir of Oliver Sacks, writing about his physician father in the 1940's. "He loved doing housecalls more than anything else, for they were social and sociable as well as medical, would allow him to enter a family and home, get to know everybody and their circumstances, see the whole complexion and context of a condition. Medicine, for him, was never just diagnosing a disease, but had to be seen and understood in the context of patients' lives, the particularities of their personalities, their feelings, their reactions."[166]

If Kraus had cared about money, he would have joined Rudi's shipping business. As he said himself, "I would have never become a doctor today. I couldn't have done what I did today. Somebody would have sued the pants off me." He mentioned the name of a well-known doctor who specialized in chronic pain. "He has two women in his office who do nothing all day but handle the insurance companies. Can you imagine?"

Instead of becoming a doctor, with Kraus' encouragement, Ann became a vet, where she applies her father's immediate mobilization treatments on horses. Not only was Kraus still practicing when Ann graduated medical school, he also walked her down the aisle when she married a fellow veterinarian. Kraus' joy was immense, although he found himself thinking sadly of Kennedy; again recalling the time Caroline burst into the treatment room, bubbling with happy news for her handsome young father.

Time was finally catching up. In 1990, while running to catch a plane for a medical conference in Phoenix, eighty-five year old Kraus found himself short of breathe in a way he never before felt. It was the early stages of emphysema. For the first time, he felt really old. Just at that time, too, Kraus' office building was sold and he needed to move. The new space came with a five-year lease. Kraus hadn't signed the lease when he left for the Phoenix conference. It was sitting on his desk when he returned. Kraus read the lease carefully again. Could he realistically assume he would be practicing when he was ninety? "I decided that was optimistic," he said. Reluctantly, Kraus decided to retire.

The next year, Jim McCarthy and several other lifelong friends held a special celebration in honor of Kraus' eighty-sixth birthday at Mohonk Mountain House. One hundred friends, some from as far away as California, gathered at the dinner. Jim McCarthy served as the toastmaster, "There's never been a turnout like this," McCarthy began, "Hans is multidimensional, a man for all seasons." Friends from different aspects in his life took turns speaking about him. Jon Ross added his toast: "Hans is an extraordinary man, who has done extraordinary things, but the incredible thing is that in no way does he perceive himself as someone special. And that just underscores his larger-than-life charisma for me." Among those present was Bob Boyle: still doing his Kraus exercises, still feeling great. Afterwards, Boyle wrote a heartfelt article about Kraus that appeared in the very stylish *New Yorker*.[167]

Kraus ordinarily hated big public displays, but this time, the outpouring of affection touched him. And then it was his turn to rise from his chair and say a few words. "I've reached the venerable age when people say nice things about you," and he insisted that his age was the only reason for the praise. But retirement was a big adjustment for Kraus, who had worked since a teenager in his father's office. Kraus thought it was too bad that now he finally had free time, he couldn't use it to climb.

Kraus mostly occupied himself by spending time with friends, meeting medical colleagues for lunch, reading medical journals and writing more articles about the importance of exercise. He also had more time with Madi for the opera and concerts. And, he started working on an autobiography. Remembering his experience attempting early drafts of *Backache, Stress and Tension,* he harbored few allusions that he was a writer; he found that well-crafted medical articles were one thing, but writing a book was another. Still, it was the best strategy Kraus could come up with for passing on his medical knowledge. Then Kraus went for his annual check up.

His doctor, Larry Sonkin, a protégé of Gene Cohen, was also a longtime friend.

"What have you been doing with yourself for the past year, Hans?" Sonkin asked him.

"Not much," Kraus replied.

"Why don't you meet an acquaintance of mine who runs the pain treatment clinic for a major Manhattan hospital?"

Norman Marcus's background was impressive; he'd received his medical training at some of the best schools in the country, after which he joined some of the best hospitals, then started the first pain treatment clinic in a leading New York hospital, before he moved to Lenox Hill Hospital, another major Manhattan teaching hospital.

Marcus' approach was thoroughly establishment. His work and philosophy reflected AMA wisdom that chronic pain specialists should seek to manage pain and focus patients' expectations on realistic goals of *coping* rather than farfetched and unrealistic pipedream hopes of *curing*.[168] Marcus knew Kraus by reputation and respected Sonkin's opinion. To Marcus's credit, he was open to considering new ways to help his patients. Still, Marcus harbored low expectations for the meeting.

When the two doctors met for lunch at the New York Athletic Club, Kraus began by asking Marcus what he did.

"I treat people with chronic pain," Marcus replied, politely. *Maybe this lunch was a waste of time after all.*

"How do you do that?" Kraus asked.

"We teach our patients how to manage their pain, deal with it, and live with it," Marcus replied, patiently. *Kraus is supposed to know these things. Why is he asking these questions?*

"Why don't you get rid of the pain?"

"Because it's chronic pain. That's the definition of chronic pain. You *can't* get rid of it," Marcus explained. *Maybe the old guy is starting to lose it.*

"How do you know you can't get rid of it?"

"Because the pain is *chronic*," Marcus said. *Geez, you'd think he'd know something like this!*

"Yes, but how do you know that? How do you that the pain doesn't come from a place where you *can* get rid of it, like the muscles?"

"Because we treat the muscles," Marcus said. *Of course we do. Anyway, what does this have to do with chronic pain?*

"How do you treat the muscles?"

"With aerobic exercises," Marcus replied. *Is there really any other kind? What's he getting at?*

"Why do you use aerobic exercises?"

"Everyone uses aerobic exercises." *Hey, that's a really good question. Why do we use aerobic exercises? I'm head of the clinic, too; I should know.*

"Yes, but how do you know that these are the right exercises?"

Marcus looked at the old man blankly. *Uh, I didn't realize there were right exercises or wrong exercises.*

"How do you know you're not dealing with conditions that won't respond to aerobic exercises, like tension, spasm, stiffness, weakness or trigger points," Kraus persisted, "but which would respond to other types of exercise?"

"Well, actually I don't, but this is the standard way of treating chronic pain patients." Marcus said, shifting in his seat. *Wait a second…that's another really good question!*

"This might be the standard way of treating it, but that doesn't mean it works," Kraus said.

Marcus thought of the low cure rates at his clinic. *Hey, Kraus makes a really good point. I know what we're doing isn't working. But we don't know what else to do. So we keep doing it.*

"I think you may be missing an opportunity to cure people who weren't properly diagnosed and treated." Kraus replied.

Stunned, Marcus listened closely as Kraus explained his approach. By the end of the lunch, Marcus had asked Kraus to join his staff. Kraus was enthusiastic, until he saw the application. "An inch thick, requesting four recommendations," he said. "Of course I could give them recommendations, but really!"

Kraus was disgusted at the thought at that point in his career. "I didn't want to be a part of any organization that functioned like that," he said. As an alternative, Marcus suggested instead that Kraus volunteer at his clinic a couple of times. Kraus wouldn't have to go through the application process and hassle with bureaucracy, he could work with patients again, maybe prevent some unnecessary surgery…but he then couldn't be paid, and that might be a problem…

What a great deal! Kraus thought, and leapt at the chance.

51

Tuesdays with Hans

✦

1991, New York

The more time Kraus and Marcus spent together, the more Marcus's admiration for Kraus grew. Their original plan of spending two hours a day on Tuesdays at the Lenox Hill clinic soon grew to ten hours each Tuesday. Marcus quipped, "You've heard of 'Tuesdays with Morrie'? For me, it was Tuesdays with Hans."

At the Lenox Hill clinic, Marcus picked the worst patient cases for Kraus to review: veterans of multiple failed back operations disabled by chronic pain, which had extracted a heavy financial and emotional toll, pushing aside relationships, careers, hobbies, and general enjoyment of life. None of the patients had seen significant improvement after completing the classic treatments at Marcus's clinic. When Kraus called these patients to describe his approach and offer to treat them, he told them in his characteristic way: "These new treatments might help you, but then they might not." All chose to try.

Thick files existed on each patient, but Kraus approached them as though starting completely fresh. This meant starting with a physical exam of their muscles. Marcus was used to short—later he would term them "meaningless"—physical exams: some desultory tapping knees for reflexes, and a little strength testing. He watched, amazed, as Kraus painstakingly tried to identify tender muscles that might represent specific muscle groups causing the pain—probing, prodding and palpating each muscle in turn. When Kraus asked the patients when a doctor last touched their muscles, he wasn't surprised when they looked blank; none could remember.

Marcus said, "I saw that the way Hans examined patients itself was revolutionary." Kraus had seen the newer generations of doctors make diagnoses based mostly on high-tech techniques at the expense of "old fashioned" physical exams; a problem affecting all of medicine, not just the treatment of chronic pain.[169]

Oliver Sacks, watching his physician father giving a physical exam in the 1940's, recalled, "I loved to see him percuss the chest, tapping it delicately but powerfully with his strong stubby fingers, feeling, sensing, the organs and their state beneath. Later, when I became a medical student myself, I realized what a master of percussion he was, and how he could tell more by palpating and percussing and listening to a chest than most doctors could from an x-ray."[170]

Then there was the set of detailed questions Kraus asked each patient about habits, hobbies, work, lifestyle, and personal relationships. Kraus wasn't trying to pry, but instead he hoped to discover unconscious sources of stress. Kraus' insights left Marcus shaking his head.

Overall, when Kraus talked about muscles, Marcus struggled to keep up despite his credentials. It made Marcus realize how little he understood about muscles and their impact on other body systems. "It was humbling," he admitted. "Muscles just are not emphasized in medical school and medical training. They're over fifty percent of the human body, yet there is no science of muscles, no real interest; maybe because there's no prestige in them." Marcus would later point to the 2003 edition of the *Journal of American Academy of Pain Medicine*. "Even though the group acknowledges that seventy to eighty percent of back pain is related to muscles," he said, "there was not one presentation, not a single article in it on muscle pain."

Marcus had begun to realize that if he were serious about understanding Kraus' approach, he had work to do. He pulled his old anatomy books off the shelves, pored through Kraus' articles and books, and listened hungrily to Kraus when he described his experiences and theories. And when the results from the initial group of test patients who went through Kraus' treatments came back, Marcus was delighted. Some patients didn't improve at all, but others were cured.

All in all, it was a huge improvement from the results from his clinic before. But Kraus was dissatisfied. He was used to "miracle cures," and there weren't enough in the sample by Kraus' standards. He had expected better. Moreover, he was puzzled by the inconsistencies.

Why should there be such glaring differences, since he had designed the treatments himself, and either he gave the injections or supervised Marcus in the trigger point injections? The only exception was the K-W exercises, when the physical therapists at Marcus's clinic, rather than Kraus, supervised the patients. Could the explanation lie there?

Marcus was skeptical. "How could the way you do exercises make such a big difference?" Marcus insisted to Kraus, "Movement is movement. Exercise is exercise."

But Kraus persisted. And when they talked to the clinic physical therapists, they found one who had decided—on his own—to make "improvements."

Marcus still wasn't convinced. "The changes were so small," he pointed out, "How could they matter so much?"

But one more time, Kraus and Marcus put these patients, without charge, through Kraus' program. This time, they made sure all the physical therapists stuck exactly to the K-W exercises as Kraus intended. For Marcus, that was the turning point, because this time, the rest of the "failed" patients showed the same improvement.

Marcus said, "Up until that point, I didn't really get it, and didn't think the exercises really mattered. I saw what happened when someone who was well trained and well intentioned decided to make 'minor changes' to improve the exercises. That experience turned me around and made me realize the science and elegance of Kraus' exercises—and that the exercises themselves and *how they were done* had fantastic meaning and importance. And, in fact, when we started to follow the K-W exercises without deviation, we started seeing some really dramatic results."

One of the most striking stories at Marcus's clinic was that of a woman who had lived in terrible pain for seventeen years. The original cause of her pain was long obscured, but it had been exacerbated by multiple failed spinal fusion operations, which kept building scar tissue around her spinal column. Marcus said, "Like all her previous doctors, I thought her condition was untreatable and un-curable, that there was simply nothing you could do for her. When she first came to us at the clinic, we put her on twenty milligrams of morphine every four hours, and it just took the edge off her pain.

"When I re-examined her with Hans, we found she had these trigger points all over [in four muscle groups and eight different muscles]. As Hans pointed out, we knew she had an untreatable condition [from the spinal fusions and scar tissue]. But we could treat her pain from the trigger points. Over six weeks, we gave her trigger point injections and K-W exercises. At the end of her treatments, she was pain-free. We took her off the morphine, and she went back to work."

This woman's case wasn't unique: Marcus recounted story after story of seemingly miraculous cures from chronic pain. At Marcus' clinic, Kraus produced so many of his miracle cures that the extraordinary risked seeming ordinary, or that the cures were too good to be true: there was the woman who had been living for years on disability, unable to hold a job; after being cured by Kraus' treatments, she mortgaged her house, raised money to fulfill her dream of owning a bagel store, and became so successful, she bought a second store. There was a patient who had lost a year of his life to time spent in hospitals from five abdominal operations—including one that removed part of his intestine—after previous doctors misdiagnosed as gall bladder disease; he too was cured. There was also a patient who had suffered fourteen years of chronic pain from two failed "laminectomies," in which doctors removed bone from vertebra; he was also cured. And there was a woman battling cancer, whose previous doctors assumed that her terrible pain must be from the cancer, and hadn't even considered treating pain from another source; once Kraus and Marcus treated that pain, it too, went away.

One of Marcus's biggest surprises was watching Kraus cure chronic pain patients, such as the previous woman, whom previous doctors had diagnosed with conditions unrelated to muscles. "Regardless of where the pain was coming from, we saw it often had a muscle component," Marcus said, before listing examples: cancer, headaches, abdominal pain, impingement syndrome, and rotator cuff tears. "I realized that diagnoses can be traps. And that muscles can mimic or mask a lot of other problems," Marcus said.

52

The Legacy

✦

1992–1996

Kraus was soon working at Marcus's clinic on a regular part-time basis. Particularly as Kraus approached ninety and grew frailer, the work and the patients grew even more important. Kraus loved the second chance to heal more patients, and found that Marcus and the clinic kept him reinvigorated.

Although Kraus had been worried about his legacy, he didn't have to be: He had his patients, who never forgot him. When Kraus sent notices to his old patients that he was at Marcus' clinic, the response was overwhelming: emotional notes, calls, visits, even a sizable group who made appointments, either because they had stopped doing their K-W exercises and old conditions had re-emerged, or new ones had developed.

For Marcus, working with Kraus was a great success for his patients, but less so for his clinic. He praised Lenox Hill for being forward-thinking enough to establish the only in-patient pain center, but he also saw that Kraus' approach didn't translate well economically from the controlled setting of a solo practitioner's office to the demands of a large clinic with financial targets. As he explained, "It was harder to remain profitable because we were getting patients better. Many other pain centers were full because they had repeat patients, the same patients coming back again and again. But we were *curing* patients. We faced bottom line issues [that they didn't] since we constantly needed a new stream of patients."

Marcus's cure rates boomed, but his rate of internal referrals plummeted. Relationships inside the hospital grew strained, and run-ins with hospital administrators grew common. Kraus had grappled with the AMA during the years of his private practice, and that continued after he joined Marcus' reinvigorated clinic at Lenox Hill. Looking around at the chronic pain community, Kraus commented, "They lost their common sense. When you get a Ph.D., do you need to turn in your common sense?"

Kraus shook his head in frustration as he recalled some medical conferences he attended and some of the medical articles he had read: Chronic pain doctors prescribing bed rest,[171] who didn't believe in exercise,[172] stretching,[173] trigger points, or trigger point injections.[174] Chronic pain doctors who supported back surgery, despite their high failure rates, not just to fuse spines, but taking it further, to insert devices releasing various medications[175] in different strengths and delivery methods,[176] acting as nerve blocks,[177] administering electroconvulsive therapy,[178] providing electrical nerve stimulation,[179] or creating electrical currents in the brain cortex.[180]

But that wasn't all. Kraus read medical articles or listened to presentations about brain surgery for chronic pain[181] that cut out part of the brain's message relay center, implanted a brain "pacemaker" for electrical stimulation, or embedded devices to release morphine into the brain,[182] with potentially devastating side effects if something went wrong.[183]

Trying to explain the dramatic increase in spinal fusion operations in the U.S., which had more than doubled from the 1980's to the 1990's despite their high failure rates,[184] Kraus sighed: "When x-rays first came out and doctors could see the bones and the spine, we really lost some of our intelligence as doctors. We became mechanistically oriented. We can see what's in the body, but we forgot that x-rays don't show muscles. We thought that what we saw was all there was to see. Unfortunately, we also forgot that what we were seeing could be normal. When more sophisticated tests, like CAT scans and MRIs came out, we were really cooked. That's when doctors essentially lost their minds about this."

Adding perspective, Marcus commented, "For instance, degenerative spines are normal [as people age], not necessarily diseases, not necessarily the reason for patients' complaints. In most cases, arthritis or narrowing of the space, or what was going on with the discs, has nothing to do with the pain. But because we could see them, we assumed they were the trouble."

Kraus didn't doubt most doctors are sincere. Or that factors *outside* the medical profession also contributed to the explosive growth in back surgery. For instance, the media unwittingly positioned back surgery as progressive and desirable by focusing stories on controversial new drugs or attention-grabbing new surgical procedures, rather than dull exercises. When the *New York Times* ran two major articles in 2001 on chronic pain, both featured high tech drugs.[185] When Norman Marcus tried in 2004 to publish a back pain article on exercise in a leading medical journal, he was turned down: his approach, he was told, was "too old fashioned."

And patients, as Kraus was surprised to discover as far back as the 1950's, sometimes even preferred surgery or drugs to dull exercises. Partly, it seemed intuitive that new advances would be "high tech," but surgery also offers the "benefits" of ceding accountability and generating sympathy. When Kennedy had decided against back surgery when doctors first recommended it to him in 1942, a close friend bluntly told him he was crazy. "Of course I don't know a damn thing about the circumstances, but to me, it doesn't look like the best thing to do. As far as I can see, you're merely putting off the inevitable, because you'll probably have to have the operation sometime anyway."[186]

Within six months of working with Kraus, Marcus, the firm skeptic, became a fervent convert. He reassessed everything he had previously done in chronic pain throughout his professional life, discarded all of his previous assumptions and beliefs, re-trained his clinic's nurses and physical therapists, and overhauled his clinic's administration. Within a year, Marcus had adopted Kraus' approach in entirety, even learning to palpate muscles, identify trigger points, and give trigger point injections. "Norman gives the injections as well as I do, maybe better," Kraus said proudly.

Many people find it hard to admit they took a wrong turn in the road, and would rather keep going in the wrong direction rather than ask directions and admit the wrong turn. In the context of the high ego profession of medicine, admitting a wrong turn would be many times harder. This is what Marcus did. It took a lot of character and humility. On top of that, for the next several years at Lenox Hill, Marcus had to deal with hospital bureaucracy and financial pressures in a way that Kraus never did.

Kraus found great solace in his work at Lenox Hill, and the legacy of treating even more patients. For that, Kraus was quick to credit "the other Marcus" in his life. Kraus loved to comment about the same name coincidence of the two men who played such significant roles in his life. *Was it a coincidence?* he would ask.

The first Marcus brought Kraus great sorrow and guilt. The second Marcus brought Kraus great satisfaction and gratification. "I can die knowing that my medical knowledge will be passed on," Kraus said, contentedly, in November of 1995.

Indeed, four months later, Kraus was dead of cancer. In the obituary that ran in *Sports Illustrated*, Bob Boyle recalled his friend, "an extraordinary man." Boyle wrote, "Madi Kraus, Hans' wife of thirty-eight years, says her husband wanted no memorial service. In a sense, he has no need of one: His legacy lives on throughout the world of sports."[187]

Boyle could have added that Hans' legacy lives on in the hearts—and backs—of thousands and thousands of his patients, too.

PART VI

CONCLUSION:
THE STORY BEHIND
THE STORY 1994–1996

53

The Debt

✦

1994, New York City

As it turned out, one of those patients was me, the author of this book. I kept myself out of the narrative, but my story intersects with that of Hans, and has direct bearing on his story—more precisely, how Hans and I came to know each other, how I came to write this book, and what sustained me and drove me during the ten years it took to write and publish this book about him. This is the story behind the story.

It's also the story of a huge debt I owe to Hans. This book is at least partial payment.

The story behind the story started with a back injury; my back injury. As usually happens, the triggering event for the back pain was mundane (like Bob Boyle's stretching to pick up a piece of paper, or Kennedy's shoveling a bit of dirt); in my case, I over-trained for competitive swimming when I was in college at Harvard. As the injury healed, it was exacerbated, I see now, by the kind of stress many college seniors face at that pivotal point; when they grapple with issues like re-defining relationships with parents, what to do after graduation, and how they try to find meaning in their lives.

Doctors at the Harvard health services and Massachusetts General prescribed a range of traditional treatments for my back: drugs, bed rest, traction, and hospitalization. One doctor coolly informed me that I might have muscular dystrophy, because the pain and tenderness were so widespread, he explained, he didn't see how it could be an injury. He seemed unaware that his words might not have been a big thing for him, but it was a very big thing for the twenty-year-old listening. It was a scary couple of days until the doctor decided, after all, that the first diagnosis he had ruled out—torn muscles—was the correct one.

Despite all the time off from classes in my senior year due to the injury, I managed to graduate in the normal timeframe. But the injury never healed, and developed into a classic case of chronic pain, running a course similar to Bob Boyle's.

Years later, when I read accounts of his or other people's back pain, I knew well what they meant—the pain makes you feel as though knives are slicing into you, that your body is so stiff and brittle, that if you move, it will snap in half. When I read about Kennedy's pain, and how he had to hobble about on crutches and work in the White House stretched out on his bed, I knew well what that meant, too.

In my early twenties, I read a magazine article about "Kennedy's back doctor," who then headed a practice at a prestigious Manhattan hospital. But the article wasn't about Kraus. The subject was instead Dr. "G," the doctor who had been Kraus' back-up when Kraus went on the climbing trip with Gino Solda in August of 1963, and who had treated Kennedy only once, unsuccessfully, for a minor golf injury, which had been to Kennedy's knee and not even his back. To the adage that medicine is part science and part art should be added that it is also part marketing. Dr "G," like Janet Travell, was superb at marketing.

Knowing nothing at all about Hans Kraus at this point, I made an appointment with the man who was Kennedy's back doctor, according to the article. Dr. "G" breezed into the examining room. Extremely charming and debonair, he made me feel his time was valuable and that I was fortunate he would treat me. Dr. "G" proceeded to diagnose trigger points, and prescribed trigger point injections and follow-up physical therapy. Dr. "G's" trigger point injections took the edge off the pain, and he declared them a great success. With his reputation and credentials, I believed him.

It never occurred to me to ask Dr. "G" why he couldn't get rid of my pain, though. For the next fifteen years, I lived in constant pain. Some days weren't bad; some days were. I loved sports and being active, and was resolved not to let my back pain get in the way of how I lived my life. But that grew harder and harder.

Ironically, I first heard of Hans through climbing rather than medicine. I started climbing at the Shawangunks in 1990, and like Bonnie Prudden, despite chronic pain I managed to learn during "good periods" when my back wasn't "acting up." Often my back would go out: while reaching up for a hold, or sitting still for long stretches while belaying. Plenty of afternoons I ended up sitting at the base of the cliff, on the ground with the book I made sure to keep in my backpack, while my friends climbed on the rock above.

It may seem strange to persevere with an activity that brought discomfort and sometimes piercing physical pain, but climbing brought a sense of peace to my heart, and balm to my soul. When Hans later told me how the Shawangunks had saved his life, I understood that. When I entered the vertical world, there was terror, certainly, but also astonishment, at this fantastically beautiful universe I hadn't known existed. Everything in this new world was on a grander scale than my urban office daily life: the settings, the emotions stimulated, the insights inspired, and the issues confronted, like the most basic ones of life and death.

After climbing I felt rejuvenated and stronger, better able to see past the jumble of daily stresses and demands. As I would write in an article for *Climbing Magazine*, trying to explain the pull, "There must be safer, saner ways to restore the spirit than by climbing, but I hadn't found any yet." It hurt to climb, but for many years, it hurt more not to.

Over the years, as back pain often does, my back grew worse; the "good periods" were shorter, the "bad periods" happened more frequently. Desperate, I called Dr. "G" again. To my surprise and delight, Dr. "G" was still practicing. He again diagnosed trigger points, and again prescribed trigger point injections and physical therapy. Remembering my previous experience, I didn't dare hope to be cured; just helped, a little, would be enough.

Dr. "G" and his assistant gave the trigger point injections, and I remember thinking that my memory had been playing tricks. I had remembered large needles and painful injections. Now this time around, the needles looked almost ordinary, and the injections barely hurt. The problem this time around was that they also didn't help, at all.

Pain, like old age, narrows your life. By then, I had, one-by-one, cut out the activities that I loved. I had needed to cut way back on my climbing, too; partly as a way to stay connected with the rock, I started writing about it. While I kept my corporate job, I worked at nights and weekends, sending my first article in cold to *Climbing Magazine*. To my delight, a few days later, the Senior Editor, Mike Benge, called to tell me that the magazine wanted to run the piece.

More articles followed, for other sports and adventure magazines like *Outside, Runner's World,* and *Rock and Ice*. I started with short pieces and worked my way up on the writing ladder toward features—wordsmithing travel pieces, biographies, advice "how-to's," sports competitions results—anything that gave me the chance to write about climbing or the outdoors. Then in 1994, *Rock and Ice* asked me to write a series of profiles on leading Shawangunks climbers. One of the subjects they wanted me to cover was Hans Kraus.

Soon afterwards, I first met Hans. When I interviewed him for the *Rock and Ice* article in his Manhattan apartment, he was thoroughly charming and delightful, his answers coming readily, almost without pause. I got what I needed for my story, but I was convinced there was a deeper, even more interesting story that lay beneath his professional exterior. We chatted after we had finished the interview. He was pleased I was a climber and loved the Shawangunks. Then, as I was gathering my things to leave—stuffing pad, pen, and tape recorder into my briefcase—Hans asked me if I had back pain.

He had been observing the way I moved, I realized. I gave him a short account of my experience, and he began asking me questions. Suddenly I saw that he had become the interviewer, and at the end he made me a proposal.

"You should come by Marcus's clinic, where I can treat you. I think I can cure you."

I demurred at first, told him I would think about it, and thanked him for his time that day with me. At first, I was inclined not to take up Hans' offer. The treatments cost plenty of money–Hans was apologetic that he couldn't treat me for free, as he would have, in his own practice. And they were inconvenient, requiring time out of the office, during a period when business wasn't abundant and I was striving for a promotion. After Dr. "G's" unsuccessful treatments, which had also been expensive, inconvenient, and had required time out of the office, I wondered; did I really want to put myself through all that again?

But most of all, after the last round of treatments, I had given up hope. I had made my peace with back pain, and living a different kind of life than the vigorous one for which I longed. Okay, I had told myself, if I couldn't run, ski, or climb, I could take leisurely walks, attend concerts, movies, ballet and theatre, read, be with friends, enjoy good food and conversation. Okay, well, it was the kind of life I envisioned for myself in my eighties, or nineties. Not my thirties. But I had come to grips with it. I didn't want to get my hopes up once more, and then face the painful process of acceptance all over. I didn't want to open that door again, and then have it shut again, wham, in my face.

Meanwhile, I was still working on the article and continuing to interview people, including Bob Boyle and other patients. Again and again, they recounted the same story: Hans had cured them; it was a miracle. They shuddered to think what their lives would be like without having met him and his treatments.

This sounded too good to be true. Cynical New Yorker that I was, I was sure there was a lot more to the story. Were these people saying these things because they knew it was for an article? I had instantly liked Hans, and could imagine wanting to contribute to the nice picture I was surely painting of him. Had they, like Bob Boyle, become close friends to Hans and perhaps lost perspective? Had they unintentionally dramatized the results over the years? Had their memories unwittingly "improved" reality over the years in a couple of key details?

What if I called someone out of the blue, someone who had supposedly experienced a Kraus miracle, but who wasn't expecting my call? Billy Kidd, for instance? Would Billy Kidd's story really be as dramatic?

I didn't know Billy Kidd, but I heard he lived in Colorado, and when I called long distance information, it turned out his phone number was listed. When the phone rang, Kidd picked it up himself. I introduced myself and launched into my explanation: "I'm writing an article about Dr. Hans Kraus for the magazine, *Rock and Ice*. I heard you were a patient of his; could I take a minute to interview you?

Silence. Several seconds passed. Complete, dead, utter silence.

My stomach sank.

Well, something like this eventually was bound to happen. There was bound to be someone whose relationship with Kraus wasn't so reverential. Whose treatments had been disappointing, or maybe even simply *okay*. Maybe this was Kidd. Maybe Kidd didn't even remember Kraus. I was about to apologize profusely for bothering him and tactfully hang up, but Kidd starting talking.

"You caught me by surprise for a moment," Kidd explained. "I haven't seen or spoken to Dr. Kraus in years. But I often think about him. Take as long as you'd like. I owe my gold medal to Dr. Kraus. It's been so many years, but he left a deep impression on me."

Then Billy Kidd told me the story of *his* particular miracle. I sat there—and how can I write this and make this sound real?—I sat there and tears ran down my cheeks. And I decided to let myself hope. Once more. This would really be the last time, but I would give it a shot. And I let myself hope one last time.

The next day I called Hans. And I asked him if he would treat me.

I finished the article for *Rock +Ice* on Hans and sent it off. My appointment was the next week. And I remember hoping, fervently, "Have one more miracle cure left for me, please, just one more left for me."

54

One Last Kraus Miracle

✦

1994–1995, New York City

At Marcus's clinic, Hans examined me, and like Dr. "G," he found trigger points across my hips, back, and upper legs. Also like Dr. "G," Hans prescribed a series of trigger point injections, followed up by physical therapy three times a week. That's where the similarity between his and Dr. "G's" treatments ended.

Sitting in the clinic's waiting area before my first treatment began, I looked around anxiously. Down the hall, from behind a closed door, I could hear the sound of a man sobbing. It looked like the same office where Hans and Norman Marcus had previously examined me. I had the awful feeling that I was headed there next; I was.

I lay in a hospital gown on the examining table as Hans poked me carefully. When he reached a tender spot and I jumped with pain, he nodded, and wrote an X on my skin with a marker. When done, he shuffled to the stainless steel tray where lay the tools of his trade: syringes, packages of oversized needles in different sizes, vials, cotton pads, and wooden tongue depressors.

I heard clinking and clattering, and then turned to see Hans hobbling back toward me. He was carrying the longest, fattest hypodermic needle I had ever seen. It looked like an ice pick. Maybe it was. Hans wielded the needle like a heavy weight, and walked shakily toward me. Neither inspired confidence. Given his physical condition, I had assumed—wrongly, as it turned out—that Hans wouldn't give the injections himself.

He put his hand gently on my shoulder, and spoke in a calm tone to reassure me. "Zis vill hurt!"

Then with all of his force, he jabbed the needle into an area marked with an X, stabbing again and again, driving deeper and deeper. I was stunned by the force, and tried tricks to keep from screaming—biting into the towel, breathing through the pain, counting to ten over and over again, emptying my mind and trying to keep it blank.

Then it was over. The towel had a neat set of bite marks; I was limp from the pain. I thought of the famous shower scene from the movie, *Psycho*, when the Anthony Perkins psychotic character jabs in maniacal glee into the Janet Leigh character.

Hans was pleased. He seemed pleased with himself, or maybe he was pleased with his work.

He turned proudly to Marcus. "Gut, gut. See, climbers have high pain tolerance." Hans had been pleased with me.

My muscles were so sore and swollen from the trauma of the injections, that for several days afterwards, I walked with a clumsy, ugly gait. People on the street stared at me; others rudely asked what kind of disease I had. I had a crude inkling of how much harder life is for people with physical disabilities.

Then it was time to start again with more injections in a different muscle. This lasted for four months, two days of injections each week, followed by three days of physical therapy consisting of the K-W exercises. And then, to my immense disappointment, I wasn't miraculously cured.

Somehow, I imagined right after the treatments, I would be able to crank several pull-ups, run a fast mile, perform a full split, climb several grades harder. None of this happened. It turned out that the trigger point injections were not immediate magic. After I completed them, I was not immediately healed. I had forgotten about the part where over the course of years muscles not used will weaken. On top of that, as Hans pointed out, unless I learned to deal with stress, the trigger points would return. Like most back pain sufferers, including JFK, it turned out that stress played a large role in my chronic pain. I had a lot more work to do.

At least the painful part of the treatments was over. Then followed several months of follow up physical therapy: biofeedback; other exercises to learn to isolate the muscles that I tensed unconsciously when under tension; and of course, the K-W exercises, which I did religiously twice a day.

This took about two years—the same amount of time, I realized later, when I researched this book, as JFK's treatments. But finally my pain was gone. There was still more work though: now it was a matter of building up muscles, which had atrophied over the years from lack of use. I realize that's the point where JFK was when he died.

Then, miraculously, my story, like that of so many other Kraus patients, ended happily. I, too, wouldn't want to imagine what my life now would be like if I hadn't met Hans, and if he hadn't treated me.

I went back to sports, working out at the gym, running, stretching. And rock climbing. Two months after Hans died, I met my husband while climbing in the Shawangunks. Nine months later, we went out to Colorado to snowboard and married on the side of a mountain in a gentle snowfall. As I write this, that was eight years and two children ago. We have built a wonderful life that includes staying active, trips to the Shawangunks, and respect for nature. And we hope to pass these values onto our daughter and son.

It's exactly the kind of vigorous, active and full lifestyle I had so badly dreamed for, but couldn't achieve before Hans. Now I share it with a remarkable man I wouldn't have met, with a family I wouldn't have had. They're a lot of what has inspired me over the past ten years, as I've tapped away on the computer keyboard in the small hours of the night, or craned over print-outs of chapter drafts on long family car rides when we visit family or go skiing, with my husband driving and my children (usually, really) peacefully sleeping or playing together in the back seat.

You could call this book repaying a family debt.

Ten years later, if I feel my back muscles start to ache or tense, I would still do my Kraus exercises. But I can't recall the last time I needed to. It took several years, but I no longer think of myself as "a bad back." It's so distant, physically and emotionally, that I usually forget. More than that, even when writing this section, I had to stop and think hard, really dredge up what it was like to live with back pain. It's all so remote, like it never really happened to me, or a story I read someplace. I know Hans wouldn't mind; in fact, he would be tickled pink. He loved to hear that kind of thing.

The few times I've made references to having had back pain many years ago, usually uttering something in sympathy to someone who complains of back pain, I'm met with a blank stare, and then their disbelief: "You? Really? I can't imagine."

It turned out, after all, that Hans had one more miracle cure left for me.

55

Death

✦

May 1995–March 1996, New York

For a year after the treatments ended, Hans and I didn't keep in touch. I thought of him often, but was busy writing other articles. Hans was busy at Marcus' clinic and writing his autobiography. Then, one evening in May of 1995, I received a call from Hans out of the blue. He had tried writing his life story, but it wasn't coming out the way he wanted. Would I consider writing it?

Hans also mentioned casually that a few weeks before, during a routine physical exam, Larry Sonkin—Gene Cohen's protégé, and the same doctor who suggested he meet Marcus—had discovered prostate cancer. An optimistic prediction for how much time he had left was two years; but probably a lot less. If I was interested, we needed to start immediately.

For the next ten months, my life revolved around Hans. Our relationship began as biographer and subject, but soon evolved into a close friendship. He was old and dying, I was young enough and still formative. He was hungry to talk, I, to listen. We met twice a week, for several hours, during the week in Manhattan and during the weekend at his house in Gardiner. We didn't have a script. Sometimes I had questions and specific topics in mind, but these were starting points, to get conversational juices flowing. Sometimes Hans reminisced, sometimes philosophized about politics, gay rights, history, religion, climbing, skiing, living and dying.

At one point, thinking about how I understood both his climbing and his medical message, he said, "You know, just as Bob Boyle was the perfect person to write *Backache, Stress and Tension*, you're the perfect person to write this book."

We grew very close. When I visited upstate, sometimes I stayed overnight. I often joined Hans and Madi, and whoever else happened to be visiting, for a meal. Family members were regular drop-ins: Ann, Mary, Franz and Sisi all visited frequently. Hans had also amassed a large circle of devoted friends from climbing and medicine, and they and his neighbors were always in contact with him as well. For a man who could be self-contained to a fault, who often insisted he liked to be alone, Hans had built up an extraordinary number of close relationships over his lifetime.

The months wore on. Hans grew sicker and sicker from the cancer. It became clear that the initial prognosis of two years was too optimistic. It turned out he had ten months. Hans had wanted badly to see the book come out before he died. He thought about it constantly, and told me so, sometimes applying not a little bit of pressure, in his blunt, Hans-like way. I understood, but I discovered there was a pace to how quickly I could conduct research and write.

Once I started, I had fresh appreciation for other writers. I learned a lesson: It's hard to write a book, even a bad book. And I wanted this book to be very good. At stake was Hans' medical message that meant so much to so many of his patients. These included, of course, me.

As fall turned into winter, and Hans' condition clearly took a turn for the worse, our time together sometimes was just simple conversation. One gray fall evening we sat in Hans' living room in Manhattan. He had just finished reading some things I had written, including some autobiographical stories. They had been tough to write, and Hans looked at me.

"Are these true?" he asked. I nodded. I had never shown them to anyone before.

He continued to look at me. "You're a great writer. And this will be a great book. Do you know how I know? Because you write in blood and tears and sweat."

Hans died with the same blunt, unadorned, in your face courage that had characterized his life. He accepted that his fate was to die of cancer, and as a doctor, he knew what that meant physically. This had to have been a hard reality for a man who gloried in his exceptional strength.

Hans said, "I know I haven't lived in vain. Climbing was very important for my spiritual and intellectual life, but my real work was medicine. Lots of people got better when they wouldn't have, so I'm really very much at peace. Anyway, there's too much fuss about death here. You don't die, you pass away, that sort of nonsense. You *die*."

Hans galumphed at the absurdity of the notion. "We are all very much afraid to recognize that what we are doing is only temporary."

To be close to someone dying, who is also articulate about it, is a gift to the living. I had been close to others who died, including my father two years before, and a favorite aunt whose hand I held in the ambulance while she slipped further and further away. As I held her hand and stroked her head, my Aunt Belle, like a second mother in some ways, said, "My feet are so cold, I can't feel my feet. I'm so cold." Then the body often falls apart at both ends. You might throw up, have diarrhea, and throw up again. And you're cold, so cold, that it's in the marrow of your bones. You understand the old symbolism of death coming after you with long, icy, bony fingers.

Dying, like birth, is a messy, painful business. It's nothing like the pretty Hollywood picture of dying, with an elegant sigh, a gentle fall of the head, blown dry hair carefully arranged, make up neatly in place. Watching that happen to someone beloved is always heart wrenching, particularly for a person as physically exceptional as Hans. At least outwardly, he was accepting. It was harder in some ways for his friends and family than it seemed to be for him. Although I assumed then, as now, that was part of his inner strength. Part of his mindset as a climber. *You accept the consequences.* The consequences, now, of a long, well-lived life, was that he was ninety and his body was shutting down.

Over the course of his last couple of months Hans was on cancer medication and serious painkillers. He had decided that at his age he would not treat the cancer aggressively. The goal was to make him more comfortable; perhaps buy a couple of months, but not to fight the encroaching malignancy.

By November, Hans had stopped going to Marcus's clinic. By January, he and Madi stopped going to Gardiner on weekends and the opera during the week. Hans was spent, and those activities sapped rather than added to his energy. He was by then in the winnowing away part of the dying process. By February, it was clear he had a few months, if that.

I was trying to write as fast as possible, but I had wildly underestimated the time commitment and hadn't fully appreciated all the different kinds of research required. I knew how badly Hans wanted to see the book. I thought that at least one chapter could help, and chose the chapter on Marcus, the soul of Hans' story.

Hans was very happy to read it. "Alpha," he said, closing his eyes with sigh, and smiling. We were in his apartment in Manhattan on a Tuesday night. It was after dinner, Hans in the armchair that had become his usual abode. I sat on the sofa next to him—hard mattress, of course. I leaned over to Hans and he squeezed my hand, "Write whatever you need to. I trust you."

Like I had done with my Aunt Belle, I held his hand, and stroked his head. There's not much more you can give as a present to the dying, except your presence and your touch.

In the first week of March 1996, I was out west skiing on vacation. From phone calls with Madi, I knew Hans had taken a turn for the worse and was near death. I returned to New York as soon as I could. After the cab picked me up at JFK Airport and dropped me off at my apartment, I dumped my bags in the middle of my living room floor and called Madi to tell her I was on my way. It was only a couple of minutes' to their apartment.

Hans had wanted to die at home, surrounded by family. Madi was there, with Franz, and Ann. Hans drifted in and out of consciousness, one of us going in frequently to hold his hand. At one point, we sat in the dining room nearby. Franz had brought over sauerbraten and polenta he had made himself. We ate a little, pushed food around the plate a lot more.

Hans didn't call out in pain, although once he apologized for doing so. Mostly, he lay there quietly, patiently, waiting. Franz slipped into a headset a cassette of Hans' favorite piece of music, Mahler's second symphony, *The Resurrection*. Gently, Franz placed the earphones on his older brother who had been like a father to him. After several hours, Hans died peacefully, holding his daughter's hand, in the early morning of March 6.

Hans had wanted no memorial service or funeral. He wished, like Rudi, to be cremated, and his passing to be marked as simply as possible. Hans' ashes were carried one last time up the rock face of High Exposure by an old friend, and scattered from the top, into the air.

APPENDIX
K-W Tests and K-W Exercises

DISCLAIMER: The K-W tests are provided below for their historical value and literary interest; i.e. for informational purposes only. Before undertaking any exercise program, one should consult a physician. The author disclaims any liability for any problems, loss, or injuries that might arise from these or any other exercises or exercise program.

K-W Tests
Hans Kraus used the six K-W tests below to determine whether the postural muscles of Kennedy—and those of all his other patients, including the book author—were strong and flexible enough to support their body weight. The exercises are presented in Kraus' own words.

1. Hip Flexor K-W Strength Test
Lie flat on your back on the floor, hands clasped behind your neck, legs straight and touching. Keeping your knees straight, lift your feet so that your heels are ten inches above the floor. **You pass if you: Hold position for ten seconds.**

2. Hip Flexor and Stomach Muscles K-W Strength Test
Lie flat on the floor, hands clasped behind your neck. Have someone hold down your legs by grasping your ankles; or if you're by yourself, you can hook your ankles under a heavy chair that won't topple. **You pass if you: Do one sit-up.**

3. Stomach Muscle K-W Strength Test
Life flat on the floor, hands behind your neck, knees flexed, heels close to your buttocks. Make sure your ankles are held down, as in exercise #2. **You pass if you: Roll up into sitting position once**.

4. Back Muscles K-W Strength Test
Lie on a stomach, pillow under your abdomen, clasp your hands behind your neck, lying flat on the floor. Have someone hold lower half of your body steady (by placing one hand on the small of your back, the other on your ankles). Lift your trunk. **You pass if you: Hold steady for ten seconds**.

5. Low-Back Muscles K-W Strength Test
On your stomach, fold your arms under your head; make sure there is a pillow under your abdomen. Have someone hold your back steady with both hands. Lift your legs up, keeping your knees straight. **You pass if you: Hold position ten seconds**.

6. Back Muscles and Ham-Strings K-W Flexibility Test
Stand up straight, feet together. Relax, lean over, and try to touch the floor with your fingertips without bending your knees. **You pass if you: Touch the floor. NOTE *** If you fail**: It is because these muscles are shortened and tense. It is **not** because your arms are too short or your legs too long!

K-W Exercises
Hans Kraus prescribed the specific K-W exercises depending upon his findings of the patient's K-W tests. For more information about the K-W exercises, you can contact the Norman Marcus Pain Institute (212–532–7999; 30 East 40th Street, New York, NY 10016) or visit the clinic's website (www.nmpi.com).

Acknowledgements

Writing this book would have been impossible without the immense amount of help from the Kraus family. I am indebted to Madi Kraus and Franz Kraus, who generously provided access to family papers and photographs, and who have been unstinting with their time and support. Both are remarkable individuals in their own right. My thanks also to other Kraus family members, Ann, Mary, Sisi, and Leslie Scott Kraus.

Special thanks in particular go to Mike Wallace, Jim McCarthy, Dr. Norman Marcus, and Jim Clash. Mike Wallace was extremely gracious to respond to a "cold" interview request. And then, as his "thank you," he agreed good naturedly to submit to being sent a rough manuscript version of the book and provide feedback. Jim McCarthy was invaluable from the start, and continued to be throughout the book's development. Not only did Jim provide hours and hours of recollections—but as wouldn't surprise anyone who knows him—also provided characteristically pithy and colorful quotes, along with his forthright and openhearted support for the project.

Meanwhile, Dr. Marcus spent many hours providing advice and insight into the book's complex medical issues. This by itself has been extraordinarily valuable, but I have a personal debt to Dr. Marcus as well, for along with Hans, he had treated and cured my own long-standing back problems. Dr. Marcus also remained extraordinarily patient during the quite considerable time he put into the interviewing process for the book, and then remained good-natured as he reviewed and critiqued manuscript drafts with his characteristic humanity and humor.

Another special thanks to Jim Clash, accomplished writer, former co-worker from another lifetime, and adventurer with his own impressive history of venturing into the unknown. For over a decade, Jim has provided long-standing encouragement and support, as well as sharing valuable insights based on his own experiences into the art and process of what it is actually like to write a book.

For additional medical background, I would like to thank Alexander Melleby, Dr. Gene Cohen, Dr. Larry Sonkin, Dr. Bruce Grynebaum, and Dr. Mark Starr. I have the highest regard for the hard work, long hours, and dedication of the medical profession, and want to express gratitude to several doctors in particular, who in addition to Norman Marcus, have made extraordinary contributions to my family through their superb technical doctoring as well as their exceptional human touch: William Schweitzer, Nicole Noyes, and the thoroughly remarkable, Edna Pytlak.

For their time, support and enthusiasm, I'd like to thank Dick Williams and Rich Gottlieb, icons of Rock and Snow. For sharing climbing reminisces and insights, I would like to thank: Bonnie Prudden, Arthur Sulzberger, Jr, Jon Ross, Burt Angrist, Nick Clinch, Yvon Chouinard, Ken Prestrud, Barbara Rogers, Ted Church, Dick Dumais, Kim Massie, Howard Friedman, Betty Woolsey, Muriel Wiessner, and Laura Waterman. Thanks also to Hans' patients: Ken MacWilliams, Bob Boyle, Billy Kidd, Katharine Hepburn, Mary Wallace, Janice Mayer, Lynn Rhodes Mayer, Sally Mendel, Hanzi Steiner, and to Hans' office therapists, Viera Novak Moy and Ellen Ronis.

I am extremely grateful to my remarkable editor, Molly McGrath, who not only did a fantastic editorial job, but also managed the tough task of making the editing process painless and even enjoyable.

Special gratitude for their time and thoughtfulness is owed to manuscript readers: Norbu Tenzing Norgay, Marsha Wunsch, Robert Mads Anderson, and Vicki Mavis. I am also indebted to the ongoing support and enthusiasm of Alison Osius and Duane Raleigh at *Rock and Ice* Magazine, Jeff Achey at *Climbing Magazine*, Philip Erard, Lloyd Athearn, and John Harlin at the American Alpine Club, as well as Terry English, Jane Taylor, Glenn Hoagland, and the Mohonk Preserve.

Thanks also to Stella Hershan for sharing her memories of life in Nazi Germany, Tony Uzzo for his trust and frankness, Cathy Utzschneider for her hospitality when I was doing research at the Kennedy Library, Jay-me Brown, Gilberto D'Urso, Robert Diforio, Stuart Tower, Tom McCarthy, Lorna Britton, Nancy Jeffrey, and Pierre Salinger.

Also, my thanks to Shawangunks climbing partners for their inspiration and support over the years on Hans' routes: Steve Wunsch, Guy Haas, Jon Osser, George Mack, Patty and Rui Ferreira, Ajax Greene, Bob Phelan, Chris Zellner, Bev Keith, Viorel Nikolaescu, Seng Liew, and Arnold Villa, who gets a double thanks for salvaging my first computer after it crashed with early climbing article drafts.

Special thanks, always, to my favorite climbing partner—my husband, John, another thoroughly remarkable man, on and off the cliffs. And to my children, Grace and Mattias, ages 5 and 3 as I write this, I express a different type of thankfulness, for making it crystal clear what it's all about.

SELECT BIBLIOGRAPHY

Anderson, Christopher. *Jack and Jackie*. Avon Books: New York, NY. 1996.

Anderson, Mark M. *Hitler's Exiles*. The New Press: New York, NY. 1998.

Berg, A. Scott. *Lindbergh*. G.P. Putnam's Sons: New York, NY. 1998.

Bishop, Jim. *The Day Kennedy Was Shot*. Funk & Wagnalls: New York, NY. 1968.

Bradley, Benjamin C. *Conversations with Kennedy*. W.W. Norton & Company: New York, NY. 1975.

Clinch, Nicholas. *A Walk in the Sky*. The Mountaineers: Seattle, WA. 1992.

Collier Peter and Horowitz David. *An American Drama, The Kennedys*. Summit Books: New York, NY. 1984.

Curran, Jim. *K2: Triumph and Tragedy*. Houghton Mifflin: New York. NY. 1987.

Dallek, Robert. *An Unfinished Life*. Little, Brown & Company: New York, NY. 2003.

Dumais, Williams, *Shawangunk Rock Climbing*. Chockstone Press: Denver, CO. 1985.

Ellmann, Richard. *James Joyce*. Oxford University Press: Oxford, UK. 1982.

Fay, Paul B. *The Pleasure of His Company*. Harper & Row: New York, NY. 1963.

Gallagher Hugh Gregory *FDR's Splendid Deception*. Dodd, Mead & Company: New York, NY. 1985.

Gay, Peter. *My German Question: Growing up in Nazi Berlin*. Yale University Press: New Haven, CT. 1998.

Gulick, Charles, A. *Austria from Hapsburg to Hitler*. University of California Press: Berkeley, CA. 1948.

Gruber, Ruth Ellen. *Upon the Doorposts of Thy House*. John Wiley & Sons: New York. NY. 1994.

Hamilton, Nigel. *JFK: Reckless Youth*. Random House: New York, NY. 1992.

Hersh, Seymour. *The Dark Side of Camelot*. Little Brown & Company: New York, NY. 1997.

Howe, Nicholas. *Not Without Peril*. Appalachian Mountain Club Books: Boston, MA. 2000.

Kauffman, Andrew and Putnam, William L. *K2: The 1939 Tragedy*. The Mountaineers: Seattle, WA. 1992

Keegan, John. *The First World War*. Alfred A. Knopf: New York, NY. 1999.

Keegan, John. *The Second World War*. Penguin Books: New York, NY. 1989.

Kohler, Annette Kohler and Memmel Norbert. *Classic Dolomites Climbs*. The Mountaineers: Seattle, 1998.

Klein, Edward. *All Too Human, The Love Story of Jack and Jackie Kennedy*. Simon &Schuster: New York, NY. 1996.

Klemperer, Victor. *I Will Bear Witness: A Diary of the Nazi Years, 1933–1941*. Random House: New York, NY. 1998.

Kraus, Hans. *Backache, Stress and Tension*. Simon & Schuster: New York, NY. 1965.

Kraus, Hans. *Hypokinetic Disease: Diseases Produced by Lack of Exercise*. Charles C. Thomas: Springfield, IL, 1961.

Kraus, Hans. *Principles and Practice of Therapeutic Exercises*. Charles C. Thomas: Springfield, IL. 1949.

Kraus, Hans. *Sports Injuries*, Playboy Press: New York, NY. 1981.

Lasky, Victor. *The Man and the Myth*. Dell Publishing: New York, NY. 1985.

Lincoln, Evelyn. *My Twelve Years with John F. Kennedy.* David McKay Company: New York, NY. 1965.

Nuland, Sherwin B. *How We Die.* Vintage Books: New York, NY. 1995.

Nuland, Sherwin B. *The Doctors Plague.* W.W. Norton. New York, NY. 2003.

McCarthy, Joseph, Powers, David, and Kenneth P. O'Donnell. *Johnny, We Hardly Knew Ye.* Little, Brown & Company: New York, NY. 1983.

Morton, Frederic. *Thunder at Twilight: Vienna 1913/1914.* Collier Books: New York, NY. 1989.

Manchester, William. *Portrait of a President.* Little Brown & Company: New York, NY. 1962.

Matthews, Christopher. Kennedy & Nixon. *Simon & Schuster.* New York, NY. 1996.

Morris, Jan. *Trieste and the Meaning of Nowhere.* Da Capo Press, Perseus Books Group: Cambridge, MA. 2001.

Parker, Barry. Einstein. *The Passions of a Scientist.* Prometheus Books: Amherst, NY. 2003.

Perret, Geoffrey. *Jack: A Life Like No Other.* Random House: New York, NY. 2001.

Potts, Willard. *Portraits of the Artist in Exile, Recollections of James Joyce by Europeans.* University of Washington Press: Seattle, WA. 1979.

Prudden, Bonnie. *How to Keep Slender and Fit After Thirty.* Random House: New York, NY. 1961.

Rachlin, Edward. *Myofascial Pain and Fibromyalgia: Trigger Point Management.* Mosby: Baltimore, MD. 1994.

Rees, Laurence. *The Nazis.* The New Press: New York, NY. 1997.

Reeve, Richard. *President Kennedy, Profile in Power.* Simon & Schuster: New York, NY. 1993.

Reeves Thomas C. *A Question of Character*. C. Prima Publishing: Rocklin, CA. 1992.

Roper, Robert. *Fatal Mountaineer*. St. Martin's Press: New York, NY. 2002.

Sacks, Oliver. *Uncle Tungsten*. Alfred A. Knopf: New York, NY. 2001.

Salinger, Pierre. *P.S.: A Memoir*. St. Martin's Press: New York, NY. 1995.

Sorenson, Theodore. *Kennedy*. Konecky & Konecky: New York, NY. 1965.

Swain, Todd, *The Gunks Guide*. Chockstone Press: Evergreen, CO. 1990.

Travell, Janet, *Office Hours Day and Night*. World Publishing Company: New York. 1968.

Travell, Janet; David G. Simons. *Myofascial Pain and Dysfunction, The Trigger Point Manual*. Williams & Wilkins: Baltimore, MD. 1984.

Waterman, Laura and Guy. *Yankee Rock + Ice*. Stackpole Books: Harrisburg, PA. 1993.

Williams, Richard. *The Gunks Select*. Vulgarian Press: High Falls, NY. 1996.

Woolsey, Elizabeth D. Woolsey. *Off the Beaten Track*. Wilson Bench Press: Wilson, NY. 1984.

ABOUT THE AUTHOR

Susan E.B. Schwartz contributes to national adventure and sports magazines, including *Outside, Climbing, Rock and Ice*, and *Runner's World*. An American Alpine Club Literary Committee member and former Board member, she is a rock climber, scuba instructor, shipwreck divemaster, and marathoner. A Harvard College graduate, she lives in Connecticut with her husband and children.

NOTES

PART I

[1] US Centers for Disease Control, 2005

[2] *The Wall Street Journal*, 3/17/05, p. D6, quoting New England Journal of Medicine

[3] *Trieste*, Jan Morris. P, 43

[4] www.chipublib.org/004chicago/diasters/infant_mortality.html

[5] *Austria from Hapsburg to Hitler*, Charles A. Gulick, p. 910

[6] *Myofascial Pain and Fibromyalgia: Trigger Point Management*, Edward S. Rachlin, M.D. p. 385–387

[7] *Off the Beaten Track*, Elizabeth Woolsey, p. 123

[8] *Off the Beaten Track*, Elizabeth Woolsey, p. 104–106. Also see, *My German Question: Growing up in Nazi Berlin*, Peter Gay, p. 119

[9] *The Nazis*, p. 109. Also see *Radcliffe Quarterly*, recollections of Suzanne Ehrentheil Learmonth, fall 1998, vol. 84, No. 2

[10] *The Nazis*, p. 113, recollections of Stella Hershan

[11] *Shawangunks Rock Climbing*, Richard Dumais, p. 26

[12] *Hitler's Exiles*, Marta Appel, p. 33

[13] *New York Times*, 4/14/05, http://www.nytimes.com/2005/04/14/nyregion/14holocaust.html?pagewanted=2&ei=5094&en=75c41ea36ad6eca8&hp&ex=1113537600&partner=homepage

[14] *New York Times*, 4/14/05, http://www.nytimes.com/2005/04/14/nyregion/14holocaust.html?pagewanted=2&ei=5094&en=75c41ea36ad6eca8&hp&ex=1113537600&partner=homepage

[15] *Lindbergh*, A. Scott Berg, p.385

[16] *Lindbergh*, A. Scott Berg p. 362

[17] *New York Times*, "Brandeis At 50 Is Still Searching, Still Jewish, and Still Not Harvard," p. 1, Section A, 10/17/98

[18] Interview with Bonnie Prudden

[19] *Lindbergh*, A. Scott Berg, p. 386

PART II

[20] *Off the Beaten Track*, Elizabeth Woolsey, p. 63

[21] Millbrook

[22] The Old Route

[23] *K2, The 1939 Tragedy*, Andrew J. Kauffman and William L. Putnam, p. 117

[24] *Rock and Ice Magazine*, 12/04

[25] *Yankee Rock and Ice*, Guy and Laura Waterman, p. 55

[26] Retribution (5.10), first ascent in 1961 by Jim McCarthy.

[27] See Kraus and Weber's three papers describing their K-W tests: *Physiotherapy Review*, "Evaluation of Posture Based on Structural and Functional Measurement," November/December 1945, vol 25, No 6; "Quantitative Tabulation of Posture Evaluation Based on Structural and Functional Measurements," September/October 1946, vol 26, no. 5; and "Fundamental Considerations of Posture Exercises: Guided by Qualitative and Quantitative Measurements and Tests," vol 27, no 6

[28] Results reported in numerous medical articles, including *The Research Quarterly* 25:2 (May 1954) pp. 178–188

[29] *Sports Illustrated*, 7/16/56

[30] Three Pines (5.3)

[31] *Off the Beaten Track*, Elizabeth Woolsey, pp. 94–95

PART III

[32] *Yankee Rock and Ice*, Laura & Guy Waterman, p. 137

[33] *Yankee Rock and Ice*, Laura & Guy Waterman

[34] *Sports Illustrated*, 7/16/56, p. 60

[35] *Climbing Magazine* 12/88

[36] Results reported in the *Research Quarterly*, 25:2 (May 1954) pp. 178–188

[37] "Prevention of Back Pain," *Journal of the Association for Physical and Mental Rehabilitation*, vol 6, no.1 Sept-Oct 1952, based on presentation of the 6th annual Scientific and Clinic Conference of the Association, Milwaukee, Wisconsin, 7/8–7/12/52

[38] Classic 1953 study conducted by Morris, Hady, Raffle, Roberts and Parks

[39] *U.S. News & World Report*, 8/2/57, p. 75

[40] Personal correspondence from Dr. W. W. Bauer, AMA—Director of the Department of Health Education, to Hans Kraus, November 10, 1961

[41] *U.S. News & World Report,* 3/19/54, p. 35

[42] *U.S. News & World Report,* 3/19/54, p. 36

[43] *Sports Illustrated,* 9/26/55

[44] *Newsweek,* 7/55, p. 35

[45] *Sports Illustrated,* 8/15/55

[46] *Newsweek,* 9/26/55

[47] *U.S. News & World Report,* 8/2/57

[48] *Cosmo Magazine,* 4/56

[49] Personal correspondence, Richard Nixon to Hans Kraus, 9/16/55

[50] *U.S. News & World Report,* 8/2/57. p. 74

[51] *U.S. News & World Report,* 8/2/57. p. 74

[52] *U.S News & World Report,* 8/2/57, p. 77

[53] *Sports Illustrated,* 7/16/56, p.60

[54] *Sports Illustrated,* 8/5/57, p. 29–30

[55] *Sports Illustrated,* 8/5/57, p. 30–31

[56] *Sports Illustrated,* 8/5/57, p 33–34

[57] *U.S. News & World Report,* 8/2/57, p. 73

[58] *Sports Illustrated,* 8/5/57, p. 33–34

[59] *Cronaca di Feltre,* 8/22/59

[60] *20/20,* 12/93

[61] www.chron.com/content/chronicle/special/jfk/related/0803autopsy.html

[62] *Office Hours Day and Night,* Janet Travell, p. 333

[63] *New York Times,* 7/14/1960

[64] Kennedy childhood medical records, John F. Kennedy Library

[65] Kennedy college medical records, John F. Kennedy Library

[66] Kennedy's naval records, John F. Kennedy Library

[67] Formerly sealed Oral History, Dr. Janet Travell, John F. Kennedy Library

[68] *A Question of Character,* Thomas Reeves, p. 39

[69] *My Twelve Years with John F. Kennedy,* Evelyn Lincoln, p. 13, 54

[70] *Jack: A Life Like No Other,* Geoffrey Perret, p. 203–204

[71] *The Pleasure of His Company,* Red Fay

[72] American Medical Association Archives of Surgery, 11/55

[73] Formerly sealed Oral History, Dr. Janet Travell, John F. Kennedy Library

[74] Formerly sealed Oral History, Dr. Janet Travell, John F. Kennedy Library

[75] Formerly sealed Oral History, Dr. Janet Travell, John F. Kennedy Library

[76] *Myofascial Pain and Dysfunction: The Trigger Point Manual,* Dr. Janet Travell and Dr. David Simmons

[77] *Profile of Power,* Richard Reeves, p. 147

[78] *New York Times*, 8/2/97

[79] George Washington University archives, www.gwu/edu/gelman/archibes/collections/travel.html

[80] *Johnny, We Hardly Knew Ye*, Kenneth O'Donnell and David Powers, p. 117

[81] *New York Times*, Section C, p. 3, 10/6/92

[82] www.ibsgroup.org/other/NYTimesNov172002–3.htm

[83] *Office Hours*, p. 358

[84] *Washington Post*, 8/2/97, p. B04

[85] *FDR's Splendid Deception*, Hugh Gregory Gallagher, p. 178–179

[86] See various Travell personal correspondence, John F. Kennedy Library archives

[87] *New York Times* 11/17/02, p. 1, Profile of Power, Richard Reeve, p. 180. 20/20 12/93

[88] *New York Times* 11/17/02, p. 1, 20/20 12/93

[89] http://www.ibsgroup.org/other/NYTimesNov172002.htm

[90] *New York Times*, 1/7/61

[91] Formerly sealed Oral History, Dr. Janet Travell, John F. Kennedy Library

[92] Personal Correspondence, Evelyn Lincoln to Hans Kraus

[93] Interview with Gene Cohen

[94] Formerly sealed Oral History, Dr. George Burkley, John F. Kennedy Library

[95] *20/20* 12/93

[96] Formerly sealed Oral History, Dr. George Burkley, John F. Kennedy Library. http://geocities/jfkinfo3/testimony/burkley.html

[97] *Profile of Power*, Richard Reeves, p.242

[98] *New York Times*, 1/7/61

[99] Formerly sealed Oral History, Dr. George Burkley, John F. Kennedy Library

[100] http://www.aarclibrary.com/publib/jfk/arrb/master_med_set/pdf/md67.pdf

[101] Formerly sealed Oral History, Dr. George Burkley, John F. Kennedy Library

[102] Letter from Evelyn Lincoln to Hans Kraus, July 29, 1993

[103] Formerly sealed Oral History, Dr. George Burkley, John F. Kennedy Library

[104] http://www.aarclibrary.com/publib/jfk/arrb/master_med_set/pdf/md67.pdf

[105] "K" Medical Files (President John Kennedy's White House Back Records), Dr. Hans Kraus, 10/61

[106] "The President Is Fine," *Columbia Journalism Review*, Richard Norton Smith, www.cjr.org/year/01/5/nortonsmith.asp

[107] Formerly sealed Oral History, Dr. George Burkley, John F. Kennedy Library

[108] *Kennedy & Nixon*, Christopher Matthews

[109] *Washington Post*, 12/25/61

[110] Personal correspondence, Dr. Eugene Cohen to Dr. Hans Kraus

[111] "K" Medical Files (President John Kennedy's White House Back Records), Dr. Hans Kraus

[112] Formerly sealed Oral History, Dr. George Burkley, John F. Kennedy Library

[113] *Profile of Power*, Richard Reeves, p. 273

[114] Formerly sealed Oral History, Dr. George Burkley, John F. Kennedy Library

[115] *Conversations with Kennedy*, Benjamin C. Bradlee, p. 228

[116] *Fatal Mountaineer*, Robert Roper, p. 158, St. Martin's Press, NY 2002

[117] "K" Medical Files (President John Kennedy's White House Back Records), Dr. Hans Kraus

[118] *An Unfinished Life*, Robert Dallek, p. 230–235

[119] "K" Medical Files (President John Kennedy's White House Back Records), Dr. Hans Kraus

[120] *Look Magazine*, 12/18/62

[121] *JFK: Reckless Youth*, Nigel Hamilton, p. 215

[122] *P.S.: A Memoir*, Pierre Salinger, p. 127

[123] www.aarclibrary.com/publib/jfk…

[124] *P.S.: A Memoir*, Pierre Salinger, p. 128

[125] *P.S.: A Memoir*, p. 128

[126] "K" Medical Files (President John Kennedy's White House Back Records), Dr. Hans Kraus

[127] "K" Medical Files (President John Kennedy's White House Back Records), Dr. Hans Kraus

[128] *The Dark Side of Camelot*, Seymour Hersh, p. 439

[129] "K" Medical Files (President John Kennedy's White House Back Records), Dr. Hans Kraus

[130] *The Kennedys, An American Drama*, p. 310

[131] *My Twelve Years with John F. Kennedy*, Evelyn Lincoln

[132] CNN Segment, Dr. Sanjay Gupta, 10/3/04

[133] *Los Angeles Times*, 1/19/94

[134] *My Twelve Years with John F. Kennedy*, Evelyn Lincoln, p. 338

[135] *The Kennedys, An American Drama*, Peter Collier and David Horowitz, p. 171

[136] *The Man and the Myth*, Victor Lasky, p. 65

[137] *The Kennedys, An American Drama*, Peter Collier and David Horowitz, p. 158

[138] *Jack: A Life Like No Other*, Geoffrey Perret, p. 351

[139] *Jack: The Struggles of John F. Kennedy*, Herbert S. Permet, p. 61; *A Question of Character: A Life of John F. Kennedy*, Thomas C. Reeves, p. 47; *JFK: Reckless Youth*, Nigel Hamilton p. 164

[140] *Pleasure of His Company*, Red Fay; p. 172. See also *Profile of Power*, Richard Reeves, p. 44

[141] *Journal of the American Medical Association*, Dr. M.T. Jenkins, Chief of Anesthesiology, Parkland Memorial Hospital, May 27, 1992–Vol. 267. No. 20

[142] K" Medical Files (President John Kennedy's White House Back Records), Dr. Hans Kraus

[143] K" Medical Files (President John Kennedy's White House Back Records), Dr. Hans Kraus

[144] *An Unfinished Life*, Robert Dallek, p. 694, Los Angeles Times, Michael Beschloss 1/19/94

[145] Personal correspondence, Dr. George Burkley to Dr. Hans Kraus, 11/30/63

[146] *Johnny, We Hardly Knew Ye*, Kenneth O'Donnell and David Powers, p. 1–2

[147] Personal correspondence, Evelyn Lincoln to Dr. Hans Kraus

[148] 20/20 11/12/93

PART V

[149] *Back Talk* 7/78, p. 1

[150] Based on follow-up study of 11,809 participants

[151] *Wall Street Journal*, 3/1/05, p. D6

[152] *Wall Street Journal*, 3/1/05, p. D6

[153] *Spine*, 1996 Mar1; 21 (5): 626–633

[154] *Back Talk*, 7/78, p. 2

[155] *Sports Illustrated*, 6/15/81, p. 349

[156] *Yankee Rock and Ice*, Jon Waterman, p. 194–195

[157] Gargoyle or Gray Face

[158] *Myofascial Pain and Fibromyalgia: Trigger Point Management*, Edward S. Rachlin, MD, p. 385–392

[159] *20/20* 12/03

[160] *An Unfinished Life*, Robert Dallek, p. 213

[161] *An Unfinished Life*, Robert Dallek, p. 205

[162] *The Kennedys, An American Drama*, p. 61

[163] *JFK: Reckless Youth*, Nigel Hamilton, p.104

[164] Choate Medical Records, John F. Kennedy Library

[165] *FDR's Splendid Deception*, Hugh Gregory Gallagher

[166] *Uncle Tungsten*, Oliver Sacks, Alfred A. Knopf, NY, 2001, p. 93

[167] *The New Yorker*, 12/30/91

[168] van Tulder MW, Koes BW, Metsemakers JF, et al, Fam Pract. 1998; 15 (2): 126–32. Also, *Therapie* 2001 Nov-Dec; 56 (6): 697–703 (ISSN: 0040–5957); *Therapie* Nov-Dec; 56 (6): 697–703 (ISSN 0040–5957)

[169] *New York Times*, "Restoring the Physical to the Exam," 1/29/02, Section F, p. 6

[170] *Uncle Tungsten*, Oliver Sacks, p. 93

[171] www.spine-health.com/topics/conserv/overview/con02.html

[172] International Association for the Study of Pain, 1995, p.54 "There is, however, little scientific evidence to support the value of any specific form of back exercise."

[173] International Association for the Study of Pain, 1995, p. 49

[174] International Association for the Study of Pain, 1995, p.45, also p. 48: "No proven benefit in the treatment of acute low back symptoms."

[175] Clin J Pain 1996 Sep; 12 (3): 174–9 (ISSN 0749–80470), See Minerva Anestesoil 2000 Oct; 66 (10): 713–31 (ISSN 0375–9393)

[176] Continuous Epidural Analgia; Dolin SJ, Bacon RA, Drage M Disabil Rehabil 1998; 20 (4): 151–7. Also see about time released, Hale ME, Fleischmann R, Salzman R et al, Clin J Pain 1999; 15(3) 179–83; Medscape Pharmacotherapy 2001

[177] J Clin Anesth 2002 Feb; 14 (1); 39–41 (ISSN: 0952–8180); Acta Anaesthesiol Scand 2001 Oct; 45 (9): 1100–7 (ISSN: 0001–5172)

[178] Curr Pain Headache Rep 2002 Feb; 6 (1): 17–22 (ISSN: 1531–3433)

[179] Cochrane Database Syst Rev 2001; (3): CD003222 (ISSN 1469493X)

[180] J Neurol Sci 2000 Dec 15; 182 (1): 1–4 (ISSN: 0022–510X)

[181] Hawaii Med J 2000 Mar; 59 (3); 96–8 (ISSN 0017–8594)

[182] Schweiz Rundsch Med Prax 1998 Feb 25; 87 (9); 314–7 (ISSN 1013–2058)

[183] Arch Med Res 2000 May-Jun; 31 (3): 258–6 (ISSN 0188–4409)

[184] National Center of Health Statistics, National Hospital Discharge Survey 1984, 1987, 1990, 1992, 1993, 1994; AAO Department of Research and Scientific Affairs

[185] *New York Times Magazine*, 12/16/01, p. 70, See also *New York Times* 1/22/02, "Misunderstood Opoids and Needless Pain"

[186] Letter from Lem Billings to JFK, 6/24/42. Source: *Reckless Youth*, p.493

[187] *Sports Illustrated* 3/18/96

978-0-595-35752-9
0-595-35752-0